British Poetry since 1939

Twayne's English Authors Series

Kinley E. Roby, Editor

Northeastern University

TEAS 409

British Poetry since 1939

By Bruce K. Martin

Drake University

Twayne Publishers • *Boston*

British Poetry since 1939

Bruce K. Martin

Copyright © 1985 by G.K. Hall & Company
All Rights Reserved
Published by Twayne Publishers
A Division of G.K. Hall & Company
70 Lincoln Street
Boston, Massachusetts 02111

Book Production by Elizabeth Todesco
Book Design by Barbara Anderson

Printed on permanent/durable acid-free
paper and bound in the United States of
America.

Library of Congress Cataloging in Publication Data

Martin, Bruce K., 1941–
    British poetry since 1939.

    (Twayne's English authors series; TEAS 409)
    Bibliography: p. 189
    Includes index.
    1. English poetry—20th century—History and criticism.
    I. Title. II. Series.
PR502.M33   1985   821'.914'09   85–885
ISBN 0–8057–6900–5

For my mother and father

Contents

About the Author
Preface
Acknowledgments
Chronology

Chapter One
Prologue: The British Literary Climate in 1939   1

Chapter Two
Poetry in Wartime: Douglas, Lewis, and Reed   13

Chapter Three
The Empiricist Response: Fuller and Larkin   47

Chapter Four
The Naturalist Response: Hughes and Hill   82

Chapter Five
The Meditative Response: Smith and Jennings   119

Chapter Six
The Neoromantic Response:
Tomlinson and Heaney   142

Chapter Seven
Conclusion: British Poetry
into the Twenty-First Century   172

Notes and References   179
Selected Bibliography   189
Index   202

About the Author

Bruce K. Martin is professor of English and chairman of the department at Drake University, where he has taught since 1967. He received his graduate training and degrees in English at the University of Cincinnati. His scholarly interests center on British literature of the nineteenth and twentieth centuries, and on literary theory. Besides published essays on George Eliot, Thackeray, Hardy, Steinbeck, and Poe, he has written a book-length study of Philip Larkin for Twayne's English Authors Series, published in 1978.

Preface

Most American readers and poets have been taught to regard recent British poetry with condescension, if not hostility. Compared with their brilliant modernist predecessors or with their principal American contemporaries, British poets after Dylan Thomas are usually viewed as feeble and provincial. Such an attitude seems to have taken hold in the 1950s, when it became fashionable to see Britain's poetry reflecting her demise as a world power and exhibiting what A. Alvarez, in his Penguin *New Poetry* anthology (1962), termed "the gentility principle."

Yet, almost as soon as this negative view had begun to gain acceptance, a fairly steady, if quiet, protest began. Alvarez's anthology itself featured the work of those relatively few British poets said to display the acceptable form and degree of "newness" otherwise reserved by Americans. By the end of the 1960s one could find an anthologist of current British verse insisting to Americans that "There *is* a contemporary British poetry which is modern; for a while that seemed to be in doubt."[1] One could find, too, a British critic, after noting the pressure on English poets to accept a place of "demoralized inferiority" to their American counterparts, observing, "Fortunately there are not many signs, as yet, that poets are kissing this rod."[2] But perhaps the strongest indicator of at least the possibility of a shift of image and opinion came in 1974, with an American critic's writing a book on current British poets (Calvin Bedient, *Eight Contemporary Poets*) including some dismissed by Alvarez and his fellow British apologists as hopelessly stodgy, and calling for a revised account of recent British poetry.

Even so, British poetry since the death of Yeats remains largely unexplored territory for most thoughtful American readers. Sometime during the years, an interest in Auden's career after he settled in the United States gave way to an awareness of, at most, a few poems by Philip Larkin or the personality of Ted Hughes. Otherwise poetry from Britain hardly seemed to matter. Bedient's book, while perceptive and important, scarcely deals with recent British poetry beyond the relatively few figures it examines in detail.

It is in the hope of opening up this terra incognita that the following study of British poetry since 1939 has been prepared. The first section describes the situation of poetry in Britain at this period's beginning. Subsequent chapters deal in detail with varying responses to that situation, mainly through an examination of representative respondents. Throughout there has been an attempt to offer self-contained treatments of individual writers and at the same time to relate each author's career to what was happening in British poetry generally. I have tried to attend to impersonal forces, literary and nonliterary, as well as more personal factors in the shaping of poems and poetic careers during this time. The inclusion of British poets during World War II represents a special feature, as ordinarily they have been excluded from discussions of recent British poetry.

Many persons have provided help and encouragement in the preparation of this study. The Drake Graduate Research Council and the Liberal Arts College both provided financial assistance for travel to Britain. The staff of the Cowles Library at Drake, particularly the Reference Department, sought out books, articles, and bits of information vital to this study. Our department secretary, Fran Marks, endured my hideous handwriting and careless typing, to turn out a clear and useful manuscript. And my wife, Barbara, and sons, Matthew and Kirk, allowed me to do this, with no questions and no complaints even as my needs often conflicted with theirs. All of these, as well as the two to whom the book is dedicated, have my deep thanks.

Bruce K. Martin

Drake University

Acknowledgments

Grateful acknowledgment is made to those named below for permission to quote from the works listed:

From "Twentieth Century Blues," by Noel Coward. Copyright 1931, Chappell & Co. Ltd. Reproduced by permission of Chappell Music Ltd.

From *The English Auden: Poems, Essays and Dramatic Writings, 1927–1939* (1977), by W. H. Auden, edited by Edward Mendelson. © 1977 Edward Mendelson, Wm. Meredith and Monroe K. Spears, Executors of the estate of W. H. Auden. Reprinted by permission of Random House, Inc.

From *Collected Poems 1928–1953* (1955), by Stephen Spender. Copyright 1930, 1942, 1947, 1948, 1952, 1955 by Stephen Spender. Reprinted by permission of Random House, Inc.

From *The Collected Poems of Louis MacNeice* (1966), by Louis MacNeice. Reprinted by permission of Faber and Faber.

From *The Complete Poems of Keith Douglas* (1978), by Keith Douglas, edited by Desmond Graham. © 1978 Marie J. Douglas. Reprinted by permission of Oxford University Press.

From *Raiders Dawn and Other Poems* (1942) and *Ha! Ha! Among the Trumpets* (1945), by Alun Lewis. Reprinted by permission of George Allen & Unwin Ltd.

From *A Map of Verona* (1946), by Henry Reed. Reprinted by permission of Jonathan Cape Ltd.

From *Collected Poems 1939–1961* (1962) and *Buff* (1965), by Roy Fuller, by permission of Andre Deutsch; from *New Poems* (1968), by Roy Fuller, printed with the permission of Dufour Editions, Inc., Chester Springs, PA 19425.

From *The Less Deceived* (1955), by Philip Larkin, by permission of the Marvell Press; from *The Whitsun Weddings* (1964), by Philip Larkin, reprinted by permission of Faber and Faber Ltd.; from *High Windows* (1974), by Philip Larkin. © 1974 by Philip Larkin. Reprinted by permission of Farrar, Straus and Giroux, Inc.

Chronology

1939 In January W. H. Auden and Christopher Isherwood leave England for the United States. On 28 January W. B. Yeats dies in France. On 13 April Seamus Heaney born in County Derry, Ireland. On 1 September Germany invades Poland to begin World War II.

1940 Yeats, *Last Poems and Plays.*

1942 Alun Lewis, *Raiders' Dawn.* Roy Fuller, *The Middle of a War.*

1944 On 5 March Alun Lewis killed in Burma. On 9 June Keith Douglas killed in France. Roy Fuller, *A Lost Season.*

1945 Alun Lewis, *Ha! Ha! Among the Trumpets.*

1946 Keith Douglas, *Alamein to Zem Zem*—war experiences in North Africa. Henry Reed, *A Map of Verona.*

1951 Keith Douglas, *Collected Poems.*

1952 Donald Davie, *Purity in English Verse*—manifesto of style representative of the "Movement" viewpoint.

1954 On 1 October an anonymous article titled "In the Movement," describing a postwar movement in British literature, appears in the *Spectator.*

1955 *New Lines,* ed. Robert Conquest—contains early poems by Philip Larkin, Kingsley Amis, John Wain, and other key figures in the Movement. Philip Larkin, *The Less Deceived.*

1957 Roy Fuller, *Brutus's Orchard.* Ted Hughes, *The Hawk in the Rain.*

1959 Geoffrey Hill, *For the Unfallen.*

1960 Charles Tomlinson, *Seeing is Believing.*

1962 Roy Fuller, *Collected Poems. The New Poetry,* ed. A. Alvarez—its introduction attacks the "gentility" of the Movement; its poetry, by younger English and American writers—Hughes and Sylvia Plath among them—suggests an alternative direction for British verse.

1963 *New Lines II,* ed. Robert Conquest—an anthology in response to Alvarez and other detractors of the Movement. *A Group Anthology,* ed. Edward Lucie-Smith and Philip Hobsbaum—suggests another postwar alternative to the Movement.

1964 Philip Larkin, *The Whitsun Weddings.*

1966 Charles Tomlinson, *American Scenes and Other Poems.* Seamus Heaney, *Death of a Naturalist.* Stevie Smith, *The Frog Prince and Other Poems.* Alun Lewis, *Selected Poetry and Prose.*

1967 Ted Hughes, *Selected Poems, 1957–1967.* Elizabeth Jennings, *Collected Poems.*

1968 Geoffrey Hill, *King Log.*

1970 Philip Larkin, *All What Jazz*—collection of jazz reviews expressive of his antimodernist position. Ted Hughes, *Crow.*

1971 Geoffrey Hill, *Mercian Hymns.* Stevie Smith dies in London 7 March.

1972 Charles Tomlinson, *Written on Water.*

1974 Philip Larkin, *High Windows.*

1975 Seamus Heaney, *North.*

1976 Stevie Smith, *Collected Poems.*

1977 Ted Hughes, *Gaudette.*

1978 Keith Douglas, *Complete Poems.* Charles Tomlinson, *Selected Poems, 1951–1974.* Geoffrey Hill, *Tenebrae.*

1979 Elizabeth Jennings, *Selected Poems* and *Moments of Grace.* Seamus Heaney, *Field Work.*

1980 Seamus Heaney, *Preoccupations*—essays. *Oxford Anthology of Contemporary Verse,* D. J. Enright—Movement poetics and polemics revived.

1982 Ted Hughes, *New Selected Poems.*

1983 Philip Larkin, *Required Writing*—essays and articles. Ted Hughes, *River.*

Chapter One
Prologue: The British Literary Climate in 1939

While recognizing 1939 as a somewhat arbitrary dividing line within the broader history of modern British literature or the literature of the twentieth century, one must acknowledge the unusual degree to which Britain's official entry into the century's second European war signaled the end of a distinct phase of her literature. Because it can be argued that rarely have England's poets been so governed by a sense of the larger events of their time than were those writing in England immediately before World War II, it seems not at all unreasonable to view British poetry, like Britain itself or Europe as a whole, moving steadily toward 1939. The year 1939 takes on the qualities of a literary, as well as a political and social, limit to anyone looking back on the poetry dominant in England not only in the 1930s, but also in the 1920s.

With the experimental writing of the 1920s fiction and poetry approximated each other technically as perhaps never before or since. James Joyce and Virginia Woolf produced prose virtually indistinguishable from poetry, while T. S. Eliot and others composed poetic passages stylistically so near prose that in 1928 Edmund Wilson was inspired to write an essay titled "Is Verse a Dying Technique?" And although the 1930s poets partially restored traditional form, they and the novelists drew even closer in terms of concerns than had their counterparts of the 1920s.

Increasingly these writers responded to the economic and social woes of their countrymen, as the postwar slump marking the 1920s in Britain gradually gave way to worldwide depression. Britain's failure to regain prewar markets led to perennial unemployment problems, the General Strike of 1926, and a sense of hopelessness for thousands of families put permanently on the dole.

In a 1931 song Noel Coward summed up the feelings generated by the rise of fascism abroad and the severe depression at home when he asked:

1

Why is it that civilized humanity can make this world so wrong?
In this strange illusion, chaos and confusion,
People seem to lose their way ...
Nothing to win or to lose, it's getting me down.
Who's escap'd those dreary Twentieth Century Blues?[1]

Unlike its American counterpart, "Brother, Can You Spare a Dime?,"
Coward's lyric complained not so much of poverty as of what he
later called the "harsh discordancy" and "hectic desperation" of the
times[2]: the sense of the breaking up of even the illusory Old England,
a belated but full recognition of the total consequences of World
War I, and a fearful feeling of proximity to a Europe about to
explode.

The Response of the Poets

The prose writers emerging in Britain at this time offered their
own varied responses. Evelyn Waugh responded with black humor;
Aldous Huxley, with satire. Christopher Isherwood gave ominous
accounts of totalitarian Germany. Graham Greene depicted a grim
contemporary world from a religious perspective. Perhaps the most
distinctive response, though, came from George Orwell, whose nov-
els and essays represented with unerring honesty the dangers and
uncertainties confronting his countrymen as World War II
approached.

Of course, even Orwell, despite his plainspokenness and despite
his disassociation from the intellectuals of his time, became—and
remained—part of the English High Culture. Writing of the thir-
ties, the historian A. J. P. Taylor reminds us of the rashness of
assuming that "literary taste and popularity indicate what ordinary
people were thinking."[3] Rather, Taylor insists, the key to most
Englishmen's feelings lay more in newspapers and other pulp pub-
lications, and increasingly in radio and film, than in what we would
call literature. Even so, serious writers tried hard to relate to the
problems of the masses. No more striking evidence of this is to be
found than in the work of the new poets of the early 1930s.

At their center was the precocious Wystan Hugh Auden, while
other principals of the ill-defined "Auden group" included Stephen
Spender, C. Day Lewis, and Louis MacNeice. Their similar ages,
common educational backgrounds, close friendships, and shared

intensity for the writing of poetry helped create a distinct group impression. Beginning with Auden and Lewis's appearances in *Oxford Poetry 1927*, each figured prominently in anthologies intended to break new ground in English verse, notably *New Signatures* (1932) and *New Country* (1933), edited by the young poet Michael Roberts. Each published a critical manifesto on poetry and his aims as a poet that broadly resembled those of the other three. And, in the early and mid-thirties each brought out collections of poems increasingly focused on the economic and political crises of England and Europe, and distinguished by realistic detail and topical allusion.

During the early years of this loose association the Auden group confined their poetic writing to relatively short lyrics. Only Lewis, besides Auden himself, attempted anything more ambitious, as he moved through two fairly long sequences, *Transitional Poem* (1929) and *From Feathers to Iron* (1931), to *The Magnetic Mountain* (1933). This last, a long poem dedicated to Auden and punctuated with reminders of Lewis's indebtedness to him, surveys the problems of contemporary England, concluding with a vague, undefined hope for a more purposeful future.

For all of its ambitiousness, though, *The Magnetic Mountain* paled beside Auden's long philosophical poem of this period, *The Orators* (1932). There, through a variety of speakers and perspectives, Auden saw an England infected by social annd political ills yet seemingly unwilling to deal with them in a meaningful fashion. Specifically, he exposed the absence of responsible leadership in a morally sick nation. Complaining of the repressiveness and staidness of English life, he doubted that things would change under the current style of leadership, which itself was sick.

In the fourth of six odes comprising the final part of *The Orators*, Auden takes us through cities and slums where workingmen live and work almost insensibly ("Their minds as pathic as a boxer's face, / A shamed, uninteresting and hopeless race."), and then to the upper class, whom he dismisses as prudish and self-centered. After asking, "Who will save? / Who will teach us how to behave?" he proceeds to analyze current leaders. Like W. B. Yeats in "The Second Coming," Auden fears that only the "worst" can exhibit forceful leadership:

> O yes, MacDonald's a giant,
> President Hoover's a giant,

Baldwin and Briand are giants—
Haven't they told us?
But why have they sold us?
They said they were winners,
They were only beginners.
Pygmies, poor dears,
Beside the Giant Sloths and the Giant Despairs.
Mussolini, Pilsudski and Hitler have charm
But they make such a noise:
We're getting a little tired of boys,
Of the ninny, the mawmet and false alarm.

Though later dropped by Auden from his *Collected Poems*—presum-
ably for being too direct and too topical[4]— the ode is nevertheless
instructive for capturing the impatience underlying the entire *Or-
ators:* an impassioned certainty about the problems of contemporary
society coupled with uncertainty about their being solved.

In his impatience and in the manner in which he voiced it, Auden
unquestionably was the leader of the young poets associated with
him. More than any of them he managed to alert readers and writers
to the possibilities of English poetry. Roy Fuller, then a young
aspiring poet, recalls his excitement at learning from Auden's ex-
ample that the traditional resources of English poetry need not be
reactionary, that they could be used for a poetry as "contemporary"
as that produced in freer forms by Eliot and Pound.[5]

No doubt a good deal of Auden's impact stemmed from his
attacking capitalism at a time when the established economic system
seemed to be collapsing. Also, the candidly Freudian quality of
many of his lyrics provided a welcome respite from the mid-Victorian
prudishness still coloring most elements of British public culture.
Nevertheless, because Auden's Freudianism, like his Marxism, was
unorthodox, and because they both were colored by a distinctly
Auden style, his appeal was at least as much technical as ideological.

Starting with his first collection, he presented a concrete, direct
style. Perhaps this is related to what has frequently been described
as the "clinical detachment" of his most characteristic writing,[6] as
well as his ability to convert his Marxist borrowings into "a series
of coherently generalizing images."[7] In analyzing the Audenesque
style which proved so attractive to the 1930s, Bernard Bergonzi has
credited such things as Auden's penchant for the definite article,
the bizarre or unexpected simile, and the personified abstraction—

all of which proved appropriate to what Bergonzi terms the "classificatory vision" conducive to broad-scale political and social analysis.[8]

But, these tendencies, as Bergonzi notes, were to some extent shared by all of the poets making up the so-called Auden Group, and even by many novelists of the period. Perhaps of more significance to determining the source of Auden's peculiar appeal is the affinity of much of his writing with popular song lyrics of the time, as well as with various techniques of the cinema. Certainly Cole Porter, Noel Coward, and the movies inspired much that is in Auden's poems and plays of this period, helping him to create what one critic has called a "satirical newsreel of the thirties."[9] His protean manner of adopting various masks and voices, as well as various other oddities of diction perhaps related to his earlier embrace of Gerard Manley Hopkins's poetry,[10] helped make his poetry additionally striking.

Even so, as Auden's editor Edward Mendelson points out, it was not until 1932 that his writing became "explicitly political."[11] This shift into politics, as well as the didactic impulse accompanying it, was typical of young British poets during the 1930s. Orwell attributed their political commitment to a desperate need to believe in something after the cynical 1920s had debunked everything else.[12] Relatedly, Spender has noted how, despite the leftist leanings of many war poets, the gap between the literary elite and political writers had widened in the 1920s, to the point where as an Oxford undergraduate he felt ashamed of his interest in politics;[13] no doubt the thirties were liberating for him. And Bernard Bergonzi speculates that the young poets' sense of having been too young to fight in the Great War, certain shared schoolboy codes of morality, and their common experience of teaching school may have created in them the need to instruct and the need to participate in politics through their writings.[14] Whatever the factors behind such a development, in Auden's case it resulted in an increase in not only topicality but the wry humor for which he is celebrated.

Following a two-month visit to Spain in 1937, Auden wrote several cryptically Freudian ballads—"Johnny," "Miss Gee," "Victor," and "James Honeyman"—which have been seen as a rejection of the public role and political action.[15] Even his "Spain, 1937," despite its powerful rhetoric and watershed impression, may not reflect so much a commitment as supposed when it first appeared.[16]

Certainly "Musée des Beaux Arts," written in late 1938, represents Auden's acknowledgment, and perhaps his celebration, of the primacy of civilian normalcy in human affairs. Relatedly the chilling "Epitaph on a Tyrant," written about the same time, treats totalitarianism almost more as an unpleasant fact of life to be recognized than as a force to be countered by individual endeavor. Where one so fearful of Hitler might be expected to be heartened by the earnest preparations for armed action taken in early 1939, Auden, given his gradual move away from public and political allegiances, could be inspired only to write a poem like "The Unknown Citizen," stressing the indifference to individual happiness of all governments, including the more democratic ones.

The general outline of Stephen Spender's career during the 1930s resembles that of Auden's. Certainly he learned much from Auden. For example, Auden's easy appropriation of urban technology into his writing enabled Spender to write poems celebrating the greater beauty of a fast-moving train ("The Express") or of a slowly descending airship ("The Landscape Near an Aerodrome") than that of their counterparts in nature. Of course, Spender commanded a much narrower range of styles and devices than Auden; his poems seem almost wholly lacking in the wit or satiric bite characteristic of much of Auden's best writing. Nevertheless, he frequently produced poems of intense beauty and poignancy, and for this was immensely popular in the 1930s.

Where Auden captured the absurdity of that period, Spender captured its hurt and its pathetic confusion, a confusion that he confessedly shared. Exhorting young men of the middle class, whom he addressed as "comrades," to act on behalf of universal brotherhood, he characterized their time as "this day when grief pours freezing over us, / When the hard light of pain gleams at every street corner, / When those who were pillars of yesterday's roof / Shrink in their clothes ..." ("After they have tired of the brilliance of cities"). Elsewhere, in "The Uncreating Chaos," in a manner worthy of Yeats he pictured things as falling apart.

Unlike Yeats, however, Spender could find a visit among schoolchildren an occasion not for aesthetic theorizing, but for sympathizing with the trapped child of the slum (" ... The stunted, unlucky heir / Of twisted bones, reciting a father's gnarled disease ..."—"An Elementary School Classroom in a Slum") and for pleading for his release with his captors, an indifferent adult society. The social and political conscience of the young Spender seems nowhere more at work than in *Vienna* (1934), where he recited with a sometimes frightening intensity the various crises troubling Europe after Hitler had become Chancellor. Spender has since recalled being torn after 1933 between the sensitive intellectual's terror of another war and an equally strong impulse to expose the Nazi terror to a largely ignorant public: "One had the sense of belonging to a small group who could see terrible things which no one else saw."[17]

Yet, for all of this pressure to take sides against Hitler, and for all of Spender's concessions to such pressure—for example, the increase of Marxist materials in his writings, or his trip to Spain in sympathy with the Loyalists—perhaps even more than Auden he failed to commit himself to a fully political posture. Though briefly joining the Communist Party, he had foreseen the difficulties of such a move as early as 1933, when he had pronounced poetry and communism necessarily antithetical.[18] The strongly anti-Nazi *Vienna* was generally judged unsuccessful and never reprinted, and his allegiance to the Communist party never more than partial and highly qualified.

Certainly a concern with the individual and the personal persisted in Spender's poetry even during his most political phase. His poems on Spain, where he ostensibly was serving the Loyalists, invariably concentrated on the horror of the war and suffering common to both sides and ignored the political dimension of the struggle.

While in some respects more attuned to Marxism than Auden or Spender, C. Day Lewis in his writing after *The Magnetic Mountain* betrayed increasing uncertainty about political involvement. While Auden and Spender were in Spain, Lewis stayed in England writing poems for *Overtures of Death* (1938). Some of them—notably "Maple and Sumach," "February, 1936," and "Landscapes"—begin as commentaries on nature but quickly yield to an awareness of horrible events elsewhere; the resulting mood is one of severe depression. While an occasional poem attends solely to politics (for instance, "The Bombers") or social issues ("Sex Crimes"), in most we see Lewis struggling to remain private and finding himself repeatedly interrupted by a nagging conscience.

As for Louis MacNeice, of the Auden group he seems to have been temperamentally the least fitted to the demands of his age. Measured against the whole of his work, the outburst of social discontent in "An Eclogue for Christmas" (1933) appears almost an aberration. Where Lewis in his poems sought a satisfactory ideology, with a classical fluidity reinforced by classical allusions, MacNeice with a gentle wit emphasized the simple, commonplace experiences, the sights and sounds of everyday life. All of his poems at least imply a wariness of ideologues, whom he characterized as "theory-venders, / The little sardine men cramped in a monster toy / Who tilt their aggregate beast against our crumbling Troy" ("Turf-stacks"). By temperament and conviction unattracted either to what he terms the "Brazen Tower" of political thought or to the Ivory Tower of purely personal experience, MacNeice, of all the Auden group, changed his stance the least during the 1930s. As a poet of "the shape and substance of what is actually happening around him"[19]— and not of documentation, or myth, or parable—he had the least difficulty in reiterating his empiricism, and the least need to retreat from ideology.

While Auden and his associates together best typify what was happening in British poetry of the 1930s, they were by no means the only significant poets to emerge during that time. In contrast with them, at least some talented newcomers reacted to the contemporary social and political crisis in a decidedly conservative manner. The most notable young right-winger of the decade was probably Roy Campbell, a South African who saw in fascism the only hope for saving Western culture, and who fiercely attacked as naive and blind those other poets and intellectuals drawn to the Republican cause in Spain.[20] Of the new poets taking a more radical posture than the Auden group, the most talented were John Cornford and Christopher Caudwell (Christopher St. John Sprigg), who both died in Spain fighting for the Republic. Caudwell gained fame as a Marxist literary theorist especially critical of the Auden poets' cautious political venturing. Scorning them for their loyalty to the "bourgeoise" notions of individualism and personal liberty, Caudwell saw nothing but self-delusion or dishonesty in their professed concern with revolution.[21] Of course, the thirties saw the appearance of other younger poets—notably George Barker and William Empson—whose posture toward contemporary political and social issues is difficult to discern from their poetry.

But the most spectacular newcomer of the 1930s, who ultimately would eclipse even Auden, was the Welsh wunderkind Dylan Thomas, whose *18 Poems* appeared before he was even twenty. By the decade's end he would bring out two other collections, which, along with *18 Poems,* include most of the poetry he would ever publish. Many of his finest lyrics—"I see the boys of summer," "The force that through the green fuse drives the flower," the "Altarwise by owl-light" sonnets, and "After the funeral"—were thus available to readers of the thirties.

While newcomers may appear to have dominated poetry in the decade or so before World War II, at least three of the older poets wrote and published much during that time. If no longer exciting the wonder of young poets as they had during the 1920s, Ezra Pound, T. S. Eliot, and William Butler Yeats continued to be regarded as formidable. Certainly none of the three was unaware of political developments around him, and each responded in a manner both characteristic and crucial to the broad outlines of his career.

Politically Eliot is not easy to relate with the other authors discussed thus far. For his failure to condemn fascism during the 1930s—and for his tendency on occasion to quibble with those who did—he has been condemned by some as a fascist. Others have insisted that he was merely avoiding being mistaken as a "liberal," and that his seeming indifference to the horrors of totalitarianism was of a different order from that of right-wing sympathizers.

Where Eliot might be said to have moved increasingly toward a fixed, suprapersonal lodestone of belief and consciousness as his religious sensibility unfolded, Yeats in the last years before World War II—which were to be the final years of his life, as well— moved in an increasingly personal, or at least an increasingly esoteric, direction. His relationship to modernism was somewhat tangled, in that he was much older than Eliot or Pound—and in a sense had already had one career as a late romantic poet before they had even begun to write—and in that he ignored much of their experimenting by clinging to many older poetic forms and practices.

Of course, in his deployment of images and in his ruminations on art and poetry, Yeats was closely aligned to Eliot, Pound, and the entire imagist-symbolist basis of modern poetry. His devotion to the image as the central element of the poem, his distrust of externally (or empirically) derived meaning in poetry, put him at odds with the didactic bent of much new poetry of the 1930s. Whether any poet as sensitive to Irish affairs as Yeats could ever care about the political disputes of young Englishmen is questionable; certainly his aloofness from such disputes is a function in part of Ireland's long-standing isolation from European politics. And, although his concern with Irish culture necessarily had its political dimension, the period of his most active political involvement, spurred by events related to the Irish Civil War, had passed by the time totalitarianism was spreading through Europe.

For his indifference to Europe's political crisis, Yeats, too, was occasionally branded a fascist. A look at his writings after 1925, however, suggests that such a label was even more untenable with him than with Eliot. In that year he published *A Vision,* the culmination of his long search for a personal symbology; his reconsideration of that symbology resulted in an extensively revised version, published in 1937. His volumes of verse published during the intervening years—*The Tower* (1928), *The Winding Stair* (1933), and *A Full Moon in March* (1935)—all contain poems suggesting a poetic sensibility much more radically apolitical than Eliot's. Such lyrics as "Sailing to Byzantium," "Among School Children," "Byzantium," and the various Crazy Jane poems show Yeats struggling with the personal riddles of aging, memory, and the body-soul duality, and with his role as an artist in resolving such dilemmas: in other words, with those problems which in Yeats's view eventually become preoccupations of every thoughtful person, whatever his politics. On such a plane Yeats's radically personal concerns and Eliot's radically impersonal meet.

The Critical Stalemate

None of the Auden group was unaware or unappreciative of the later writings of Yeats. Auden's memorial tribute was simply the most beautiful evidence of the hold Yeats continued to exert over his earlier disciples.

Yet Yeats's later efforts—and perhaps their own responses to them—proved puzzling to Auden and his associates. For instance, Stephen Spender, writing in 1934 of "W. B. Yeats as a Realist," praised "the passion, the humanity, the technical perfection, the strength, the reality and the opportunism" of Yeats's later work, but complained of Yeats's tendency to substitute a "magical system" and "aristocratic faith" for a solid philosophy of life in his poems, and thus to blur their humanity.[22] Though insisting that "Yeats has found, as yet, no subject of moral significance in the social life of his time"—and presumably the young Spender could think of many—he at the same time found irresistible the beauty and purely "rhetorical" power of the poems. In this single essay we see Spender moving between the didactic stance of the orthodox Auden poet and the imagist position whereby the poem becomes its own subject and argument. The confusion here illustrates the basic irresolution informing Spender's own work and that of many other poets immediately prior to World War II.

The ambivalence of Spender's feelings about Yeats resembles that of the other Auden poets about their modernist masters, and relates to the confusion in each of these poets' theoretical manifestos issued in the mid-thirties. Such confusion and ambivalence are in part the outcomes of the rather radical confrontation of sharply opposed critical theories that occurred in the twenties and thirties. Auden, Spender, and the others came of age at a time when the basic questions arising from such a confrontation could not be ignored, as conflicting pressures from persuasive advocates helped shape their sensibilities as poets and as critics.

Spender's discussion of Yeats's realism reflects uncertainty over whether modern poetry ought to proceed on its own way, according to its own peculiar aesthetic principles, or whether it ought to reflect the social and political realities outside it. Of course, this fundamental dispute—between art and life, between the aesthetic and the ethical notions of literature—goes all the way back to Aristotle and Plato. And the efforts with which Renaissance theorists—such as Sidney in his *Defense of Poesy*—had tried to reconcile the two views of literary art were not unlike those of Spender struggling to defend Yeats even as he attacked him.

The resulting uncertainty over the claims of life and art, and of personal and impersonal theories of poetry—an uncertainty compounded by the international and personal factors already mentioned—was perhaps the key legacy of British poetry immediately prior to World War II. A number of other, more specific issues also had arisen by the time the war began. Because the 1930s had been the first period during which British poetry was forced to face modern mass culture, the questions of to what extent poets ought to acknowledge that mass culture, address its consumers, draw on it, or even become part of it would have to be considered. Also, partly because Pound and Eliot had attacked some British literary traditions as insular and parochial, and partly because England could no longer claim any sort of supremacy among nations, the question of the degree to which British poets should strive to be British or should pursue more international connections would become a key issue.

Chapter Two
Poetry in Wartime: Douglas, Lewis, and Reed

The impact of World War II on England and on her culture is much more difficult to determine than that of World War I. Certainly modern mass warfare was much more imaginable in 1939 than it had been in 1914; a good deal of the Great War's horror had related to its novelty. Also, World War I had profoundly altered the tone of British writing by producing—and killing off—a talented group of distinctively wartime writers, by creating guilt and disillusionment among those who either survived or had been too young to fight, and by ultimately undermining the whole facade of moral and economic superiority that had informed the world of their Edwardian predecessors. The war shocked all British systems, but especially the cultural and intellectual order on which even the most rebellious writers had depended. Because the British never fully recovered from that shock, no later crisis could possibly match the catastrophic force of 1914–18. As Keith Douglas put it, "[H]ell cannot be let loose twice."[1]

While the novelists and poets of 1914 had scarcely written about even the possibility of England's being involved in a great European war until such involvement became reality—having been accustomed, like all other Englishmen, by a century of noninvolvement to regard such a development as nearly impossible—most British writers of the 1930s, and especially the poets, could think of little else to write about, having been conditioned by years of disillusioned reflection on the war and its failings. Recent history contains few more pathetic illustrations of war's horrible effects on the sensitive mind than that of Ivor Gurney, a shell-shocked contemporary of Wilfred Owen and Isaac Rosenberg, who, refusing to believe that the war had ended, continued to write war poems until his death in the late 1930s, when another war was, in fact, beginning. Yet Gurney represented but an extreme of the refusal, or the inability, of most of his contemporaries to let go of the earlier war. This, in

turn, caused a generation of slightly younger poets to be preoccupied
with that war and its continuation in literature, and to regard their
times as a "long weekend" years before historians coined the phrase.[2]

War and the British Literary Climate

This more expectant, and ultimately more accepting, attitude
toward war reflected in part a difference in the nature of the struggle
against Hitler from that of 1914–18. This time war hit Britain in
a way it had not since the Civil War of the seventeenth century.
After several months of what American journalists dubbed the "Pho-
ney War"—with the Germans occupied in Poland, the French set-
tled behind their Maginot Line, and the British concentrating on
blockading Germany and evacuating London—and after a disastrous
British expedition to protect Norway from Nazi attack, the Germans
swept across Western Europe in a remarkably short time, and pre-
sented the British with their first genuine threat of foreign invasion
in 900 years.

Dunkirk, the Blitz, Churchill, "London Pride," "England's Finest
Hour"—all belong to a sort of folklore surrounding the Battle of
Britain. Unlike British battles of the 1914 war, this one involved
the entire population: every social class, every age group, and almost
every region of the nation. Not until the war was three years old
had as many British soldiers died in battle as women and children
at home.[3] The bulk of the suffering, of course, occurred in London,
where air raids became an expected nighttime event from the sum-
mer of 1940 until the following June. Compounding the death and
destruction was the disruption of metropolitan life—of traffic, mail
delivery, shopping, telephone service, and virtually every other facet
of communication and commerce upon which a modern city depends.

Like travel and business-as-usual, the prewar culture of London,
and of Britain generally, was temporarily halted by the fierce and
lengthy Nazi air attack, as well as by the threat of land invasion.
This situation became especially chaotic for the literary world, as
publishing routines were interrupted and facilities often destroyed,
and as writing became an impossibility amid heavy bombardment.
Aspiring authors were further discouraged by the shutting down of
channels open to them before the war, as paper restrictions put the
squeeze on new book titles, and as many magazines ceased publi-
cation and it became illegal to start new ones.[4]

After recovering from the initial shock of the disorders attending the Blitz, however, the literary world adapted and began a modest development despite such hardships. For one thing, several new publications, begun before the ban went into effect in May 1940, partly filled the void created by those forced to shut down. Most significant among these were *Horizon,* edited by Cyril Connolly, and *Poetry (London),* under the editorship of the legendary M. J. Tambimutto. Colorful and wild-looking, Tambimutto published many of the best poets of the war years and became a sort of guru to the literary subculture flourishing in the pubs of Soho as the war lengthened. Publishers found they could circumvent the ban on new magazines by disguising such publications as anthologies; thus the Penguin *New Writing* series and other similar ventures quickly became a standard medium for rising literary stars, especially poets. And, because the end of the Blitz restored an at least tolerable atmosphere for writing and created a greatly increased demand for books—a demand compounded by the loss of twenty million volumes destroyed in the Blitz[5]—Penguin's and other cheap paperback series prospered. The employment provided many writers by the British Broadcasting Corporation and by the Ministry of Information further modified the uncertainties of war that had earlier threatened their literary activities.

Not all of these developments proved entirely salutary. Most writers working for the BBC or the Information Office were demoralized by the intellectually demeaning tasks to which their talents were directed, and by the condescending attitude of bureaucrats.[6] George Orwell's celebrated resignation from the BBC resulted from his feeling that he was "just an orange that's been trodden by a very dirty boot,"[7] a feeling no doubt shared by many others. And, despite the rise of new periodicals and the anthology and a wartime reading public peculiarly eager for stimulating material, literature continued to work against extreme restrictions on paper. In a year when official publications consumed 100,000 tons, less than 22,000 were allotted for books of all kinds, and presumably but a small fraction of that for what could reasonably be termed literature.[8] Nor did the quality of the new fiction and poetry printed on that meager paper allotment please many discriminating critics. Surveying five years of wartime literary activity, Cyril Connolly remarked on the irony of the government finally—after books were becoming "as bad as they are ugly"—recognizing the value of such activity: "The State now sits by the bedside of literature like a policeman watching for a would-be suicide to recover consciousness, who will do anything for the patient except allow him the leisure, privacy and freedom from which art is produced."[9] Given the conditions under which writers had been struggling, such a decline was hardly surprising.

Even so, much poetry was written and published during this period. While the number of fiction titles published annually fell sharply during the war's first three years, poetry production declined much less sharply and even rose after 1942.[10] Obviously this was partly owing to the greater ease of dashing off a poem than a novel, especially under the trying and distracting conditions of war. Such an advantage enjoyed by the poet was compounded by paper restrictions and by the anthology vogue already described. Readers ordinarily accustomed to reading and preferring fiction to poetry probably found it decidedly more convenient to take in the shorter lyric form, thus producing a sharp, if temporary, growth in poetry's following. Whatever the reasons, there were plenty of poets and plenty of poems published in England during the war.

While the death of Yeats and the posthumous publication of his *Last Poems and Plays* (1940) had marked the end of an era, most of those established poets who remained continued to write. Eliot, of course, completed the final three of his *Four Quartets* during the war, with "Little Gidding" (1942) especially reflecting his wartime experiences in London. After publishing Cantos XII–LXXI in 1940, Ezra Pound spent most of the war in Italy, publishing virtually no poetry, although his confinement upon being arrested by the U.S. Army in 1944 inspired the *Pisan Cantos* (1948), generally considered some of his most humane writing. During this time Edith Sitwell modified her eccentric technique somewhat and reached a peak in reputation as a poet with such lyrics as "Still Falls the Rain," "The Poet Laments the Coming of Old Age," and her "Three Poems of the Atomic Age." Relatedly, as the fervor for extreme modernism and political realism waned, the poems of such neotraditionalists as Edwin Muir and Robert Graves began to command serious critical attention. In this poetry of the war years each still relatively young member of the Auden group continued the inward journey begun in the late thirties, although some, notably Louis MacNeice and Stephen Spender, troubled over past failings and errors more than did the others. None, including Auden himself, would again write such acclaimed poems as those of the 1930s.

As for Dylan Thomas, who had outshown the Auden group so dazzlingly, he devoted most of his wartime attention to scripting and directing documentaries and to widening his reputation as a teller of stories and imbiber of drink among the literati frequenting London pubs. His writing of verse became sporadic; of the roughly two dozen "new" poems in *Deaths and Entrances* (1946), his only collection since before the war, less than half were not written during 1939 or 1945. Despite so slender and uneven an output, some of the pieces of this period—"A Refusal to Mourn the Death, by Fire, of a Child in London," "Fern Hill," and the "Vision and Prayer" series—are among Thomas's most beautiful.

Many new poets appeared during the war, and most have been forgotten by even the most eclectic anthologists. Foremost among those new writers to enjoy wide recognition, followed by rapid eclipse, were the group known as the New Apocalyptics. Claiming to have been inspired by Dylan Thomas—who quickly denied all connection with them—the Apocalyptics were hailed as leaders of "a new Romantic tendency, whose most obvious elements are love, death, an adherence to myth and an awareness of war."[11] Such a program—and it was proclaimed in various forms by several of the poets themselves, as well as by their enthusiastic anthologists— proved pretentious and vague, as did much of the poetry written under the New Apocalyptic banner. Of these writers John Lehmann has complained, "They only succeeded in being plaintive when they attempted to be passionate, and when they tackled larger themes their sentiments sounded inflated and insincere."[12]

Of the Apocalyptics only one, Vernon Watkins, achieved solid, permanent recognition. However, other poets of more lasting distinction—George Barker, David Gascoyne, and Kathleen Raine— began to be recognized in the early 1940s. And, while most of the distinctively "war" poets of this time failed to write poetry commanding any permanent reputation, the work of at least three merits reading even today.

Keith Douglas

Certainly no young British poet in the early 1940s projected a keener awareness of the significance and the hazards of writing at that time than did Keith Douglas, who was killed in France in 1944, at the age of twenty-four. The peculiarities of World War

II and its implications for the would-be author Douglas explored at length in a 1943 essay, where he complained of so-called "war" poets wholly lacking in the sort of experience that had shocked Wilfred Owen, Siegfried Sassoon, and Isaac Rosenberg into creating a new kind of war poetry for a new, modern kind of war. "It seems there were no poets at Dunkirk; or if there were, they stayed there," Douglas complained, as he went on to scorn even the most technically accomplished of the younger writers for having had "no experiences worth writing of."[13]

This sense of living in the shadow of the earlier war and of its poets—a sense not unlike what the Auden group had felt before the modernist giants—is reflected in many of Douglas's poems, even those to which he brought the direct feelings of battle. While his strongest poems came out of the thirty months of fighting he experienced and observed in the Middle East, and while several of these have repeatedly been recognized by critics and anthologists as among the most masterful writing of his time, it appears that not even experience itself could overcome the powerful sense of inferiority Douglas felt toward his generation's war and its war poetry. One of the most interesting poems that he wrote during, and about, his long spell as a tank cavalry officer is ironically titled "Gallantry." In it he comments on the irreconcilability of civilian and military modes of behavior, as reflected in the deaths of three soldiers, one of whom Douglas describes as "the doomed boy ... / whose perfectly mannered flesh fell / in opening the door for a shell / as he had learnt to do at school." Continuing this note of incongruity for the rest of the poem, he closes with an especially self-conscious remembrance of Owen, noting how "the bullets cried with laughter, / the shells were overcome with mirth, / plugging their heads in steel and earth." More directly, in another poem he interjected "Rosenberg I only repeat what you were saying." Such lines clearly support Paul Fussell's notion that World War I was the real source of all war writing in the twentieth century.[14] Elsewhere Douglas generally managed to subdue his self-consciousness in writing about the war, and while he might even mock the earlier war as "a bogy to frighten children and electors with,"[15] he never denied it or its poetry the title "great," in contrast with what his generation was able to pursue. His judgments of inferiority make one marvel that he could write at all about his war without the paralyzing sense of an Owen or a Rosenberg looking over his shoulder, and make those truly distinctive and excellent poems he did manage during his relatively few years as a writer all the more impressive.

To be sure, Keith Douglas brought remarkable qualities of character and intellect to the task of overcoming such feelings. His celebrated disobeying of orders to rejoin his regiment in battle at El Alamein typifies the singular behavior of this singular poet. A scholarship student at Oxford before the war, Douglas had already, by his eighteenth birthday, distinguished himself as a talented painter, a classical scholar, a poet published in the respected *New Verse,* and a rebel against arbitrary authority. Having spent much of his childhood by himself—as an only child whose father had left him and his mother when he was eight—he had developed the imagination and self-discipline that were to serve his vocations as poet and soldier.[16] His two years at Oxford before being called up were a time of intense involvement in writing and painting, in editing the student magazine *Cherwell,* in friendships, and in love affairs. Though highly aware of his barely middle-class status—his mother had to earn most of the money to maintain their humble household—he could nevertheless write in a notebook that "The allegiance of the rabble defiles that to which it is given."[17] His distrust of authority was coupled with an attraction to discipline; thus he liked the military but not militarism.[18] This paradoxical element of his makeup becomes ironic in view of his fellow soldiers' verdict that he was brave but not "military."[19] Relatedly, his Oxford tutor Edmund Blunden recalled Douglas as "one of the most outspoken of people ... but ... infallibly gentle and attentive."[20]

Not counting his school writings, Douglas wrote fewer than one hundred poems, of which only about half were published during his lifetime. The irony of this latter figure is compounded by the fact that scarcely a dozen of the poems written during his military service, when he did his best work, appeared in print before his death. The rest came out later—some as a sort of appendix to his posthumously published narrative of desert warfare, *Alamein to Zem Zem* (1946); some in various periodicals, especially *Poetry (London),* as Tambimutto had been an early Douglas champion and mentor; some in the *Collected Poems,* which did not appear until 1951; and others, most recently, in the *Complete Poems* (1978).

Although barely ten years separate his earliest known poems from his last, Douglas projects a not inconsiderable variety, as well as some notable shifts, of concern in his writing. The school poems predicted most of the subjects of his mature work, while concentrating on some that he later would abandon. Thus the riddle of youth and age, of time's passing, occupies a number of the early pieces. Such titles as "Youth," "Dejections," "On Leaving School," and "Pleasures" suggest the quasi-romantic tone, as well as the seemingly forced emotion, of much Douglas juvenilia. Of course, he could, during these early years, write poems on love ("Kristen," "Love and Gorizia"), on nature ("A Storm"), and on art and poetry ("Images," "Famous Men"). He could explore the puzzling and often painful relationship of one's private personality to the larger, impersonal world ("Distraction," "Point of View") and could even manage a war poem (".303") when only fifteen.

With Oxford and the army, however, the unsettling political situation, the sadness of war, and the implications of such things for the individual came increasingly to dominate Douglas's writing. Even in poems ostensibly concerned with topics he had earlier pursued—such as love ("Tel Aviv," "This is the Dream") or the self-world relationship ("The Hand," "The Sea Bird," "These grasses, ancient enemies," "Devils," "Dead Men," and many others)—Douglas made war his unmistakable setting. And, once he reached Egypt, that exotic setting itself became the subject of a number of poems.

The aspect of his writing that impressed readers and critics from the very beginning is its technical virtuosity. A meticulous craftsman, who worked and reworked poems, Douglas exhibited a dazzling precociousness. Desmond Graham, his biographer, notes how "Auden, Edith Sitwell, the early Yeats, Pound and Eliot had been imitated and absorbed by the time he left school."[21] Such care and craft are evidenced in "Famous Men," which Douglas later guessed to have been written when he was fourteen or fifteen.[22] There, in three short, three-line stanzas he tells how dead heroes are not—and perhaps cannot be—adequately compensated. Then, in an arresting fourth stanza—in marked contrast with the quiet, almost nonimagistic quality of the others—he concludes: "And think, like plates lie deep / licked clean, their skulls, / rest beautifully, staring." The disturbing simile, the poem's first overt reference to the dead men's bodily state, and the irony of their repose forcefully suggest the totality of their helplessness, their pathetic dependence on the poet himself for recognition. That he ultimately recognizes only the beautiful tableau of their skulls, and not their virtues or accomplishments, provides the finishing measure of their decline, and a skillfully executed closure to the poem.

The kinds of skills evidenced in "Famous Men" are to be found to some extent in most of his early poems, including some decidedly less distinguished than that one. Prosodic exactness and the placement of sharp images became staples of his writing while he was yet a teenager. All his early poems reflect a concern with prosody, often used very subtly, as well as the willingness to subject his writing to the discipline of carefully arranged stanzas and rhyme. Thus, in an early villanelle ("Villanelle of Gorizia")—a form to which he often turned—he weaves through the poem the image of a street being "repeated with sunlight." The use of such an image in a generally quiet context links the young Douglas with the young Auden, who surely served as a principal model. Equally effective are the piling up of images such as "winking cup and wine" or "hands snow-red" to create a mood of romantic apprehension ("Mummers"), or such details as "a thousand aery shimmers" and "glebe and woodland" to set up a Tennysonian fairyland ("Youth"). While such poems seem deliberately stylized, they suggest a near-mastery of the particular styles being exploited. In most of the other early poems, except for the rather obvious link with Auden, or an occasional image suggestive, say, of Keats or Eliot,[23] Douglas seems to have assimilated his models surprisingly well.

In keeping with the Audenesque quality of much of his writing in the 1930s, he could put images to witty use. Highly suggestive of such wit is "On Leaving School," an early sonnet developing the speaker's uncertainty toward the freedom he is about to enjoy. Douglas rescues the poem from the ordinariness of its subject and its not very striking octave by beginning the final section: "One of us will be the kettle past care of tinkers, / Rejected, one the tip-top apple, the winking / Sun's friend." Such gentle humor protects the poem from the meaninglessness of adolescent complaining into which it might otherwise fall and helps create a more mature basis for sympathy with its young speaker.

An even more sustained show of wit occurs in "Encounter with a God," perhaps Douglas's strongest school poem. In a mock-Japanese setting Douglas has a god, Daikoku, "Rotund ... / with a round, white paunch," visit a poetess eager to write in praise of his beauty. After he tells her he is not beautiful but is drunk and will not be in her poem, she proceeds to write anyway: "How

intricate and peculiarly well- / arranged the symmetrical belly-pur-
ses / of lord Daikoku." Her determination to make him beautiful,
his refusal to be so, and the quaintness of her description help debunk
the reverential attitude she would invoke.

While Douglas continued to read and to write with intense in-
terest, for the most part he did not develop very strikingly as a poet
until he went to the Middle East. His essay quoted above reveals
what a premium he placed on meaningful subject matter as an
impetus to solid poetry. Such emphasis is revealed, too, in a 1943
letter, where he renounced his early poetry as "innocent" and there-
fore lyric. "A lyric form and a lyric approach will do even less good
than a journalese approach to the subjects we have to discuss now,"
he insisted.[24] Certainly his writings at Oxford and during his first
year in the army continued the smooth style of his earlier work; if
anything the poems of that period further refine the Audenesque
clarity of the previous writing. However, despite their undoubted
technical refinement, one finds among them few really exciting
pieces. With the exception of "Russians," "To Curse Her," "Time
Eating," and "Simplify Me When I'm Dead," there is surprisingly
little of interest there, and these exceptions suggest the preemin-
ence—for Keith Douglas, at least—of the significant subject in
leading to the significant poem.

The exceptional poems indicate the weaknesses Douglas needed
to overcome if he was to grow as a poet in the total sense he valued
so highly. "Russians," which was inspired by a Russian regiment
reported to have been frozen in Finland, is refreshingly concrete in
the context of most of the other poems he was writing at this time.
He grounded the poem in the scene of ice, wind, and dead soldiers'
meaningless gestures, he played on the ironies of their fate, and,
after whimsically trying on various ways of considering the frozen
Russians, he concluded, "Well, / at least don't think about what
happens when it thaws." Whatever its shortcomings, such a poem
improves greatly on the vague complaining or semiphilosophizing
of much of his other early writing.

Similarly, "To Curse Her," compared with Douglas's many other
love poems, combines rhetorical strength and imagistic sharpness
to suggest the disappointed lover's frustration and anger. In the
first of three stanzas he states the paradox of handsomeness and
falseness presented by his girlfriend. "I could cover / that face with
praise till I've stretched over / a figurative mask of words / for its

beauty," he tells her, as he ends the stanza by calling for a truce. However, having honored her beauty, he perhaps feels dissatisfied at having neglected her deceitful side, for he proceeds to search, in the second stanza, for the appropriate classical comparisons by relating her voice to that of the sirens and her hair to Cressida's, and in the third stanza to despair of "doing justice" to her "perfidy." In a final outburst of pain he can only wish her "Cressida's ruin and decay / known for a strumpet, diseased and outcast." These last lines convey powerfully not only his frustrated sense of betrayal and his feeling of inadequacy in expressing that sense, but his attachment to her even after the betrayal. His greater ease in describing her beauty than her deceitfulness signals to us—and probably to him, too—the hold she continues to have over him. In the tradition of love poetry to which Douglas is relating—in the hands of a Donne or a Marvell—such a conclusion might appear comic or even self-mocking. Here, though, the feeling is more one of pure pain, which may be one reason that Douglas made no attempt to publish this poem while placing in print much less powerful and more conventional love poems at about the same time.

"Russians" and "To Curse Her," whatever their flaws, nevertheless avoid the blandness plaguing much of Douglas's early writing, a blandness perhaps due to the desire to emulate W. H. Auden. No doubt Audenesque clarity without the substance of the early Auden resulted in much dead writing by young poets throughout the 1930s and 1940s. However chary Douglas later became of taking on the role of Owen or Sassoon, the ghost of Auden seems to have been the one he really needed to exorcise.

"Time Eating" and "Simplify me when I'm dead," both written shortly before his departure for the Middle East, mark a decided advance toward such exorcism. Throughout his late teens we can see Douglas straining for a credibly metaphysical dimension in his writing. "Time Eating" represents one of his strongest efforts up to that time at nailing down such a dimension and at sustaining the central metaphor needed to depict it. An elaborate, Latinate exploration of "Ravenous Time"—with its "ruminative tongue," "volatile huge intestine," and "catholic belly"—fill the first three quarters of the poem. In the fourth the poet suddenly reveals his situation—that of the recently abandoned lover—and connects it with the poem's conceit by noting that while time can remake such things as the lizard's tail and the snakeskin, his love is unique and

cannot be remade. "That you gobbled in / Too quick," he tells
time. By itself this complaint might smack merely of the self-pity
characterizing most other Douglas poems concerned with love. In-
stead, his long delay in even mentioning love or his personal plight,
and the ornateness by which the controlling metaphor is developed,
make the poem singularly interesting, its speaker an object of some
admiration, and his dilemma, once it is revealed, convincing and
serious for the reader.

As for "Simplify me when I'm dead"—perhaps the last poem
Douglas wrote before leaving England for Egypt, and one of his
most celebrated—it marks the beginning of his truly mature phase
as a writer. There, in addition to the clarity and prosodic exactness
found in much earlier poems, the balance, the contour, and the
unstrained metaphysical element toward which he had been working
since his school poems all come together in a moving and eloquent
statement of values. Literally the poem represents its speaker's re-
quest that after his death he be reduced to the essentials of his
character so that they can be judged objectively. The poem displays
a concern with death that is related to Douglas's expectation ex-
pressed in many of his war poems, and in conversations with friends
at numerous times, that he would die in battle. This poem surely
relates, too, to what Vernon Scannell has described as "[the] par-
adoxical view of time as thief and donor, the sense of a man carrying
his death within him"[25]—a sense that runs throughout Douglas's
poetry but seems to have been compounded by the war—for it is
punctuated by references to processes and causal developments hav-
ing the potential both to detract and to add. Douglas asks his
survivors to "remember" him by forgetting particulars ("incidents,"
he terms them) and concentrating on the ultimate question: whether
he deserves "mention or charitable oblivion." Time is viewed not
only as the medium of death and decay, but, almost happily, as the
only means by which his request can be fulfilled, since "Time's
wrong-way telescope" invariably reduces and simplifies. What he
is basically asking, then, is that his friends, or whoever cares about
him, wait long enough for time to do its job on them.

The eloquence of the poem stems from its own simplicity and
dignity. After opening with the simply stated request, "Remember
me when I am dead / and simplify me when I'm dead," he compares
such simplifying to the "processes of earth" that permit a "learned"
appraisal of the skeleton, and then argues the advantages of such

"distance" over "momentary spleen / or love" for an equally intelligent appraisal of character. The correspondence of the poem's three-line stanzas to its major syntactical divisions, the relationship of its rhyme schemes (*a/b/a a/b/a*) to the six-liners of which Douglas was so fond, the subdued quality of the poem's metaphors, and the quiet repetition of the opening lines at the end—all suggest not only the poet's control of his poem but the speaker's control of his situation, his understanding of what he wants and why. Likewise the Yeatsian images Douglas allows himself in describing the stripping processes of nature—which "leave me simpler than at birth, / when hairless I came howling in / as the moon came in the cold sky"—show powers of wit and irony, as well as considerable self-awareness.

In general, the later poems exhibit a strengthening of the skills combined in "Simplify me when I'm dead." While Douglas could still lapse into some of the faults of his earlier writing, even in the inferior poems of his final two years he showed a sense of how things ought to be. If particular poems failed, they generally came off as unsuccessful, rather than confused, as before. The poetry of Douglas's overseas service seems increasingly concrete and focused even as it achieves a metaphysical quality.

Two closely related poems—in fact, one is derived from the other—illustrate what Douglas was up to at this time. Written while he was hospitalized in Palestine in late 1941, both "Adams" and "The Sea Bird" begin with the speaker's discovery of two birds, one dead and the other alive, in the cliffs along the Mediterranean. In the first version the speaker's wonder at the spectacle of the live bird in flight—"electric, brilliant blue / beneath he is orange, like flame— / ... / incendiary in tint"—leads to a comparison of the bird with an acquaintance named Adams. Moving through a brief catalog of ways in which Adams resembles the bird—in alertness, in appearance, in the ability to command homage—the speaker begins recalling, with increasing intensity, a particular instance of those qualities in Adams working on him, to the point where "he sucked up, utterly drained / the colour of my sea" and where Adams now threatens to destroy for him any present reality he can call his own so that he prefers to identify with the dead bird if only the specter of Adams will leave him alone. A fanciful and seemingly happy analogy thus turns into a nightmarish discovery, which threatens to obliterate his sense of his own personality.

Despite the interest and emotional impact of "Adams," Douglas showed in "The Sea Bird" that he could make a perhaps more interesting and certainly better-integrated poem from the same foundation. Retaining the first five stanzas but for a few changes that remove unnecessary ambiguities from the earlier version, he this time has his speaker concentrate wholly on the live bird and on the way by which it momentarily threatens to absorb the seemingly objective reality around the speaker. Such a threat continues "till [the bird] escapes the eye, or is a ghost / and in a moment has come down / crept into the dead bird, / ceased to exist." These last lines, raising the whole issue of what it means to exist, only compound the speaker's growing wonder at the trickiness of physical and mental vision. Clearly a tighter poem—Douglas added to the original five stanzas fewer than half the lines he had added in "Adams"—"The Sea Bird" suggests our proneness to be tricked not only by what is clearly past or distant, or by that which intends to absorb us, but by what we assume to be' present or near, or which has no such intention. In this we find a much more complex and troubling speculation on the nature of time and change that had fascinated Keith Douglas as a schoolboy.

Other paired poems of this period—such as "These grasses, ancient enemies" and "Syria," the two pieces titled "The Offensive," and "Tel Aviv" and "Jerusalem"—evidence an equal power of reconstruction. Two other poems written during Douglas's Palestinian hospitalization especially suggest how far his talent had come. Desmond Graham sees a definite relationship between "Negative Information" and "The Hand" in that the second deals from the perspective of intellect with the same situation that the first treats from that of the imagination.[26] The use of tracks in the sand as an image in both poems certainly supports this notion. In "Negative Information" such tracks—like all "curious indentations" the mind receives in its constant hunger for patterns, like the "fantastic moon" the speaker recalls entrancing his judgment one night, and like the many deaths he has heard of in the war—are emblematic of all the misleading data, negative and positive, with which life presents us. "To this, there's no sum I can find," he concludes:

> the hungry omens of calamity
> mixed with good signs, and all received with levity,
> or indifference, by the amazed mind.

Such amazement at so much misleading, or enigmatically inconsistent, impressions gives way in "The Hand" to bemusement at our obsessive searching for pattern and meaning, which Douglas terms "proportion," in each other's behavior. The poem's controlling metaphor is suggested in its title: the hand is discussed first as an emblem of balance and symmetry, and then as a means for internalizing the outside world, and for "drilling the mind, still a recruit, / for the active expeditions of his duty / when he must navigate alone the wild / cosmos." As in the other poem, military experience here furnishes Douglas with telling examples and metaphors. This one ends, though, with a rather abrupt shift to the viewpoint of those outside the particular mind that has been so drilled, to those others who watch his "tracks" and "look for the proportions, the form of an immense hand." Because such searching, which has a metaphysical dimension beyond the physical and social ones, proceeds on the dubious assumption that the hand's proportion is, in fact, analogous to the mind's or can be assimilated intellectually, the poem ends in noting the futility and illogic of such a search. Aware of such illogic, the speaker seems neverthelesss stymied at being unable to suggest an alternative way of proceeding.

These poems show Douglas at the most refined and controlled stage of his unfortunately brief writing career. His zest for writing and his sense of the kind of poetry he wanted to write seem to have been reinforced by his contact with the rather impressive colony of British writers-in-exile based in Alexandria during the war. While such contact can only have been sporadic, and while Douglas may have remained standoffish much of the time, the acquaintance of such poets as Lawrence Durrell, Bernard Spencer, Olivia Manning, and Terence Tiller cannot have harmed his literary or his social sensibilities. Certainly he must have impressed them in his writing and in his manner, as Olivia Manning could write in 1943 that "Among the younger men whom the army has brought out here, Keith Douglas stands alone.... [H]e is the only poet who has written poems comparable with the works of the better poets of the last war,"[27] and Durrell reputedly modeled the character Johnny Keats in *The Alexandria Quartet* on Douglas.[28]

Probably the chief reason for Douglas's distance from the English literati in Egypt concerned his preoccupation with soldiering. Most of the writers he met in Alexandria were either civilians or soldiers longing for contact with the civilian life they missed. Douglas,

however, seems to have been forever aware of the proximity of the
battlefield, a proximity that tended more to attract and fascinate
than to alarm him. Not long after his arrival in Egypt he began to
write of the Middle East, and especially Egypt, as a region of almost
incredible variety and contrasts. What many other British writers
who had landed there found disgusting or uncomfortably foreign
Douglas seems to have assimilated quickly as exotic and exciting
material for reflection and for poetry.

Several poems written in the summer of 1942 capture this ex-
citement. Pieces such as "Devils," "Christodoulos," and "Behavior
of Fish in an Egyptian Tea Garden" revel in the mix of beauty and
filth, aspiration and degradation, and joy and suffering character-
izing that part of the world. To Douglas the North African campaign
can have meant only the grafting of further paradox onto an already
heavily paradoxical mode of existence.

One of his strongest poems, "Cairo Jag," confirms this view. Its
first two sections represent but another Douglas look at the two
worlds of the city, that of exotic romance and that of unspeakable
filth. Both of these Cairo can subsume. But what it cannot subsume,
what shocks even the most hardened Egyptian imagination, is the
genuinely "new world" not far from the city, a world where:

> the vegetation is of iron
> dead tanks, gun barrels split like celery
> the metal brambles have no flowers or berries
> and there are all sorts of manure, you can imagine
> the dead themselves, their boots, clothes and possessions
> clinging to the ground, a man with no head
> has a packet of chocolate and a souvenir of Tripoli.

Such a world's only vegetation is inorganic, its only life lifeless, its
only thought unconscious.

"Cairo Jag" reflects the singular view of warfare for which Doug-
las's war poems have been praised. One critic applauds his refusal
to write propagandist war poetry or to deal in pity or sentimen-
tality.[29] Ted Hughes sees Douglas using war as a means of denying
that truth is necessarily beauty and of asserting that "the truth of
a man is the doomed man in him or his dead body."[30] And Roy
Fuller notes the absence of the "civilian element" in Douglas: "The
reluctant draftee, the actual or potential *paterfamilias,* the essential

pacifist with views at some point along the red end of the spectrum—such attitudes are not to be found in Douglas."[31]

Nowhere is this apolitical and amoral viewpoint more evident than in Douglas's episodic combat narrative, *Alamein to Zem Zem*. There, after acknowledging that the rich and powerful cause wars, he refuses to recognize any injustice in this, but instead insists:

It is exciting and amazing to see thousands of men, very few of whom have much idea why they are fighting, all enduring hardships, living in an unnatural, dangerous but not wholly terrible world, having to kill and to be killed, and yet at intervals moved by a feeling of comradeship with the men who kill them and whom they kill because they are enduring and experiencing the same thing.[32]

This insistence upon a glorious comradeship transcending national considerations is echoed in his frequent accounts of fraternizing with "the enemy." Careful not to allow patriotism to interfere with his "pure" image of soldiery, he insists on the distinction between the ordinary German soldiers ("decent fighting men," he terms them) and their leaders ("thugs and perverts"), and on the soldiers' ignorance of Nazi atrocities.[33] Yet he refuses to comment on the morality of the Allied cause. His fixation upon the military experience per se comes out, too, in his often lengthy and detailed descriptions of dead soldiers, which reflect more curiosity and fascination with rendering the details of corpses' expressions and postures than pity for the dead men.

Nevertheless, sometime in late 1942 he had begun to develop in his poetry a decidedly critical stance toward the war, which in its final stages intensified to a horror bearing comparison with that expressed by the celebrated poets of World War I. While determination, and occasional zest, to do battle remained an element in his writing, such attitudes were increasingly challenged by a more skeptical, less warlike posture. Some poems ("Dead Men," "The Trumpet," "Gallantry," "Sportsmen") display a fascinating mixture of the two viewpoints. Others, such as "Enfidaville" and "Mersa," turn on the pointless destruction of civilian existence brought about by the war.

In only a few instances, though, does Douglas project the logical conclusion to such questioning of war, which is a sense of personal guilt for his involvement in it, and these came relatively late. One of them is perhaps his best-known poem, "Vergissmeinnicht," where a British soldier finds and reflects on the body of a German three weeks dead. Specifically, he notices beside the corpse an inscribed photo of the dead soldier's girlfriend and reflects on the ironic combination of lover and warrior contained in the body. More explicit in the matter of personal responsibility is the sequence of three lyrics titled "Landscape with Figures," which gradually moves in on corpses contained in a group of tanks destroyed in battle, and on the hellish state of mind experienced by the speaker-observer.

Douglas's most intense expression of personal guilt, though, and one of his strongest antiwar statements come together in "How to Kill." Originally titled "The Sniper," it eerily outlines the steps and sensations involved in shooting an unsuspecting enemy soldier. Douglas tells of sighting the intended victim, of observing that "He smiles and moves about in ways / his mother knows," and instantly making "a man of dust / of a man of flesh." This rapid diffusion of the "centre.... and waves of love" into "vacancy" amuses the speaker, as he observes, "How easy it is to make a ghost." Then, in a final stanza, he compares the combination of subtlety and sudden totality of such killing to "The Weightless mosquito touch[ing] her tiny shadow on the stone."

Analyzing what he has done and objectifying it through metaphors appear nothing new for the speaker; one senses that behind this poem are numerous attempts at understanding the chore of killing to which he has been frequently, and routinely, obligated. However, while the coolness of his analysis contributes to our horror at the event—a horror in part directed against its agent, who readily admits "This sorcery I do"—it relates, too, to his judgment that he is "damned" for his deeds and to the residual sympathy for his victim that lies behind such judgment. A sort of numbness seems to have set in, so that he no longer speaks of where he is, say, in "hell," as in "Landscape with Figures 3," but only *what* he is, "damned," which seems to us—and to him—a much more profound matter. Such self-indictment, because it condemns him as irredeemable, permits him to subject his deed and its consequences to such seemingly cold-hearted dissection.

These later war poems are remarkable not only for their indisputable technical virtuosity, but for the deep feelings they reflect, feelings rather distant from Douglas's earlier attitude toward soldiery. His regiment left North Africa for England in November

1943, to prepare for participation in the Normandy invasion. Two of his very last poems, "Actors waiting in the wings of Europe" and "On a Return from Egypt," refer to his uncertainty in further soldiering. Relatedly, the four fragments of the final book of poems he was projecting, to be titled *Bête Noir,* suggest a return to the deeply personal level of his prewar writing, though also an advance beyond its vagueness.

Thus the neutral and sometimes enthusiastic anticipation of battle seems to have left Keith Douglas, or at least his poetry. In this the great poetic subject for which he had waited at Oxford ultimately failed him. But his ongoing search for a more satisfying technique, and for his real subject, resulted in several magnificent poems and in a model of dedication for all who would write poetry in an age of war.

Alun Lewis

Unlike Keith Douglas, Alun Lewis, a Welshman also killed in 1944, exhibited little sense of a coherent or developing literary career. Where Douglas's writing suggests a talent that had matured and, to judge by the tantalizing *Bête Noir* fragments, would probably have grown even more, Lewis's output was erratic and uneven in quality. He wrote some poems of genuine distinction, though fewer than Douglas, but they are scattered throughout his canon, they exhibit little evolution, and his final writing represents no guarantee that he would have continued to write excellent poems had he survived the war.

Nearly five years older, Lewis seems to have exhibited little of Douglas's adolescent precocity as a poet, though he, too, showed academic brilliance. Where Douglas was the only child of a family line that had known better times and even aristocratic connections and that had fallen recently, Lewis's family consisted of generations of coal miners in southern Wales, with his schoolmaster father and professor uncle representing a fairly recent attempt to rise above the rather bleak circumstances to which family tradition might have consigned them. By the time Alun Lewis entered the army, at the age of twenty-four, he had not only completed a college degree and done a year's graduate work in London, but had gained a teaching certificate and taught a year in the village of Pengam. Roughly a year after joining the army Lewis married Gweno Ellis, whom he had met while at Pengam, and he spent over two years in the army in England before being sent overseas to India and Burma. A most reluctant volunteer—he seems to have been a pacifist until the war's beginning—and hardly an enthusiast for military life, Lewis persisted in the complex of civilian values and outlooks that, as has been noted, the more adventurous and less settled Douglas had managed mostly to avoid.

In this regard the respective identifications of the two soldier-poets are revealing. Douglas tended to view himself as an unworthy successor to Owen, Rosenberg, and Sassoon, the terrifying poets of the earlier war. Lewis, however, preferred to identify with a quite different sort of poet who had died in World War I, Edward Thomas. Not really a Georgian and certainly not a militarist, Thomas had brought to the writing of poetry, and to his writing of poems during wartime, a peculiar sensibility and longing that make it difficult to relate him to other poets of the Great War, and that perhaps account for his singular and lasting reputation. At any rate Lewis adopted the quiet, restive Thomas as a model and persisted in this identification. Lewis's best-known lyric, "All Day it has Rained," turns on an overt reference to this connection, for after developing, in a characteristic catalog of realistic details and in irregularly measured and rhymed lines, the boredom of a company of isolated soldiers in the English countryside on a wet, dull day, Lewis recalls with affection some children he had watched when he had visited the town "where Edward Thomas brooded long / On death and beauty—till a bullet stopped his song." This abrupt conclusion to his line of memory and association and to his poem marks Lewis's return to the ominous reality of war framing the nonchalant talk of the camp and the men's preoccupation with the dull weather.

The issue of his identification with Thomas fully occupies another, longer poem, "To Edward Thomas," where Lewis recalls again the older poet's home environment and his puzzling over the paradox of the seemingly quiescent Thomas who had agonized so much. After describing in detail the natural setting which at times had pacified Thomas and which, he felt, could inspire him as well— "for that moment Life appeared / As gentle as the view I gazed upon"—Lewis recounts his later meditating on Thomas's frustrations and weariness as a poet. His conclusion is that Thomas had been called by a "voice" stronger than nature, that had grown clearer ("More urgent as all else dissolved away") and that he had "possessed" fully at the time of his death. The riddle of Thomas's ambivalence and suffering Lewis here adopts as his own, as he chooses to believe that in the end Thomas had found the peace he had long been seeking.

Lewis's affinity to Edward Thomas suggests an aspect of his central style in which he differed markedly from Keith Douglas, namely his penchant for realism. From the beginning of his writing Lewis worked to establish solidity through the massing of realistic details. In this he early achieved an objective Douglas moved toward only gradually, and never completely, and he looked to a poetic type predating that of the Auden group's writing, which frequently tended toward romantic generality. The earlier Lewis poems, of course, were rooted in his Welsh homeland. They frequently offer explicit geographic reference in such titles as "The Rhondda" and "The Mountain Over Aberdare," and feature such clusters of locale as "Hum of shaft-wheel, whirr and clamour / Of steel hammers overbeat, din down / Water-hag's slander" ("The Rhondda"), or "Massive above the dismantled pitshaft / The eight-arched viaduct clamps the sky with stone. / Across the high-flung bridge a goods train rumbles" ("Destruction").

Such cataloging functions throughout Lewis's writing, especially in poems he wrote in India and Burma, and constitutes a key element in most of his stories. He depicted the squalor of an Indian village by noting "the long-nosed swine and the vultures / Groping the refuse for carrion, / And the burial cairns on the hill with its spout of dust" ("Karanje Village") and established the despair of hospitalized soldiers through a panorama of what they could see from their beds:

> Soft shadows warm those bones of rock,
> And the barefooted peasants winding back,
> Sad withered loins in hanging dirty folds,
> Mute sweepings from the disappointed streets,
> Old shrunken tribes the starving dusk enfolds.
> The wind sweeps up the rifle range and blows
> The Parsis' long white robes, there where they go
> Under the wheeling kites, bearing a corpse
> To the high tower that the vultures know.
>
> ("In Hospital: Poona (2)")

Realism and surrealism combine, as the view from the hospital reflects the viewers' feelings.

This insistent tie to locale relates to a tendency toward overt ideology in much of Lewis's writing. While few of his poems are formally didactic, most evidence fairly clear ideological commitments; and although—or perhaps because—his poetry really never aspires to the philosophical profundity of Douglas's, its ideology tends to be more explicit. In Alun Lewis's poems social realism, not surprisingly, is linked to social protest. His working-class origins, as well as his growing up in a time of almost unrelieved economic depression in Wales, probably dictated that he would respond to life with a keen eye toward social conditions, and with some anger toward their alleged perpetrators and much pity for their victims. In "The Rhondda" he moves through the life of that Welsh city's industrial classes in unrelievedly negative terms, remarking finally how "the fat flabby-breasted wives ... scrub, make tea, peel the potatoes / Without counting the days." The monotony and quiet despair of such people's lives occupy his attention in several other poems and, in at least one, "Destruction," subverts the ostensible purpose of the poem. There the speaker contrasts the city's grimness with his girlfriend's romantic outlook in such a way that his meditation becomes fragmented between his feelings for the girl and his social rebelliousness. Although Lewis may have intended such a fragmented character as his subject, it appears more likely that he allowed his own preoccupation with social conditions to capture the poem from an initially romantic intent.

Certainly he found it difficult not to reflect with pity on the common individual or his problems. In contrast with the often coolly detached Douglas, Lewis could never view a situation except in terms of what it meant for particular persons affected by it. This predisposition toward empathy frames all of his war poems, including those composed in the East, and largely accounts for the greater sense of individual characterization in his poetry than in Douglas's. Where in a typical Douglas poem, when the speaker is not concerned solely with his own problems, other people are rendered in distant groups or very impersonally, Lewis is much more prone to develop the *other* people in his poems as distinct characters possessing concrete feelings.

Of course, Douglas's attitude permitted him the wit and irony Lewis never achieved, qualities often needed in Lewis's writing. And certain Douglas's poems equal Lewis's in characterization. However, Lewis to a much greater extent depicts war, for example, certainly not as a glorious adventure, and not even as a chamber of horrors, but as a tiresome intrusion into the commonplace pleasures and pursuits that make up most people's lives. Almost all of his war poems in some manner deal with regret at having to forgo the rooted existence of home, family, and love. The proneness of his poems to dwell on feelings of separation and loss, at various stages in the military career, contrasts curiously with the general absence of such feelings in Douglas's writings. In this there is none of the "officer" or even aristocratic mentality often ascribed to Douglas, but rather a democratic or at least equalitarian view of persons affected by the war.

While many poems illustrate these tendencies, in only a relatively few did Lewis manage to maximize his strengths as a writer while minimizing his weaknesses. Two such poems, "Dawn on the East Coast" and "After Dunkirk," depict the sensibility of the civilian in military uniform, and both utilize realistic detail. The first is more typically Lewis, however, in that it is fairly short and concentrates on a particular incident. Lewis frames his description of this incident, the death of a soldier in a storm, with a brief panorama of the Suffolk coastal region. "From Orford Ness to Shingle Street / The grey disturbance spreads / Washing the icy seas on Deben Head," he begins, as he quickly notes the storm's arrival in the countryside and shifts his attention to a "soldier leaning on the sandbagged wall,"—with his "single self-centred monotonous wish" to see "[a] girl laying his table with a white cloth"—and to his sudden drowning, which snuffs out his wish: "Two carbons touching in his brain / Crumple the cellophane lanterns of his dream." The careful play between exterior and interior produces a movingly understated account of the young man's death.

"After Dunkirk" constitutes a more ambitious effort. Again Lewis combines realistic detail and surrealistic phrasing, and again the poem's emotional impact turns on the force of civilian memory, almost a constant in Lewis's writing. Here the speaker-protagonist describes the development of other soldier-civilians' view of the war and of warfare in such a way as to suggest what his experience and reflection have taught him. Reputedly inspired by Dunkirk survivors Lewis actually met during his own training,[34] the poem begins with the speaker's remark that after a lifetime of silence and inward weeping, he now wishes to speak. What compels this "confession" is a faith that has been sorely tested by war's progress against the soul, by politicians' oversimplifications, by propaganda ("Rumours of rape in crumbling towns"), and by the whole mythos of warfare leading to "Despair of man that nurtures self-contempt / And makes men toss their careless lives away.... " Such faith has been worn, too, by camp life, which Lewis portrays in a vivid catalog and finally terms "The difficult tolerance of all that is / Mere rigid brute routine," which makes one "Less home-sick, fearful, proud, / But less a man." Then comes what Lewis terms the "test of self," whether any residue of that germinal faith can survive the brainwashing of military life. Apparently the Dunkirk returnees convinced Lewis that they—and he—would have "new resolution ... to live again." The key to such resolution is the renewed remembrance of those they have loved, "When the worn and beautiful faces of the half-forgotten / Came softly round them ... making complete all that was misbegotten / Or clumsily abused or left neglected." Ironically the soldier's problem becomes his solution, as a resurgence of home-sickness, an ultimately resistant civilian mentality, makes the men, at least from Lewis's viewpoint, stronger soldiers. He closes with a sense of the battle's survivors—and himself—coming out of the near-despair that had threatened their basic humanness.

"In Hospital: Poona (2)," written after Lewis had been in the East for some time, is an even more personal poem, but one that also owes its positive conclusion to loving remembrance. Technically it is especially notable in that, while rarely is rhyme anything but a clumsy device in Lewis's hands, here it works quite comfortably. He recalls lying awake at night in his hospital bed, waiting until his lover back in England likewise would be "furled ... in the same dark watch" and "the whole of Wales / Glided within the parish of my care." His unfolding memories included Cardigan Bay, the great mountains of Wales, and the mining valley where his beloved lies. With daybreak, when "ten thousand miles of daylight grew / Between us," he realizes that "Time upon the heart can break / But love survives the venom of the snake."

One of his most moving pieces, a narrative titled "Burma Casualty," was written at about the same time. It concerns the ulti-mately successful struggle against despair of a young soldier who has lost his leg. The first of its four stanzas tells of his meeting Japanese snipers in the jungle, of how "a cough of bullets, a dusty cough / Filleted all his thigh from knee to groin," and of how he refused to die, despite the "great velour cloaks of darkness" threatening him. Next Lewis tells of the temptation presented by that darkness, "how it played the enchantress in a grain / Of morphia ... and offered to release / The Beast that breathed with pain and ran with pus / Among the jumping fibres of the flesh." Stanza three describes the soldier's terror not of amputation itself, but of the prospect of being more profoundly tempted (he says) by the darkness. As he falls under the anesthetic, Lewis typically remarks that "His wife's ... timeless love stooped down to raise him up," while he returns from sleep "Retching and blind with pain, and yet Alive."

"Burma Casualty" is rather noteworthy for this stage of Lewis's military career, since by the time he wrote it he was not always so prone to value life over death or to treat death's attractions as so illusory. In fact, his Indian poems generally exhibit a rather steady decline in his allegiance to the modern Western valuing of life above all and an increasing affinity with the Eastern embrace of all experience, including death. This rejection of purely Western culture was foreshadowed in "The Crucifixion," a poem Lewis had written before coming to the East, in which—looking forward to such later poems as Stevie Smith's "Was He Married?," Kingsley Amis's "New Approach Needed," and even Lawrence Ferlinghetti's "Christ Climbed Down"—Lewis attacked an object of veneration, the asceticized Jesus. And, while the strain of social protest in many of his Welsh poems as well as later ones such as "Sacco Writes to His Son" suggests a measure of Western idealism, it betrays also an embittered doubt in the efficacy of Western institutions to realize the ideal of justice behind them.

Lewis's fascination with India seems to have equaled Keith Douglas's with Egypt. He wrote to his wife of a journey through the Indian countryside as "a colossal experience ... My mind stayed in its proper place, my imagination was content to watch the Marco Polo wonders of ordinary life."[35] His poetic description of an Indian mountain range reflects this same wonder at the variety and surprise of the landscape:

> The valleys crack and burn, the exhausted plains
> Sink their black teeth into the horny veins
> Straggling the hills' red thighs ...
> High on the ghat the new turned soil is red,

The sun has ground it to the finest red,
It lies like gold within each horny hand.
("The Mahratta Ghats")

In other poems he contrasts the viewpoint or situation of the West-
erner with that of the Indian or Burmese native, to the detriment
of the former. One such poem, "Midnight in India," begins with
the observation that "Here is no mined and cratered deep / As in
the fenced-off landscapes of the West." This sense of a radical dif-
ference between East and West permeates those poems, explicitly
contrasting the manners of peasants with those of soldiers. In "The
River Temple: Wai" Lewis begins with an elaborate setting in which
to place "the bald old priest with wizened loins" and "the woman
in the blue frayed sari" pursuing their normal activities, moves on
to describe, ironically, the soldier "squatting like a peasant"—
caught in a foreign climate and forced to dream of the English
countryside for relief from the heat—and concludes that, unlike the
peasants with their certainties, the English intruder "[m]ust seek
beyond religion's gloom / The love the violent do not know, / Com-
passion of the womb." In "The Peasants" he also notes how "soldiers
straggle by" native farmers following the rounds of their primitive
agriculture. "History staggers in their wake," he comments: "The
peasants watch them die." The epigrammatic wit of Lewis's pano-
ramic observer becomes the sympathetically rendered sorrow of a
lyric speaker in the ironically titled "Home Thoughts from Abroad,"
who feels cut off from the West as he stands in a "breathless Indian
night," yet subject to "blue nostalgic moods" which prevent his
accepting the East.

The ambivalence of such poems, or at least Lewis's attraction to
the Eastern mentality, becomes more pronounced in his reactions
to Eastern religion, particularly as represented in the Hindu god
Vishnu. In "Karanje Village," after the catalog of oppressive details
and images of death cited earlier, Lewis shifts his attention to a
"little Vishnu of stone, / Silently and eternally simply Being, /
Bidding me come alone.... " In terms reminiscent of Yeats he
remarks how the god seems not to turn him away but to warn him
of "the flesh / That catches and limes the singing birds of the soul /
And holds their wings in mesh." Relatedly he makes his speaker
of another lyric ("Peasant Song") a peasant singing a prayer, ex-
pressing a mystical sense of union with the earth. However con-

descending such a portrayal of the peasant mind-state may appear, it squares with what Lewis wanted to believe about the East and what he increasingly wanted to appropriate for himself. In a letter to his wife recalling villagers' prayers he had heard, he commented, "[I]t seems that in that rhythm and clangour and steady chant, here was a rhythm of many universes and real truths."[36]

The "real truth" of death is one that Lewis from his experience of India felt especially compelled to appropriate and one that the Eastern mentality as he conceived it seemed especially able to handle. He explained to his wife: "Death is the great mystery, who can ignore him? But I don't *seek* him. Oh no—only I would like to 'place' him."[37]

Such an attitude surely prepared him to write "The Jungle," where he sympathetically presented the British soldier's wish for repose, even death, amid the lush tropical climate. Composed probably about the same time as "Burma Casualty," this impressive lyric is Lewis's version of "The Lotus-Eaters," but one wholly lacking in Tennysonian irony. Certainly it begins with a rendering of setting not unworthy of Tennyson:

> In mole-blue indolence the sun
> Plays idly on the stagnant pool
> In whose grey bed black swollen leaf
> Holds Autumn rotting like an unfrocked priest.

In the first part of the poem the collective speaker tells of coming to the jungle "[t]o quench more than our thirst—our selves." In the second part memory takes over, as the soldiers' origins ("[t]he sidestreets of anxiety and want") and the earlier build-up for war are recalled. "But we who dream beside this jungle pool," the speaker explains, "Prefer the instinctive rightness of the poised / Pied king-fisher deep darting for a fish / To all the banal rectitude of states, / The dew-bright diamonds on a viper's back / To the slow poison of a meaning lost / And the vituperations of the just."

For all their sense of weariness and abandoned causes, however, yielding to the jungle proves a difficult matter, as the poem's final two sections reflect the soldiers' inability to blend into their new setting. "Grey monkeys gibber, ignorant and wise. / We are the ghosts, and they the denizens," the speaker remarks, to suggest an unshakable self-consciousness that will continue to separate him from what he has come to want. The tone shifts from the lush of noonday to the jungle's cold night, as he feels increasingly alien in this "older world / Than any they predicted in the schools," despite his persistent rejection of that more modern world that has sent him there. The result is a painful uncertainty, a sense of displacement, an inability to make that final crossing. This poem reminds one of Alun Lewis's frequently expressed appreciation of E. M. Forster, as the gap between East and West proves impassable, and deeper than conscious desire.

A curious blend of the two cultures likewise marked the decision that sent Lewis back into jungle combat six months before his death, after he had been offered a chance to remain out of the war zone. Like Douglas, he chose to rejoin his unit in combat, despite being offered an instructor's position far behind the lines. Unlike Douglas, however, he broke no regulations in returning to his men, and he did so not out of bravery or particular love of adventure, but rather out of a desire to experience more, possibly death, and out of loyalty to his fellow Welsh soldiers.[38] Writing to his wife of this decision, he spoke of "what is instinctive and categorical in me, the need to experience."[39]

While the artistic potential of Alun Lewis's complex personality was too rarely realized in his poetry, it appears with sufficient clarity in his best poems to earn him a place among the more striking writers of his generation.

Henry Reed

Though he spent only a few months in the British army Henry Reed wrote the most celebrated poem to come out of World War II. Readers and critics have found "Naming of Parts" sharper and more ironically focused than anything by Keith Douglas or Alun Lewis. Despite such celebrity, however, Reed has published no poems besides "Naming of Parts" and the others contained in a single collection, A Map of Verona (1946). A reading of that short book in its entirety reveals a development relatable to those observed in Douglas's and Lewis's writings, and to larger tendencies of British poetry in general during the 1940s.

One of Reed's recent critics, borrowing from Walter De La Mare, has described Reed as an "Ariel-dominated" poet, mostly concerned with the aesthetics and craft of poems rather than their relationship to the life outside them, the domain of writers he terms "Prospero-dominated."[40] Certainly it is difficult to discern in the mere twenty-four poems making up *A Map of Verona* any pervasive ideology such as can be found in the writings of many other poets of the war. And certainly even the least interesting of Reed's pieces combines a delicacy of tone and prosodic caution generally absent from the work of his contemporaries in uniform writing more realistically. However, even Reed's limitations, and the variations in his writing, have ideological implications, and most of his poems betray some concern with the larger reality out of which they originated.

The contents of *A Map of Verona* can be quickly surveyed. The heading, "Preludes," comprises half of the poems. These include: a number of nondescript, vaguely romantic lyrics; a set of poems labeled "Lessons of War," of which "Naming of Parts" is the first; and a first-rate parody of T. S. Eliot titled "Chard Whitlow." Next comes a neoromantic sequence titled "The Desert." The book concludes with three somewhat longer poems based on the Tristram legend, which Reed contained under the title "Tintagel," and two based on classical subjects, "Chrysothemis" and "Philoctetes," the latter being Reed's longest single piece.

Of the dozen Preludes, the three "Lessons of the War" and the parody on Eliot are by far the strongest. The rest languish, to varying degrees, in Audenesque vagueness, as they deal with problems of love or other unspecified worries. While "Lives" may be an exception—since there Reed thoughtfully compares types of personality (the openly wild, the controllable, and the wily) to elements of nature—it improves only to a degree on the others.

The three "Lessons of the War" offer a sharp contrast to the obscurity of the remaining Preludes, as they focus on the instructing of combat troops as filtered through the mind of a young recruit. Though not rhymed and though conversational in tone, Reed's stanzas represent orderly, five-line sections, with the final line frequently operating as a quasi-refrain.

Certainly "Naming of Parts," which enjoyed a revival of attention from American anthologists during the Vietnam War, epitomizes the control, understatedness, and irony of Reed's best writing. Apparently this and the other two "Lessons" stemmed from the imitations of instructors with which Reed entertained his army friends.[41] The first stanza begins straightforwardly, with the instructor's outlining the topics of the course: "To-day we have naming of parts.

Yesterday / We had daily cleaning. And to-morrow morning, / We
shall have what to do after firing." This viewpoint is quickly un-
dermined, however, as the poem turns briefly but significantly to
nearby flowering fruit trees ("Japonica / Glistens like coral in all of
the neighboring gardens ... "). Although the stanza's final line,
"And to-day we have naming of parts," reiterates the poem's initial
focus, a tension has been set up, and it expands in succeeding stanzas
to emphasize increasingly the gap between the lifeless, mechanical
skills of warfare in which the recruit is being instructed, and the
more beautiful, organic processes of nature that he can see all around
him. As the poem progresses, nature occupies larger portions of
each stanza, so that by the end "naming of parts" seems solely an
impediment to the recruit's experiencing the beauty, force, and
legitimacy of nature.

One area in which the trainee is made to feel especially estranged
from natural existence is the erotic, which in "Naming of Parts" is
represented by the bees "assaulting and fumbling" the flowers, but
in "Judging Distances"—the second "Lesson"—becomes explicitly
human. Here Reed develops his poem through a competition of
pressures on the trainee's mind, as time and memory distract him
from an absurd present denying him his past—just as in "Naming
of Parts" it attempted to deny him his place in nature. Here, too,
nature is denied, as the instructor insists on reducing landscape and
life to abstraction. "[M]aps are of time, not place, so far as the
army / Happens to be concerned," he tells his recruits, though by
"time" he means only the perversion of expressing topography in
terms of a clock's face, and though he is wholly unable to tell why
the army need regard things in this way. The basic principle he
lays down is that things only seem to be things, and that field
reports ought to avoid unnecessary commitment to concreteness or
particularity. While sheep may be "safely grazing" in the field, he
warns, "[W]hatever you do, / Don't call the bleeders *sheep.*"

The poem turns on the trainee's attempt to apply such principles,
as repeatedly the poetry of what he observes and of the civilian
viewpoint he has brought to the army intrudes on the antipoetic
method the instructor would enforce. Thus, after observing houses
and a couple lying together under swaying trees, the recruit quickly
adjusts his account to fit the formulas of army reportage, so that
"under some poplars a pair of what appear to be humans / Appear
to be loving." But when he imagines his instructor's objection that

he has failed to record his distance from the human pair, he realizes fully the absurdity of the denial demanded of him, and responds that the lovers appear to have "finished" and that their distance is "about one year and a half" from him. In this he sadly recognizes how much military life has removed him from his own lovemaking and how much it threatens to remove him from any essentially human response. While this poem, like the other, shows the trainee's ultimately resisting such a threat, it suggests nevertheless the basic danger of the mental state into which warfare would fix him.

"Unarmed Combat," the third lesson, might appear the anomaly among them. Indeed, Vernon Scannell has seen here a much more affirmative stance and a much less certain irony than in the other two poems.[42] To be sure, "Unarmed Combat" concludes with the lyric protagonist, again an army trainee, invoking courage and determination and asserting that "we must fight / Not in the hope of winning but rather of keeping something alive":

> so that when we meet our end,
> It may be said that we tackled wherever we could,
> That battle-fit we lived, and though defeated,
> Not without glory fought.

His awareness of this "something" he values so highly and wishes kept alive grows out of listening to his instructor's introduction to the skills of unarmed combat, and from his own interpretation of these remarks in view of his past experience. With an extreme verbal ineptness the instructor begins by assuring the trainees that "In due course of course you will all be issued with / your proper issue," just as later he tells them to "give [the enemy] all you have, and always give them / As good as you get: it will always get you somewhere." The jargonish double-talk of these remarks, and of his reference to the "ever-important question of human balance" and the "ever-important" need for strong initial positioning, combines with a reliance on dubious or at least irrelevant logic—when, by a curious non sequitur, he urges them never to fear to tackle from behind, since "it may not be clean to do so, / But this is global war"—to suggest a character even less reliable than that of the instructors in the other two "lessons." The unwitting allusion to Lear in his concluding observation, that "the readiness is all," thus appears especially ironic.

The second half of the poem, taken up by the trainee's rumination on what he has been told, constitutes a much more profound interpretation of the instructor's comments. Reed's calculated efforts to render the instructor foolish and the more intelligent and thoughtful manner of the listener's response make it unlikely that we should see that response merely as a capitulation to the value system endorsed by the instructor. Rather, the trainee places his own construction on the principal concept and phrases he has heard, to subvert their original meaning.

The key here is the central stanzas, where he reveals his past unhappy relationships to institutions and systems, and to society generally. Having just been told that "you can tie a Jerry / Up without rope," he confesses to always having been the one tied up, to "[having] given them all I had, / Which was never as good as I got, and it got me nowhere," and to having waged global war "from the start." The skepticism of this response feeds his nominal agreement that balance and courage count most, as his balance appears the cautious weighing of ultimate implications, and his courage involves an insistent wariness toward the simplistic formulas handed him by others. "The readiness is all," he repeats after his instructor, but through him it becomes a readiness to maintain an integrated point of view and, even while serving a system such as the military, not to be absorbed by it. He thus anticipates Alan Sillitoe's young hero in *The Loneliness of the Long-Distance Runner*. Without such special readiness, participation in a physical triumph would spell defeat in the unarmed combat for the psyche. In this Reed's final war "lesson" is basically in keeping with the others.

While none of his other poems merit such detailed attention, they confirm the strengths of the "Lessons of the War." Reed's hilarious parody of Eliot, written when the final *Quartets* were coming out, captures the pompousness and air of false profundity into which Eliot risked falling, as it begins:

> As we get older we do not get any younger.
> Seasons return, and to-day I am fifty-five,
> And this time last year I was fifty-four,
> And this time next year I shall be sixty-two.
>   ("Chard Whitlow")

Reed's less distinguished poems further suggest his gravitation toward dramatic characterization, a trend wholly realized in his later career as a distinguished writer of dramas and radio plays. Thus the rather lengthy sequence, "The Desert," though suffering from the weakness of obscure figurative reference, which plagues most of the Preludes, nevertheless points to an interesting progression of sickness, illusion of recovery, and disillusionment, and a semblance of final equilibrium, and it hints at Reed's potential strength in the sustained portrayal of single characters. Likewise the Tintagel poems become increasingly dramatic and concrete, as they move from the distance of narration in "Tristram," through a combination of narration and enclosed statement in individual characters in "Iseult Blaunches-mains" and "King Mark," to a contoured and particularized expression of misery in "Iseult La Belle."

The two poems on classical subjects continue this progression. "Chrysothemus" expresses Agamemnon's surviving daughter's vulnerability and determination through dramatic and poignant images and highly charged rhetoric. And in "Philoctetes" Reed develops an even more complex monologue or soliloquy, reminiscent of Tennyson's "Tithonus" and "Tiresius," as he places the disillusioned suitor of Helen on the isle of Lemnos just as he is about to be rescued after nine years' exile there. "I have changed my mind; or my mind is changed in me," Philoctetes begins, while preparing to meet his rescuers. Before doing so, however, he recalls being abandoned, describes his pain and delirium, and rehearses his decision to rejoin humanity:

> I have lived too long on Lemnos, lonely and desperate,
> Quarrelling with conjured demons, with the ghosts
> Of the men and women with whom I learned to people
> The loneliness and despair....

Reed shows, too, the exile's confusion about his future, particularly his concern for knowing whom to trust after having been by himself so long. The monologue ends with Philoctetes determined but unsure, eager but cautious, and renewed but wary.

The sympathetic power of "Philoctetes" comes from the combination of rhetorical control and dramatic complexity. While we may regret that Reed has written few poems since the publication of *A*

Map of Verona, his decision to shift his attention as a writer appears in retrospect a most logical and plausible outcome of developments evident in his poetry. Clearly he was moving toward something like drama, as his poetry increasingly came to resemble spoken words determined by the specifics of personality, time, and place. In this Reed resembles Keith Douglas and Alun Lewis, as well as many other wartime poets, for he ultimately shows a distrust of the large-scale statement, empty rhetoric, and vague romanticism that had infected English poetry during the thirties and early forties. That Reed's own solution to such a dilemma was unique makes him no less a representative figure.

Chapter Three
The Empiricist Response: Fuller and Larkin

The central tendency in the work of the leading wartime poets was toward concreteness and even fictionality in their verse, and away from the vague idealization that had been fostered, in part, by the early work of Auden and his circle. In this the soldier-poets followed the Auden group themselves, who by the late 1930s had moved toward a poetry largely concerned with particular and personal problems expressed in concrete terms, and away from larger subjects. Relatedly, the prose narrative writings of Keith Douglas and Alun Lewis—specifically *El Amein to Zem Zem* and Lewis's short fiction— and Henry Reed's gravitating to the writing of drama reflect not only these talented poets' versatility, but an uncertainty about the possibilities of poetry in their time, an uncertainty shared by many of their contemporaries and by those slightly younger poets who were to emerge after the war.

A crisis had developed in English poetry, a crisis signaled by the departure of Auden and the breakup of his circle, by the death of Yeats and the absence of any comparably commanding figure to succeed him, and by the controversy surrounding Dylan Thomas and the kinds of imitation his writing had inspired. It is scarcely surprising that the young Philip Larkin, tiring of the Yeatsian poetry he had come to write at Oxford, would turn to novel-writing in the mid-1940s and would develop a (for him) new kind of poetry only out of his frustrations in attempting additional novels and stories—or that his Oxford chums in the so-called Movement of the early 1950s, Kingsley Amis and John Wain, despite their continuing interest in writing poems, would make their marks as novelists. To write honest poetry seems to have been extraordinarily difficult for anyone who had come of age during the waning of Auden's youthful phase. Even Roy Fuller, who had been born early enough to fall under many influences besides Auden's and to publish his first collection in 1939, began to turn out novels after the war's end and has continued to do so while pursuing a prolific career as a poet. Because so little of the poetry from the war and the years immediately afterward inspired the writing of poetry, most young poets seemed determined to write something else. And most of the better poetry appearing in the decade or so after the war reflected a wariness toward ideals and idealization, as well as toward the ambitious forms in which the earlier generation of poets had cast their ideals.

External Factors

Because World War II had been a truly more worldwide struggle than World War I, it was much more difficult for any of the participating nations, except perhaps those of North America, to have a wartime or, for that matter, a postwar experience very different from that of the other participants. The death, the suffering, the destruction, and the ultimate fatigue were much more widespread this time, as there had been not even the pretense of a "gentleman's struggle" or a sporting event about the war, and as technology had increased geometrically the capacity of nations to murder each other. No doubt, too, the opening of the Nazi death camps in mid-1945, as well as the dropping of atomic bombs that summer to conclude the war against Japan, compounded the international numbness that had already set in. If there was exhilaration at this war's end it had little about it of collective optimism; the most that could be hoped for was a respite, or a return to an ordinary if unexciting way of life.

The particular brand of postwar weariness suffered by the British cast their "victor" status in doubt. The claims made on Britain's tenuous material resources by military operations on three fronts, as well as by enemy assaults on the homeland, had been staggering. Of Britain's thirteen million homes nearly a half million were destroyed or rendered uninhabitable, while an additional four million were severely damaged.[1] The British lost half the tonnage of their merchant fleet, which they desperately needed to regain their prewar trade. The business and industrial areas throughout London, Coventry, Birmingham, and other midland cities were extensively damaged. And over 35,000 merchant seamen, 60,000 civilians, and 300,000 military personnel lost their lives.[2] The problem of repairing such physical and psychological damage to the nation was compounded by the disintegration of the British Empire—from the speedy Indian drive toward independence in 1947, through the humiliating retreat from the Suez nine years later, and toward the rapid winning of independence by former colonies throughout Africa, the Far East, and the West Indies during the 1960s.

The resulting loss of political status was accompanied by economic uncertainties. If World War I had proven to be a cultural and psychological watershed for the British, World War II proved to be an economic one, as the probability of never returning to economic preeminence among the nations of Europe became a certainty after 1945. Despite the social revolution brought about by the election of Clement Atlee and the Labourites that year—the first openly socialist government installed in a major democracy—and despite some lessening of austerity by the early 1950s, the recovery continued to be sluggish and uncertain. Just as these conditions forced the average person to attend to the commonplace concerns of life, the British intellectual or artist generally felt obligated to lower his vision to the immediate and the probable, and perhaps to narrow the assumed gap between himself and the rest of the populace. Given the excesses and miscalculations of the prewar years, which might be said to have led to both Auschwitz and the Hiroshima and Nagasaki bombings, the thoughtful person tended to proceed cautiously, to avoid extremes of emotion or reason, and to distrust the problem-solving capacity of either beyond the near-at-hand.

The literary manifestation of such attitudes began to take shape not long after the war's end. Certainly for British poetry that first postwar decade was Janus-like, in that there continued a strong tide of neoromantic writing, perhaps culminating with the cultish fervor accompanying the issuance of Dylan Thomas's *Collected Poems* in 1952 and his death the following year. At the same time, among a spirited if less accessible group of young writers, an equally fervent reaction developed against all that "Dylanism," though not necessarily Thomas's poetry, seemed to represent: the cult of the poetic personality, vagueness of subject and statement, and an esoteric view of the poet's and the poem's place in the world. By the late 1950s this latter contingent had clearly established themselves as a force in modern British literature, as their viewpoint appealed to the empiricist mentality already described.

Besides what they saw as the aesthetic posturing of the neoro-
mantics, and especially the Apocalyptics and their followers, these
newer writers denounced the excesses of modernism, which, they
felt, had led to undue experimentation, coldness, and obscurity in
much contemporary poetry, and had encouraged the artistic irre-
sponsibility of the neoromantics. Rather than an academic exercise,
they insisted, the writer ought to strive to produce an honest por-
trayal of some recognizably human experience or feeling. Instead of
the fanciful flights of metaphor and rhetoric that they ascribed to
much writing of the 1940s, they preferred sharp, clear images,
traditional prosodic forms, and a discourse closer to prose than the
modernists or neoromantics had courted.

Perhaps the most important group among these newer writers
advocating such developments were those who came to be called
"The Movement": D. J. Enright, Philip Larkin, Donald Davie,
Kingsley Amis, John Wain, Elizabeth Jennings, and a few others.
The seminal events determining public awareness of these writers,
and of a possible Movement involving them, included a series of
BBC readings featuring them and other like-minded poets, which
John Lehmann and John Wain hosted in 1952 and early 1953; an
unsigned essay titled "In the Movement" appearing in the *Spectator*
in 1954 and describing the central tendencies of these writers; and
a 1955 anthology, *New Lines,* edited by another sympathetic poet,
Robert Conquest, which brought the work of all of them together
for the first time. Two novels of the period, Wain's *Hurry on Down*
(1953) and Amis's *Lucky Jim* (1954), likewise appealed to the de-
romanticized, empiricist view of life and art, as they proposed com-
monsense approaches to dilemmas regarded as hidden or hopelessly
complicated in more psychological fiction. Similarly, Philip Larkin's
The Less Deceived (1955) proved not only a best-selling poetry col-
lection, but a rallying point for all who held similar attitudes.

Whether these writers constituted a conscious "Movement," as
many people have wished to believe, has produced a lively and
protracted, if largely unenlightening, series of debates among read-
ers, critics, and even the principal figures themselves. Some of the
poets have joked about the Movement as an exclusively journalistic
invention,[3] and it has been claimed, with some pertinent evidence,
that a primary function of the *New Lines* anthology was to "annex
for its participants a pigeon-hole in literary history which was be-
ginning to get over-crowded."[4] However, Donald Davie has wryly

recalled "the way all of us who were supposed to be 'in' it ... ridiculed and deprecated 'the Movement' even as we kept it going,"[5] and, as Blake Morrison has pointed out, evidence of a journalistic hard-sell scarcely means that a basis of group identity was lacking.[6] Whether they meant or even knew it, these writers constituted an at least temporarily concerted literary effort.

Certainly they produced a spirited polemic in defense of the viewpoint to which they all to some extent subscribed. Foremost among such statements were Davie's *Purity of Diction in English Verse* (1952), almost a textbook for writing empiricist poetry; Amis's "Against Romanticism" (1956), the poem that outlined the empiricist wariness of the distant or extreme; and Larkin's *All What Jazz* (1970), a collection of articles on jazz written throughout the 1960s, expressing a fierce distrust of modernism in all of the arts and of the academic coterie attached to it. Such distrust, Larkin tells us, refers to modern art's "irresponsible exploitations of technique in contradiction of human life as we know it,"[7] as he insists on the restoration of respect by the artist for his audience, rather than the condescension or distaste informing so much modernist art.

More recently, John Wain has complained of the puritanical cult of the new, fatally lacking in any concern for tradition. "[Art] has a memory," Wain observes, as in classic empiricist fashion he invokes the Burkean criterion of survival as a key to the good poem or painting.[8] D. J. Enright, in his lively introduction to his *Oxford Anthology of Contemporary Verse 1945–1980* (1980), likewise complains of many current poets' ignorance of—and thus irreverence for—the literary past, and joins Larkin in condemning the difficulty principle behind much modernist-inspired writing: "It was unfortunate that the great modernists of the early part of this century should have promulgated the theory that 'poetry in our civilization ... must be difficult,' for it was bound to find a welcome with those averse to the hard labour entailed in achieving lucidity."[9] Further, he scorns the deforming of English prosody and syntax in much modern verse by remarking that "The thud-thud of unexpectedness conventionalized is no advance on the thud-thud of conventional expectedness—the one bullies where the other lulls or insinuates."[10] In keeping with all of this, Blake Morrison has complained of the modernist emphasis on myth and timelessness, "which muffles the cry of the particular moment, the particular place"—that is, the element in which we mostly live our lives—and he offers a thoughtful rationale for the "minimalist" tendency of much postwar British poetry, including that of the Movement writers.[11]

The most prominent newer fiction and drama of the roughly fifteen years after 1945 reflected the same tendencies noted among these figures of the so-called Movement. For a while, of course, holdovers from before the war—such as Elizabeth Bowen, Graham Greene, Evelyn Waugh, and L. P. Hartley—continued to dominate British fiction. Soon, however, several younger writers began to emerge, all dealing with the credible concerns of fairly commonplace characters and doing so with the tools of traditional realism analogous to the older verse forms embraced by the empiricist poets. Besides those novelists associated with the Movement, we see Angus Wilson, Muriel Spark, and Iris Murdoch first attracting wide readership and critical attention during this time, and sharing the empiricist predilections of the poets already noted. Even the work of the "angry young men" of the fifties and early sixties—John Braine's *Room at the Top* (1957), the novels and stories of Alan Sillitoe, or John Osborne's highly influential *Look Back in Anger* (1956)—though sharing little of the middle-class, university-promulgated values of the others, exhibited the same wariness about wholesale social or political pronouncements. For all of their radical tone, such writers rarely showed more than a dissatisfaction with the status quo as it had evolved since the war; in this they represented merely a vaguely leftist version of disapproval toward the fruits of welfare statism to which Amis, Larkin, and most of the others could come from the slightly right side of the political and cultural spectrum. A dependence upon realistic particularity for effect and a distrust of extravagant rhetoric or myth marked the "angry" writing as much as that of the empiricist authors already described.

Roy Fuller

To discuss the most representative and most outstanding poets responding in the empiricist mode requires a return to World War II, to consider not only the dead soldier-poets whose work reflected a decided thrust toward empiricism, but the one surviving soldier-poet who represents an active link between the empiricism of the postwar decades and its roots in the 1930s. Roy Fuller's position among recent British poets is a singular one, for he began publishing in the late 1920s, was clearly influenced by the Auden generation of the next decade, achieved prominence during the war for his distinctive poetic voice, was sufficiently esteemed by all participants in the postwar empiricist reaction to be called a "father figure of the Movement,"[12] and has continued to write and publish verse into the 1980s—through all of which he has managed to avoid a radical alignment with any of the recognized groups that may have claimed him or to which he may have been consigned. Such is his continuing flexibility that as one prepares to place him into a category, such as empiricism, recent poems come to mind that challenge such absolute categorization. Even so, Fuller's commitments and practices clearly link him to the empiricist strain of British poetry since 1939, if not to the narrower conceptions of that strain.

Of course, Fuller himself experienced a metamorphosis, if a gradual one, over his writing career, particularly during the war years. His early poetry, such as that contained in his first book (*Poems*, 1939), reflected his dependence on Auden, especially in the widespread use of balladic forms and devices, the quasi-allegorical and mythological quality of much of his writing, and the increasingly saddened but vague reflection on the political situation as the war approached. Ironically, Fuller has been quick to disassociate himself from what he terms the "public school communists of the thirties, the Audens and Spenders and Day Lewises": "one looked down one's nose very much at them." "I admired [them] as poets, but I didn't particularly admire them as politicians," he has explained, insisting that his own active political experience, unlike theirs, was entirely nonliterary.[13] The young Roy Fuller's grass-roots communism may have contributed to his advancing beyond Audenesque vagueness, as the Marxist-materialist view of life to which he was early exposed has been seen leading to his later, empiricist outlook.[14]

Whatever the factors producing it, that outlook took hold in his poetry during the war and has remained with him since. Of his prewar poems, only "To My Brother," written very late in the 1930s, confronts a particular human dilemma directly and dramatically, without the quasi-romantic and mythological trappings attending most of the others. As frequently before, Fuller here deals with the tense world situation, but he succeeds in localizing it, first by recounting the details of his room—a pistol, the sounds from the nearby Thames, soot from the chimney, and an edition of Pope given him by his brother, who is evidently in France—and then by moving from this final detail to express his feelings for his

brother's safety during so perilous a time, for the seeming doom of
civilization felt by so many, and for the implications of Alexander
Pope's behavior amid what he had considered barbarous times. Given
Fuller's abstract and mythologizing propensities in his earlier writ-
ing, the poem remains remarkably direct and concrete.

The best pieces in his two wartime volumes, *The Middle of a War*
(1942) and *A Lost Season* (1944)—which won him his first genuine
critical acclaim—carry even more of the personal and the concrete,
the sense of life at its local and therefore limited yet personally
meaningful level. They comprise an objectified account of what
Fuller saw and felt during the war, first as a civilian in England
awaiting the draft and then as a naval radar mechanic sent to Kenya.
The title of "Soliloquy in an Air Raid" helps locate the powerfully
expressed dilemma of one trying desperately to write a poem even
as surrounding events cry out the futility of all artistic activity.
Somewhat later poems like "Royal Naval Air Station" and "The
Middle of a War" establish vividly the dull melancholy of wartime
anxiety away from combat. They do so principally, though not
exclusively, through fastening immediately on the specifics of set-
ting: "The piano, hollow and sentimental, plays, / And outside,
falling in a moonlit haze, / The rain is endless ..." ("Royal Naval
Air Station"), or "My photograph already looks historic. / The
promising youthful face, the matelot's collar ..." ("The Middle of
a War")—and by never straying too far from this level of specificity.
Likewise "Spring 1942," one of the most successful of the many
Fuller poems titled by dates, achieves its particular effect by initially
placing the scene very carefully—falling sun, thickening air, and
a chaplain quietly sitting down near the speaker—as does "Shore
Leave Lorry," which consists of nothing but a brief but intense
survey of a dark night in the African hills, concluding, "Over half
the sky a meteor falls; / The gears grind; somewhere a suffering
creature calls."

The settings and subjects of Fuller's poetry during the tense
1930s, as during the war itself, were tied closely to the larger events
surrounding him. Only after the war did he begin to achieve the
remarkably wide range of subjects that has become a staple in each
of his subsequent volumes. Repeatedly Roy Fuller has lamented the
narrowness of much twentieth-century poetry, whether through an
excessive academicism,[15] or through an overconcern with the poet's
personality and private life.[16] While having no great confidence in

poetry's power to move, or even to reach, a wide audience, Fuller nevertheless believes that a poet ought to write as if he were doing just that, and he partly credits whatever success he may have had in writing the kind of poetry he favors to his having avoided an academic literary career.[17]

Born in Lancashire into a lower-middle-class family, he missed public school and university, was articled to a solicitor at sixteen, and worked as solicitor to a building society until his retirement in the late 1960s, his only sustained contact with literary academe being a five-year stint (1963–73) as Oxford Professor of Poetry. Fuller's routine of a couple of hours of solid writing each morning before going to work, to a background of classical music, reminds one of Trollope and other self-disciplined English writers combining prolific authorship with successful nonliterary careers, and Fuller has interestingly compared himself to Wallace Stevens in having a modern business career to sustain a "secular sensitivity to reality" in his verse.[18]

While Roy Fuller has not written poems on every conceivable subject, his collections suggest that he could. Indeed the variety exhibited in each book reflects a fanciful openness to experience and its possibilities for poetry bordering on serendipity. For example, *Brutus's Orchard* (1957), perhaps his strongest collection, includes pieces inspired by Shakespeare and by lungworms, by a lunar eclipse and by the difficulties of being a poet, by a family estate opened to tourists and by the seasons, by Brutus and by the sexual proclivities of middle age, and by the protagonists of Beethoven's *Fidelio* and by Wordsworth and Coleridge. There his subjects range in seeming significance from the centuries-old philosophical question of the one and the many, to the grazing of a finger, while elsewhere he has written poems on such disparate topics as Brahms, a dead cat, Tolstoy, and a discarded condom. Each of Fuller's books of the past thirty-five years shows this same breadth of interest, as well as a corresponding variety of tones and attitudes toward the subjects considered.

Whether it is appropriate or even possible to derive overriding attitudes from the hundreds of published Roy Fuller poems is questionable. There are persistent concerns throughout his poetry—such as the ongoing crisis of modern civilization, nature, love and sexuality, aging, politics, art and poetry; in particular poems on each of these topics, attitudes might be said to accrue or emerge. However, in most instances attitudes are not clear or consistent, or they seem overshadowed by Fuller's complex contemplation of his subject. The absence of a marked system of attitudes is itself symptomatic of the empiricist response—where meaning adheres to the particular and the differences among particulars, and therefore the problems of generalizing are respected. Such respect for the transient, the contingent, and the specific Fuller expressed in the first stanza of his poem on Chekhov, where he noted with tacit approval the Russian author's vision of life as "a series of departures; / Its crises blurred by train times, bags, galoshes."

Given this vision, perhaps the only positive value of certainty rests in the concept of survival, to which Fuller has paid homage in his fanciful "Autobiography of a Lungworm." There he has the lungworm recount various mishaps and metamorphoses, including rejection by a pig, redevelopment in earthworms through the larval stage, and a triumphal return through the greedy pig's devouring of the earthworms ("the pig himself becomes / The god inside the car," Fuller wittily observes). The poem concludes with the lungworm's acknowledging his own simple but significant place in the complex whole of life, and with his describing life as "A huge doomed throbbing" with "a wiry soul / That must escape the knife." The essence of life becomes the gritty determination to survive on some level, and Fuller treats this most pragmatic of values as the sine qua non for any further ideology or action. By attending to the lowly lungworm, by finding its stages and survival emblematic of life's basis, Fuller suggests his unvarying commitment to the ordinary and practical, and to the empirically real.

Looking back at the 1930s, Fuller has commented that at that time "some of us were possessed too much of poetry's importance and too little of its necessary impersonality."[19] Relatedly, he has complained of the "tyranny of 'I' " in much recent verse, particularly among the so-called "Confessional" poets of mid-century.[20] Because of his own commitment to directness and particularity, his poetry is threatened by such tyranny. His means of escape, by which he tries to inject necessary impersonality into his writing, is the mask, favored by so many poets of this century. The particular mask taken on in his wartime poetry was that of the vaguely youthful, pensive observer, only indirectly involved in the life around him; the assignment to East Africa provided an appropriate vantage point for such observation. After the war the Fuller persona took on what one critic has termed "permanent middle age."[21] While the characters of poems since the mid-1940s have seemed no longer young, there has been little or no sense of their aging. Certainly Fuller has tended for the last fifteen years or so to write more poems in which the character discusses his aging or the passing of time, but such discussion seems mostly to confirm the impression given out by many much earlier poems. Indeed, what is surprising is to find that poems where the Fuller character speaks of himself as old were written when the poet was a relatively young man, even in his thirties. Such poems reflect Fuller's determination to create a persona never quite his own age as a vehicle for impersonality, irony, and the balanced play of opposing viewpoints.

Impersonal personality and the balance of extremes are evident in the structures of almost all of Roy Fuller's poems. For one thing, a remarkably high proportion of them either merely expose a dilemma without suggesting a solution or show a character unable to resolve his particular problem. Only infrequently does a Fuller poem turn on discovery or change of any appreciable degree.

Some of his finest pieces illustrate this tendency toward powerful exposition of situations, rather than their change, a tendency consonant with the empiricist outlook. Thus "The Legions" and "The Coast," two wartime selections, expose the soldier's troubled state of mind. The first, a sonnet, uses elements of the ancient legionnaire's experience to suggest his modern counterpart's fear of the effects of wartime exile. Asking if, once the war is over, he and his comrades will be free to turn to home—"as lean / And trapped wolves turn for their starving den"—the speaker goes on to consider the alternatives of remaining there and noting their acquired bestiality, or descending into even more primitive behavior, and concludes that "Exile has sores which battle cannot make, / Changing the sick from sound, the truth from fake." The fear in this awareness is matched in "The Coast," where the speaker's frightened consciousness appears through the disparate images composing the scene: a fountain, doves drinking, children begging, palms, moon, etc. He then thinks of "things / For which these are inadequate images" and, realizing that nothing substitutes for the "harsh and terrible / Facts of the time," finds his thoughts wandering to a second set of disparate images, all of them far from "[c]old Europe."

Two later short poems illustrate vividly the further degrees of complexity possible through Fuller's powers of metaphor and analysis. "The Day" hinges on an extended analogy, by which the seemingly incidental is elevated to horribly cosmic proportions. Specifically, Fuller notes an ordinary day, with a man off work "with a sudden pain" and a woman, "haloed by the morning sun, / Enquiring if he'd like the daily paper." He then compares such idleness to that of Byzantium when the forces of Islam first began to strike her remoter provinces, goes on to develop the sense of the day as the beginning of the man's physical and mental demise, and closes with a renewal of the historical analogy, set in chilling terms: "A day remembered by a shrivelled empire / Nursed by hermaphrodites and unsustained / By tepid fluids poured in its crying mouth." Even more recently, in "A Wife's Unease," Fuller has described the frustration of a middle-aged woman who, having in her youth chosen to marry a poet "Because she felt him nobly different" and having lost her youthful beauty, now finds herself craving the "rich / Vulgarity and thoughtlessness" she had forsworn. Having sensed from the beginning her poet-husband's "perpetual self-regard" and sensing that all he now loves of her is "[t]he self that loved him once," she belatedly and bitterly wishes "Her name upon a simple heart enslaved; / And issuing thence a troop of noble sons / That would return the doting of a dunce."

To be sure, a small number of Fuller's lyric poems do center on discovery or change. Perhaps the most interesting is "The Perturbations of Uranus," which begins with Fuller, or his character, having his attention suddenly and totally arrested by the "candid gaze" of a young barmaid. Comically he fears she will judge him by the standards of her youth and beauty, and tries to escape her allure by turning to his book (which, ironically, discusses the importance of the mind in human affairs), but he continues to glance at her and to wonder at how "the world belongs to the obtuse / And passionate." Thoroughly rattled, he retreats to the colorless street, where he can "array" his lust with the "armour" of his public role.

In the second half of the poem he tries to make sense of what has happened and to reconcile intellectual and aesthetic values with these fleshly concerns that seem to obliterate such values. The solution, at least for him, comes through emblems: first, that of the planet Neptune, whose existence was revealed to astronomers only by "the perturbations of Uranus," and second, that of art—"Crabbed lines of poetry, pigments congealed / Insanely on a little canvas"—

which trains us for "those transcendent moments of existence / In which the will is powerless" by helping to maintain a fusion of mind and body. Just as art exists for such moments of intimation, so do such moments exist for art, and Fuller's speaker realizes, almost gratefully, that the young girl and others like her "will induce again and yet again / Disturbances within the learned men"—out of which may come the wisdom to distinguish that which degrades from that which ennobles. Citing Yeats's remark that "Our art is the expression of desire," Fuller reaches the very Yeatsian conclusion that our desires must be rooted in our physical being even as they strain toward the metaphysical.

Despite the seeming finality of this conclusion, there remains something tentative in the speaker's position. One suspects that he will get caught similarly again and again, and that he knows it. The best that he can do is to sustain a sort of poise or readiness, which is sure to be upset. This tentative mode, characteristic of Fuller's empiricist wariness of finality, colors other discovery poems—such as "The Photographs" or "The Statue" from the wartime period, or "The Final Period" and "Poetic Ambition" from his later volumes—so much so that a sort of struggle between dynamism and stasis as formal principles is established, with the outcome never entirely certain.

Looking over Roy Fuller's poems of fifty years, a reader must be impressed by their loyalty to fixed poetic forms. The majority, well over three quarters, are rhymed and practically all exhibit tight stanzaic schemes. The Fuller stanza varies in length from the rhymed couplet—he has written many poems using this stanza, and many others in quatrains composed of two couplets each—to as many as a dozen lines. He seems especially fond of five- and seven-line stanzas. His poems include villanelles, sestinas, and ballads. He has written dozens of sonnets, most of which are contained in four rather lengthy sequences (*Winter in Camp, Mythological Sonnets, Meredithian Sonnets,* and *The Historian*). His tour de force in extreme formalism surely is "To X," a sequence of twenty-one narrative roundels concerning an abortive love affair, each part consisting of thirteen ten-syllable lines with lines seven and thirteen repeating the first and line eight repeating the second, and each part rhyming *abba abab abbaa*. Also noteworthy for the consistency of its form is the entire collection *From the Joke Shop* (1975), as its sixty-three poems are all limited to three-line stanzas. The line of a Fuller poem, while

ordinarily iambic pentameter or some other iambic pattern, fre-
quently consists of seven, nine, or eleven syllables.[22] And the un-
rhymed Fuller poems exhibit the same degree of stanzaic tightness
as the rhymed ones.

Roy Fuller has said of fixed forms, indeed of all formal elements,
that "they always seem to me to encourage my own writing, and
therefore I regard them as free forms"[23]—in contrast with seemingly
"free" verse, which he finds constricting. Relatedly, and with much
amusement, he has noted that most vers libre falls readily into
combinations of traditional patterns, as if the thoughtful writer
could hardly escape them.[24] And even syllabic verse, with which
he has experimented in some of his later poems, he has found to
be an extension, rather than a denial, of traditional meters.[25]

Whether these views are wholly valid is open to question. What
is more certain—and, for the purposes of this discussion, more
interesting—is that such views relate to Fuller's empiricist outlook
in their adherence to continuity and to the traditionally workable,
and in their skepticism about the possibility or desirability of rad-
ically altering the form of poetry. Such insistent formalism is related
to the fairly formal and occasionally elaborate syntax of Fuller's
poems, from the 1920s to the present, and to their generally Latinate
diction. While insisting that poetry ought not to address itself to
cliques, Fuller has not hesitated to say that his writing assumes,
and demands, a certain level of literateness and learning in its
reader.[26] While trying to avoid obscurity, he apparently views form,
diction, and syntax as the means of ordering not only the com-
plexities of language and expression with which the poem must
cope, but the often bewildering real world to which he believes it
must try to relate.

Certainly Fuller's attitude toward poetic form connects with his
general aesthetic, which he has suggested in numerous poems. The
issue of art and the making of art is never far from his consciousness,
as his many poems on particular writers (Gide, Ibsen, and Kafka
among others) and composers (Bartok and Brahms) and on the other
arts (painting, film, sculpture, photography) indicate. This preoc-
cupation is further suggested by those many pieces where the speaker
is admittedly a poet wrestling with the problems of art and of the
creative process. Some of Fuller's wittiest lines concern his discov-
ering that images he had considered brilliant at the time of their

invention later appear quite second-rate. "The muse's visitations /
Fatigue and inflame the sense," he explains:

> When we desire to say
> "Red" and our pen puts down
> "Cardinal" all the crown
> Of our head becomes alive,
> And we imagine five
> Or six continents under our sway.
>
> ("Jag and Hangover")

A "morning-after" feeling inevitably follows such intoxication, to
Fuller's consternation and his reader's amusement. Elsewhere he
addresses his muse as a young mistress wanting to leave him. "What
cozy times we've had together, / Playing the gramaphone, sipping
scotch / And soda," he imploringly reminds her, "and I very often /
Not even getting as far as the / Nylon cords behind your knee"
("Departures").

What these and other related poems reveal is a lively confrontation
with aesthetic issues, and a commitment to the empiricist posture
already described. Where earlier Fuller, in the spirit of the 1930s,
might have insisted on the necessity of realism in art (see "The Pure
Poet"), by the 1950s we see him struggling in his poems with the
complexities spawned by the notion of realism. Thus, in "Rhetoric
of a Journey," as he rides by train through his home county reading
The Eustace Diamonds, he sees Anthony Trollope's as an art "where
something is always missing" and wishes to live fully in "the bar-
barous world of sympathy and fear." But, in a manner reminiscent
of Matthew Arnold's "The Buried Life," he soon decides that one
can only speak truly to oneself, that we reveal our truest emotions
to others only through conventions, and that all art, including his
own, is necessarily "fated, immortal and false." Similarly, in "At
a Warwickshire Mansion" he acknowledges that art involves "sleight
of hand which points the blunt, / Compresses, lies." Elsewhere
Fuller examines the problematic relationship of the artist to the
public, in that the more a work approaches the ugliness of daily
experience the less of an audience it can attract ("The Painter"), and
however great the artist's concern or affection for the masses, his
interest in "images" of some sort estranges him from a genuine

awareness of the common man's experience (see "Dialogue of the
Poet and His Talent").

All of this, of course, has its political parallel. Fuller has admitted
to having softened his youthful insistence that poetry be political,[27]
and his own poems reflect a backing away from the fairly firm
Marxist stance of his youth. "Follower's Song" and "Epitaph on a
Bombing Victim"—respectively, a direct attack on the Nazis' mind-
less discipline and an analogue to Auden's "Unknown Citizen"—
both seemed to rest on a definite political creed, but after the war
we find in Fuller's poetic response to political matters an increasing
weariness and skepticism. No doubt the war itself, the subsequent
cold war, and the advent of nuclear weaponry—this last an obsession
in his writing of the 1950s and 60s—contributed to the disillu-
sionment of a poem such as "The Fifties," where he can only bemoan
"lies and armies," "rumours and betrayal," and "seasons suitable
for war."

The most poignant indication of Fuller's loss of political faith
comes in the sonnet "Times of War and Revolution," which begins
by remarking how "The years reveal successively the true / Sig-
nificance of all the casual shapes / Shown by the atlas," and ends
with the observation that "only pain / Of some disquieting vague
variety gnaws, / Seeing a boy trace out a map of Spain." Between
Spain and Korea, Fuller observes, a collective loss of memory set
in, resulting from the mid–twentieth century's seemingly perpetual
geography lesson of horror. Given Algeria, Vietnam, Rhodesia,
Biafra, Bangladesh, Northern Ireland, Lebanon, and El Salvador—
all of which have exploded into the world's consciousness since this
poem's composition—Fuller's writing appears powerfully prophetic,
as in his characteristically understated manner he traces the paradigm
of our political experience. Poetically the results of such disillu-
sionment and weariness could only be such pieces as "Reading *The
Bostonians* in Algeciras Bay," where Fuller notices his inability to
muster the idealism of his youth; "Death of a Dictator," where he
sidesteps the political ramifications of Stalin's death to concentrate
on the feelings of the dictator's children; or "Inaction," where he
confesses that a dog "pee[ing] against the mudguard of my car"
captures his concern more than "The fate of millions" discussed in
the newspaper.

However, it is in his response to nature that Fuller's empiricist
reserve is most strikingly apparent. Significantly, none of the poets

associated with the Movement of the 1950s have written much about nature; nor did the members of the Auden group. It fell to Fuller to suggest the irrelevance of such an enterprise. Throughout his collections, of course, one finds occasional poems vividly setting forth the beauty and sharpness of nature. However, beginning with a rather large cluster in his second wartime collection, *A Lost Season* (1944), Fuller began to examine the issue of man's relationship to nature. First he questioned the incursion of European civilization into African tribal society, which he feared would soon be "poisoned" by the values of industrialism and capitalism (see "The Green Hills of Africa"). Behind such fear, of course, lay a Rousseauistic faith in the natives as closer to nature and therefore somehow superior to his European counterparts. Yet, when he looked closely at nature, as in "The Giraffes" or "The Plains," he was struck only by the distance between himself and the natural world, a distance that he felt no man could close.

What resulted in his postwar poetry was the sense of a standoff, by which nature's superiority to man is seen as considerable but wholly physical. Thus, in "A Wet Sunday in Spring," he contrasts his own dependence on "the inventive temperate zone, / Raised only by the city's floors of culture," with the ability of certain insects to survive on their own in high, freezing altitudes. And in "Elementary Philosophy" he sees in nature the chief emblem of everything from which man is necessarily alienated. Fuller's ruminations on nature thus relate to his concern, expressed in several poems, with the questions of fate and heredity. Ultimately the inevitability and perpetuity of nature, compared with his own fragility and ephemerality, impress Fuller. In this there is a sort of wonder and admiration; certainly he does not intend us to be terrified of nature per se. There is little sense, however, that knowing nature can be of much use to us in the pursuit of truly human values, since in Fuller's view those values, like man himself, become not necessarily counter to nature, but separate from it.

As for those human relationships around which such values accrue, they have inspired some of Fuller's warmest and most intimate writing. Poems to his wife, to his daughter, and to his granddaughters sparkle with the wit and particularity informing his best verse. Nevertheless, behind these poems, and all his others dealing with love and human relations, are a sense of the transiency of people and their affections, and the corollary warning against idealizing in

such matters. Besides those realistic poems about love and marriage
already noted, as well as many others, perhaps Fuller's sharpest,
and certainly his most striking, caveat against the romantic view
of love comes in the wryly titled "Song in a Wood," where he has
a discarded condom bewail his abandonment of love, which
"[thought] I'd no lasting part / In the involvements of the heart."
"Yet I remain within the grove, / Symbolical of all that passed,"
he notes:

> Neighbor of moon and dove,
> While those that called themselves in love
> Go separate ways and die at last.

With a final chilling dose of black humor, Fuller has his "character"
insist:

> Love's only immortality
> I hold: the generations that
> Lovers sow carelessly—
> Being young and blind, averse
> To recognize their happy murderers.

Philip Larkin

In many respects the title poem of Philip Larkin's most recent
collection represents the quintessence of empiricism. It begins by
establishing very precisely a troubling state of mind in which the
speaker repeatedly finds himself:

> When I see a couple of kids
> And guess he's fucking her and she's
> Taking pills or wearing a diaphragm,
> I know this is paradise
> Everyone old has dreamed of all their lives ...

The reference to the younger persons as "a couple of kids" and the
rather old-fashioned supposition that the girl might be using a
diaphragm help define Larkin's character as middle-aged, while the
almost reflexive immediacy of his speculations about their sexual
relationship and the use of "fucking" to describe the young man's
manner of relating to the young woman—in a poem otherwise

scrupulously devoid of so harsh a term—mark the speaker as an envious, even embittered bystander at the sexual revolution of mid-century. His further description of the young people's supposed ecstasy as the pushing of "bonds and gestures" "[l]ike an outdated combine harvester" and "everyone young going down the long slide / To happiness, endlessly," makes a smooth transition from literal to metaphorical language while continuing the strain of clarity and concreteness begun in the opening lines.

More central to the poem's empiricism, however, is its resolution, which turns on the speaker's examining his assumptions about the young couple. This he does by drawing the parallel between his own suppositions about those who he believes have been freed from the traditional "bonds and gestures" surrounding sex, and what his elders "forty years back" may have thought about him in his seeming liberation from traditional religious beliefs and practices: *"That'll be the life; / No God any more ... He / And his lot will all go down the long slide / Like free bloody birds."* At this he experiences a sharp turn of mind, as he immediately thinks of high windows and envisions "The sun-comprehending glass, / And beyond it, the deep blue air, that shows / Nothing, and is nowhere, and is endless." In a flash he comprehends the errors of his assumptions, for just as the supposed religious revolution of his youth failed to free him from a sense of life's ultimate mysteries—represented by the high windows and the seemingly infinite "deep blue air"—so the much-heralded revolution of sexual mores in recent decades probably has done little to free young people from the complexity and mystery of intimate human relationships.

Significantly the relief from his initial bitterness and the solution to the personal problem it poses for him come through the scrutinizing of suppositions in relation to the concrete facts of his own experience. The poem ends by portraying a particular state of mind at a particular time, as the central step in the line of reasoning by which the earlier state of mind is rejected. Larkin's speaker cannot rely wholly on arguments or statistics, or any other type of abstractions—the telling references of the final lines are to things to which he cannot attach names but can only allude by suggestive imagery—but ultimately must consult what he knows to be his own experience and feeling in the present. To be sure, such a process raises the problems of subjectivity and self-knowledge, indeed of epistemology itself, but it at least ties the character's insights to a Cartesian base, which makes his conclusions more credible to him and to the reader than they would be were they wholly speculative or abstract. Important, too, is the circular quality of this poem's plot, for Larkin depicts his character's discovery not as something startlingly new or shocking, but in fact as something he had known already, had forgotten, and will probably forget again and again. Such a discovery is thus characteristic in the strictest sense, since it involves the speaker literally recognizing a part of himself. Within such modest dimensions does empiricist discovery occur.

Twenty years before *High Windows* Larkin wrote the single poem most responsible for establishing him as a principal new poet. Indeed, it was "Church Going"—as well as *The Less Deceived* (1955), the collection in which it first appeared—that identified the tone and concerns that have continued to be most closely associated with Philip Larkin even as he has achieved greater variety and demonstrated his variance from the so-called Movement. Certainly "Church Going" shares many qualities with "High Windows." It, too, begins with a concrete situation, the speaker's visit to a small country church, which is solidified through his cataloging of various details of the building and its furnishings: "matting, seats, and stone," "sprawlings of flowers," "some brass and stuff / Up at the holy end." Such a list does more than create setting. Because it is part of what the speaker is doing there, it helps characterize him as familiar with such surroundings yet as both attracted and annoyed by what he sees. Noting the "awkward reverence" with which he takes off his cycle clips, he goes on to examine the peculiarities of this particular church, to try to offset his reverential gestures with a parody of a clergyman's lectern manner, and finally to leave. At this point Larkin reinforces the inconsistency of his behavior by having him sign the book and donate a small coin, yet conclude "the place was not worth stopping for."

The visit itself comprises but two of the poem's six stanzas and reflects a habitual pattern of behavior by the speaker. What is unusual this time, however, is that he bothers, for the rest of the poem, to examine the paradox of his feelings, by considering why he should have continued to subject himself to the role of churchgoer for which he feels such scorn. While this poem differs structurally from "High Windows" by focusing on an ultimately unique event in its protagonist's life and by leading him to a conclusion he has never reached before, the emphasis once more is on his recognizing an aspect of himself and on doing so in commonsense fashion. Implicit in such a structure is the notion that the conscious, demonstrable dimension of our being can offer us much, and that to speculate on what lies very far from the conscious is largely futile. In this Larkin exhibits a more purely empiricist bent than Fuller who in many poems, especially those of his later collections, has shown a fascination for Freudianism and for the preconscious.

What the speaker of "Church Going" realizes is that his "gravitating" to churches reflects his share of a general human need for something beyond the moment and beyond ourselves, for a meaning to mortal existence—indeed the same sort of metaphysical longing acknowledged at the end of "High Windows." That from the standpoint of science or agnostic logic such hunger is irrational or can never be satisfied is rather beside the point, as Larkin insists on an honest facing of the emotional and the impulsive as part of the human personality with which we must cope. His churchgoer makes his discovery not in an urban or suburban church, but in one of the hundreds of centuries-old structures dotting the English countryside. Such a place has value, the speaker realizes, because "it held unspilt / So long and equably what since is found / Only in separation—marriage, and birth, / And death, and thoughts of these";—that is, because it lent dignity and meaning to parishoners' lives. The testing by experience—in this case the collective experience of generations of believers, as well as the speaker's own recurrent actions and feelings—again provides the basis for awareness. In the poem the sometimes caustic observations on the parochialism of religious practices and speculation on who the last worshipper might be eventually give way to appreciation for the lasting significance of "A serious house ... / In whose blent air all our compulsions meet, / Are recognized, and robed as destinies."

While "High Windows" and "Church Going" represent well the empiricist tendencies of Larkin's structuring, many other poems do so equally well. Several selections from the second of his three mature collections, *The Whitsun Weddings* (1964), likewise define their speakers in terms of an initial posture of superiority over someone else and move through a thoughtful and honest stripping away of that posture. Thus in "Self's the Man," its speaker, a bachelor, insincerely conceding at first that his married friend Arnold—"With the nippers to wheel round the houses / And the hall to paint in his old trousers ... "—is much less selfish than he, then rationalizes that Arnold, after all, chose what he wanted and so is equally selfish, and concludes that his own real advantage over Arnold is not moral but practical, in that he knows what he can stand "Without them sending a van." "Or," he adds, "I suppose I can." This telling addition reveals the depth of his uncertainty as well as his ultimate willingness to admit it.

Just as one would not engage in such an exercise were he secure, neither would the speaker in "Mr. Bleaney," a far bleaker piece, react so scornfully to the recently deceased occupant of the rented room he is moving into, were he content. He notices the room's seediness and the landlady's remark that Bleaney took her garden "properly in hand," and then proceeds to reflect contemptuously on the dead man's commonplace tastes and habits: "His preference for sauce to gravy ... the Frinton folk / Who put him up for summer holidays ..." "But," he suddenly and ruefully admits:

> if he stood and watched the frigid wind
> Tousling the clouds, lay on the fusty bed
> Telling himself that this was home, and grinned,
> And shivered, without shaking off the dread
>
> That how we live measures our own nature,
> And at his age having no more to show
> Than one hired box should make him pretty sure
> He warranted no better, I don't know.

So chilling an admission signals the reversal of his thinking from the earlier stanzas, as his glee in dissecting Bleaney as a symbol for all he disdains is replaced by the sobering recognition of his equality with—indeed his inferiority to—Bleaney, who, it seems, at least gave and received affection during his otherwise unremarkable life.

An equally moving but longer and much more positive poem exhibiting the same distance-reflection-appreciation pattern is "The Whitsun Weddings." There the main character—again Larkin's solitary, detached observer—tells of a Saturday train ride to London from some city in the north of England. Though initially noticing little but the countryside and the towns through which he passes, he soon responds with increasingly detailed and affectionate attention to wedding parties crowded on station platforms and to the newlyweds boarding the train at each stop. He reflects on the profundity of what is happening to them ("A dozen marriages got under way ... ready to be loosed with all the power / That being changed can give.") and on the "frail travelling coincidence" of his life being thrown in with all their lives. As the train arrives at its destination he experiences a "sense of falling, like an arrow-shower / Sent out of sight, somewhere becoming rain." Because his greater detachment has permitted him to feel and know better the significance and implications of the occasion ("[N]one thought of the others they would never meet / Or how their lives would all contain this hour"), Larkin's outsider feels transformed into an especially privileged insider.

"The Whitsun Weddings" reveals the closing of a gap between the observer and those he observes. This and the other poems discussed, spread over several years, should suggest Philip Larkin's persisting concern with such gaps and distances: between one generation and another, between one person's beliefs and another's, between one person's experiences and another's, between one person's perception of a relationship and another's, etc. Indeed, almost every Larkin poem rests on the perception of a gap of some sort and on the issue of its closure. And every such gap he relates to the inevitable disparity between our images or ideals and the reality in which we must live, a disparity that has caused one critic to label Larkin "[the poet] of the essential absence of life from itself"[28] and another to observe that "Larkin has all but retired *nowhere, somewhere, elsewhere,* and *absence* from competition."[29]

In the Larkin world life constantly defies desires and expectations. Children there clearly don't want to remain children forever, yet their play at being adults (see "Take One Home for the Kiddies") reveals a barbarism counter to all romantic notions of childhood. In one of his most amusing poems, "I Remember, I Remember," he pokes fun at the whole sentimental syndrome surrounding youth and growing up, especially as promoted in fiction and poetry. He, or his protagonist, pulls into the town of his birth, searches futilely for "a sign / That this [is] still the town that had been 'mine,' " and then reconstructs the scenes of his "unspent" childhood by wittily inverting the clichés of romantic poetry and the English bildungsroman:

> Our garden ... where I did not invent
> Blinding theologies of flowers and fruits ...
> The bracken where I never trembling sat,

> Determined to go through with it; where she
> Lay back and "all became a burning mist."

So caustic a view of the past—one senses a desperate desire to "remember," which gives way to the consolations of sarcasm once he realizes there is no place, and no experience of note, to remember—is itself the fruit of a disappointing adult present, which for Larkin disappoints in just about every way conceivable. If "The Whitsun Weddings" shows his character able to wrest a measure of contentment from his situation, that measure appears not easily or quickly won and, in the context of the dozens of other poems showing the disillusionments of maturity, appears certainly exceptional. Nor is old age looked on with any but a jaundiced eye, as "The Old Fools" vividly if sympathetically sees it as a "hideous inverted childhood."

The whole issue of relationships is central to the pessimism often ascribed to Larkin. While he can seemingly despair of all our activities, and while he views involvement with other persons as exceedingly risky, much of his poetry carries at least the implication that human love is worth the risk—which is perhaps not much of a concession while we're being told that there is nothing of worth to lose in such a venture. "What will survive of us is love," he assures us at the closing of "An Arundel Tomb," just as he develops, in "Broadcast," the figure of the lover listening to a radio transmission of a concert attended by his beloved and imagining her there. Relatedly, even in some of his bleakest poems ("Mr. Bleaney," for example) he rarely abandons the capacity for empathy ultimately arising in "The Whitsun Weddings" and "High Windows." There is behind these poems, and most of his others, the notion of the need for human solidarity, based on an understanding and pity that need not compromise clear-sightedness.

Even so, Larkin's poems about love are notable for their wry negativism and satire. In such poems the failure to close gaps is predominant. In its difficulties love appears almost a paradigm of life itself for Larkin, as he depicts its pitfalls at every stage. For him love affairs appear to be ending almost as soon as they begin. Certainly the ardent suitor in "Lines on a Young Lady's Photograph Album'" seems on his way to getting the snapshot, but not the girl, even as he sings her praises. And, while the man in "Latest Face" betrays a pathetic indecisiveness in backing away from a young woman he has seen for the first time, such caution seems not entirely unwise in the context of other poems, where love ultimately prompts insecurity ("Wedding Winds"), a feeling of duplicity ("If My Darling"), a sense of personal disintegration ("Waiting for breakfast ..."), embittered regret ("Wild Oats"), and downright nastiness ("Maiden Name"). In the emblematically titled "Talking in Bed" Larkin observes that in even the most solid of relationships "It becomes still more difficult to find / Words at once true and kind / Or not true and not unkind." Elsewhere he suggests the illusory nature of sexuality ("Dry Point") and the ludicrous fantasies it inspires ("The Large Cool Store"), and praises the security of a person immune to the lures of love and sex ("Love Songs in Age").

Central to the presentation of such a viewpoint is an insistent realism that has led Larkin to be called "the effective unofficial laureate of post-1945 England"[30] and the "Laureate of the Common Man."[31] While realistic detail exists as a base for behavior in his poems—and not for purposes of mere documentation or setting— his writing can be seen as a chronicle of life in recent England, with heavily trafficked streets, crowded public parks, business districts, and semidetached houses. His poems record the "split-level shopping" and "bleak high-risers" of most English towns ("Going, Going"), the British obsession with "horseracing and betting" ("At Grass"), the billboards common along city streets ("Essential Beauty"), and the consumerism of "iced lollies, / Electric mixers, toaster, washers, dryers ..." ("Here"). Through such insistent realism Larkin offers a postwar response to the challenge of mass culture with which British poetry was first faced in the 1930s. But he goes even further than the Auden group in absorbing elements of that culture into his poetic and his poetry, and in making such elements—the popular song, snapshots, the discotheque, the newsreel, the transatlantic jet, the resort poster, the Profumo scandal—the starting points of poetic activity.

A resultant feature of such writing is a strong historicism. Although he has been criticized for failing to reflect in his writing those changes occurring in England in the last quarter-century,[32] Larkin creates a poetic world that, but for intentional exceptions, is broadly contemporary—that is, recognizably postwar and recognizably British. The brief description of youthful sexuality in "High Windows," the references in "Church Going" to "suburb scrub," and the details of Bleaney's room ("Flowered curtains, thin and

frayed, / ... sixty-watt bulb, no hook / Behind the door ...") all
suggest the most recent era of British life.

And in a few poems historicism becomes blatant, as Larkin, with
equal deftness, recalls the world of salesmen traveling through the
provinces in 1929 or university dons dining perhaps a century earlier
("Livings"), the seamy underside of Victorian London ("Decep-
tions"), the life of coal miners early in the century ("The Explosion"),
and those final days of Edwardian innocence before the plunge into
the maelstrom of modernity set off by the Great War ("MCMXIV").
This last example is especially notable for its combination of pho-
tographic sweep—"The crowns of hats, the sun / On moustached
archaic faces ... the bleached / Established names on the sun-blinds
... / The tin advertisements / For cocoa and twist ..."—and fig-
urative expansion: " ... the men / Leaving the gardens tidy, / The
thousands of marriages / Lasting a little while longer: / Never such
innocence again." Such lines reveal Larkin's ongoing fascination with
the tension between the illusory permanence of the present and the
constant pressures of historical change.

The element in which such tension arises is, of course, time.
Larkin's obsessive consideration, in poem after poem, of time and
its attendant difficulties illustrates his power to treat complex phil-
osophical issues in a concrete, straightforward, and moving manner,
a power that he shares with Thomas Hardy, whose poetry he has
praised as a seminal influence on his own, and which helps define
his preeminence among recent empiricist poets. "Days are where
we live," he remarks ("Days"); to find where else we might live
besides days, or time, would be to leave life.

But time is puzzling for Larkin. Better that it should be termed
"Triple Time," as he calls it in a poem of that title, for we really
experience three senses of existence, none of which has much exis-
tential reality for us. Larkin juggles the riddle of time in a manner
reminiscent of Aristotle or Aquinas as he observes that the present
("A time traditionally soured, / A time unrecommended by event")
was not too long ago the future we anticipated as a time of fruition
and success ("An air lambent with adult enterprise") and soon will
be the past ("A valley cropped by fat neglected chances") on which
we will blame our failures.

Such understandable confusion of tenses, prompted by the illusory
nature of the present moment, relates to another kind of confusion,

in that the insight on a particular experience said to be gained by the passing of time necesssarily involves simplification and distortion:

> "Perspective brings significance," we say,
> Unhooding our photometers, and snap!
> What can't be printed can be thrown away.
> ("Whatever Happened?")

What we may be "throwing away," though, is the experience itself. If immediacy is confusing, distance is equally misleading; time never seems to afford us the proper awareness.

Such problems caused by time and temporariness in the Larkin world appear vividly in "Dockery and Son," where the central character has returned to his old college after twenty years and learned that a former fellow student even younger than he now has a son enrolled there. During the trip home he finds himself wondering at the differences between his life and Dockery's and mutters, "Well, it just shows / How much ... How little ..." as he drowses and hopes to forget the matter. Soon, however—inspired by rest, by the inescapability of the issue, and by the disquieting symbolic significance he attaches to "[j]oining and parting" rail lines reflecting "a strong / Unhindered moon"—he admits his shock at realizing "how much had gone of life, / How widely from the others." This leads him to consider, and then to deny, that Dockery knew better what he wanted. Then the possibility that Dockery was "convinced ... he should be added to" arises, but this too is knocked down as highly speculative. "To me it was dilution," he adds, as he goes on to attack all such "innate assumptions" as inadequate explanations by which we try feebly to appropriate control over what has happened to us.

For the unhappy person, such as Larkin's character, however, such explanations become all that is left. But even the contented person can know only that we cannot know:

> Life is first boredom, then fear.
> Whether or not we use it, it goes,
> And leaves what something hidden from us chose,
> And age, and then the only end of age.

Or, as Larkin puts it in another even grimmer poem, our lives consist in constantly investing hope in our ship coming in at a future time when in fact our future is relentlessly becoming our past and "Only one ship is seeking us, a black- / Sailed unfamiliar, towing at her back / A huge and birdless silence" ("Next, Please").

The bleakness of such an outlook, perhaps a necessary price for the empiricist honesty Larkin advocates and practices, surely has much to do with the emphasis in many of his poems upon continuity and custom. One admiring critic has rightly distinguished Larkin's historicity from that of John Betjeman, whom Larkin admires greatly, by pointing out that where Betjeman seems "nostalgic" for the past, Larkin does not.[33] So aware is Larkin of the transience of existence and so wary of idealizing the past that he would never concede the possibility, or even the desirability, of living in a former time. However, he would insist that we recognize the continuity of the present with the past (this is what much of his writing on time is about) and that, in avoiding the illusion of total permanence, we not fall into the equally pernicious illusion of total novelty. Just as good sense dictates that we cannot wholly remember or return to a former time, so for Larkin it suggests that we cannot and must not forget or dispel the past entirely. "High Windows" illustrates the usefulness of remembering one's personal past, just as "The Whitsun Weddings" suggests the usefulness of watching and valuing present experience.

Permanent authenticity for Larkin resides as much in unformalized rituals as in the formalized. Two of his most striking poems dealing with the importance of ongoing tradition single out such rituals for praise. "[H]alf an annual pleasure, half a rite," he calls the English custom of sea-bathing, in celebrating its continuation as a juxtaposition of the contemporary and the timeless: "Still going on, all of it, still going on! / To lie, eat, sleep in hearing of the surf / (Ears to transistors, that sound tame enough / Under the sky) ..." ("To the Sea"). Where in another context the presence of "Chocolate-papers, tea-leaves, and between / The rocks, the rusting soup-tins" might disturb Larkin, here he seizes on them as evidence of a timeless observance linking today with his own childhood and with countless earlier generations. With warm-hearted humor he concludes that

> If the worst
> Of flawless weather is our falling short,
> It may be that through habit these do best,
> Coming to water clumsily undressed

Yearly; teaching their children by a sort
Of clowning; helping the old, too, as they ought.

Likewise, in "Show Saturday" the county show inspires an even more prolix cataloging of loving detail to describe the people and "something they share / That breaks ancestrally each year into / Regenerate union." "Let it always be there," he insists, seeing such rites as vital to the rootedness upon which a healthy society, as well as the poetry of realism, depends.

Compared with Roy Fuller, Larkin seems more concerned with the puzzles of time and historical continuity in the modern world. This may be the result partly of having been born, unlike Fuller, after World War I and therefore of having missed any very direct contact with Edwardian culture. Despite Larkin's possible intentions, there does seem a strong measure of idealization of that culture in "MCMXIV," while Fuller appears much more casual in his references to the time before the war. And, while all of this is highly speculative, it seems not unreasonable to suggest that the experience of attending Oxford during the early years of World War II—when "events cut us ruthlessly down to size" and "the effort expended on one's post-war prospects could hardly seem anything but a ludicrous waste of time"[34]—and of finding his hometown of Coventry largely destroyed by German air attacks (an experience described vividly in his novel *Jill*) contributed, on the one hand, to his sympathetic acceptance of a rootless contemporary culture and, on the other, to his concern that traditions and roots not be undervalued.

Certainly Larkin's poetry is more permeated with the nitty-gritty of everyday life in England than is that of Fuller, whose descents to the kinds of realistic details noted in Larkin's writing are much rarer. While Larkin could hardly be called plebeian in the tone and taste reflected in his verse, certainly he seems abler and more willing to absorb the common man's viewpoing into the scenes and situations he creates. Perhaps this is a measure of the greater practicality and empiricism of his poetic posture. Donald Davie sees Larkin accepting post-1945 England as "the only one we have" and "[agreeing] to tolerate the intolerable for the sake of human solidarity with those who don't find it intolerable at all."[35] The remarkable commercial success of Larkin's writings—five printings of *The Less Deceived*, five of *The Whitsun Weddings*, three larger printings of *High Windows*, the reissuing of his novels and his first poetry collection,

The North Ship, and paperback and American editions of all his books[36]—suggests that he has overcome Fuller's reservations about realistic writing not having sufficient appeal for a public desiring escapist literature. Nor is this an instance of consciously selling out to anything, since Larkin's poetry scarcely portrays life as overly pleasant.

The difference in degree of contemporary realism in their writings relates, also, to basic differences in their poetic intentions. As noted earlier, Fuller, while eschewing needless obscurity, expects a certain level of learnedness in his readers. This is not to criticize Fuller, but merely to point out the difference between his commitment and that of Larkin, whose poetry is strikingly bare of such allusiveness and who has complained of modern poetry and its followers abandoning the audience British poets once enjoyed by retreating into the academic and the arcane: "At bottom poetry, like all art, is inextricably bound up with giving pleasure, and if a poet loses his pleasure-seeking audience he has lost the only audience worth having, for which the dutiful mob that signs on every September is no substitute."[37] For Larkin the villain is modernism, which he attacks savagely in his introduction to the collection of his jazz reviews, *All What Jazz,* and which he blames for alienating the common reader from poetry and for encouraging young poets essentially to write only for themselves. While he would probably acknowledge his poetic kinship with Fuller, he has written hardly any poems about poetry or art, and would probably regard doing so as self-indulgent and narcissistic. And, where Fuller might view Larkin's consideration for poetry's readership as risking concession to commercial appeal, Larkin sees such concern as a concession only to the humanity every poet shares with every reader.

Certainly Larkin's provisional acceptance of the middle- and even lowbrow worlds permits him to view those worlds more from the inside. When combined with his rather consistent skepticism about the overall direction of Britain in the age of the welfare state—a skepticism to which Fuller arrived rather belatedly—he offers an empathetic conservatism, which may be more genuinely understanding of the average Englishman and his problems than much liberal or radical posturing. And, while it is difficult, and perhaps irrelevant, to gauge the political differences between the two poets, it is notable that Larkin, conservative in so many ways as he seems to have always been, manages to close the gap between himself and his subjects much more consistently than Fuller, for all of his earlier Marxist and Communist leanings.

Fuller's poems can include, and frequently begin with, the kinds of realistic details and settings noted earlier. Since World War II, however, his poems have tended to depart fairly rapidly, and fairly far, from the degree of specificity suggested by their openings. Thus, one from the 1960s, "Road Safety," begins with the amusing self-reproach he feels upon seeing the bumper sticker urging him to "Watch my behind not hers," as he imagines himself dying in an auto crash after leering at a girl, "Like some mad three-badge stoker choked by his own / Crapulous vomit." The poem's witty reversal, by which he imagines generations of "eye- / Catching nubility" and decides to die happy, ends on a more abstract level of thought and language, with mention of "malignancies of flesh" and "bonanza mine," than probably would a Larkin poem on the same dilemma. And while in another, longer poem, "In Lambeth Palace Road," Fuller repeatedly returns to the particular London setting with which he begins, he avoids the piling up of realistic details common in Larkin's longer pieces, and moves ultimately to a beautiful but highly abstruse consideration of the poet's mythmaking powers. Even in the ironically titled "Romance"—which begins with a line of arrestingly contemporary focus, "Girl with fat legs, reading Georgette Heyer," and where his aim is to invoke the muse to return poetry to a "lower epicycle" and the realism of "end-stopped irony"— he implicitly characterizes himself as a poet too caught up in poetizing and too little involved with life at a concrete level.

Larkin's tendency, and perhaps his greater ability, to dispel distance and to concentrate on the particular is nowhere more apparent than in "Faith Healing," written after he watched a documentary on that subject.[38] Where, given his objective and agnostic perspective, one might expect at most pity for the faithful filing to the podium where the evangelist stands, or thoughtful analysis of their ignorance, instead he abandons not only agnosticism but even the vague humanism of "Church Going" and develops an emotional identification with the women, "Moustached in flowered frocks," with whom he has so little in common socioeconomically or intellectually. Through extensive details the first stanza fastens on the entourage and techniques of the faith healer, who, "scarcely pausing, goes into a prayer / Directing God about this eye, that knee." But even before the stanza is completed, Larkin leaves this potentially satirical focus, to attend to the women and to describe at length their crying, their "deep hoarse tears, as if a kind of dumb / And idiot child within them still survives / To re-awake at kindness."

Just as Larkin tends more than Roy Fuller to allow the viewpoints of outsider and insider to blend, and thus to maintain contemporary realism more consistently, so he sets up in his poetry more of a tension between competing structural principles. While a slightly higher proportion of his poems than Fuller's display change or discovery in the speaker, most of Larkin's discovery poems involve the discovery of uncertainty, a movement away from an initially fixed position or viewpoint, and thus remain faithful to the tentativeness inherent in empiricism. Equally pertinent to Larkin's commitment to this tentative mode is the way in which tensions arise in his poems between various degrees of informality in diction, between metrical and stanzaic regularity and irregularity, between the sentence and the stanza as organizing principles, and between subtlety and abrasiveness in the employment of rhymes—kinds of tensions much less prevalent in Fuller's poetry, which tends to be more epigrammatic. While at a casual glance Larkin's poems look highly traditional—and his reliance upon poetic tradition surely relates to his affection for other traditions—compared with Fuller's, his diction and prosody are much more complex and varied. In this Larkin appears much less under the restraints of poetic tradition, much more willing to subject them to the experiment of poetic context.

In other respects, however, his poetry seems more restrained, though such restraint is not always at variance with his empiricist commitment. Significantly his poems offer a much narrower range of subjects. Unlike Fuller's erudite and sometimes exotic work, Larkin's poems largely suggest variations on a limited number of themes, paralleling his preference for the circumscribed harmonies and progressions of traditional jazz to the greater freedom of the progressive type. Such narrowness of range relates, too, to Larkin's readinesss to condemn modernism and even its chief practitioners, such as James Joyce, where Fuller retains a reverence for the modernist masters and prefers to attribute excesses to their less sensitive disciples. To the modernist-progressive rubric of freedom, Larkin asks, "But freedom from what?" and responds, "One can only answer 'humanity.' "[39]

Perhaps the strongest, most obvious indicator of Larkin's greater restraint is the slightness of his poetic output. In forty years as a published poet he has brought out but four books ("interruptions of silence," one critic calls them), spaced evenly throughout the period and containing only slightly more than a hundred poems; his only two novels were completed before he was twenty-five. On the other hand, Roy Fuller, while beginning to publish only a decade earlier than Larkin, has managed three times as many poems and poetry collections, plus a dozen volumes of fiction. Each man has pursued writing as a spare-time activity, as Larkin's career as university librarian has paralleled Fuller's as solicitor in terms of its demands and distinction.

John Bayley has ascribed a "poetry of arrest" to Larkin, the silence of which ironically keeps us much more curious about the poet than does the more poet-centered writing of "confessionals" like John Berryman or Robert Lowell.[40] Relatedly Calvin Bedient has attributed to Larkin an "eloquent taciturnity betraying a reluctance to use words at all."[41] This reluctance to write much (Larkin usually attempts no more than three or four poems in a year) relates not only to his concept of a poem as the "verbal pickling" of a highly significant experience[42]—which does not necessarily occur every day—but also to the reluctance of the characters in his poems to believe or act much. Most of the time, apparently, silence says it all for Philip Larkin. His refusal to interrupt that silence very often suggests his seriousness as an artist, as well as his personal commitment to the empiricist wariness coloring most of his poems.

Such wariness contributes to the enlivening tension of Larkin's writing, a tension of conflicting attitudes he finds attractive. Indeed, a chief source of continuity in his work seems to be his vacillation between such attitudes, both within and among individual poems. The amusing sequence "Toads" and "Toads Revisited" finds Larkin subscribing to the work ethic even as he condemns it, and, in the latter poem, embracing work merely as a stay against despair. His impulse toward both action and passivity, as well as toward both belief and doubt, has been noted, as has his ambivalent attitude toward human society. Where he could declare, in "Wants," that beyond all social gestures lies "the wish to be alone" and that beyond all gestures at perpetuating the memory of oneself "desire of oblivion runs," we see him in "Vers de Société" wittily electing society over solitude. Here again, though, the choice occurs for negative reasons, as an alternative to thinking about death. Larkin rarely embraces positives; rather, he rejects the negative. Such rejection manifests itself in his frequent use of the negative prefix, as well as in his double-negative book title, *The Less Deceived,* as he wishes to measure things as cautiously as he can.

This tension between positive and negative has its cognitive dimension in the struggle between hope and awareness throughout his poetry. The image of Philip Larkin as the advocate of clear-sighted awareness, at whatever cost, should be obvious from what has been said already. For all of this advocacy, however, it is important to remember how tolerant Larkin can be of the deluded, and even of the delusion, and how often he casts awareness as at best a mixed blessing. Where in "Sunny Prestatyn" he applauds sympathetically the impulse of the defacer of the romantic travel poster, and where elsewhere he suggests repeatedly that delusion must give way ultimately to disillusionment, he never suggests that delusions of some sort are not necesssary to our well-being. Given his obsession with the passing of time, the temporariness of such well-being should hardly disqualify it as an attraction. This seems to be the direction he takes in "Essential Beauty," where he contrasts the worlds projected in billboards ("sharply-pictured groves / Of how life should be") with the reality in which we live ("where nothing's made / As new or washed quite clean"). Larkin has said that he came to view billboards with sadness.[43] If so, the sadness surely is as much for life's failure to live up to our illusions, as for our folly in subscribing to them. Larkin sees us and himself, like the speaker in "High Windows," alternatively forgetting and remembering, but in this instance remembering is too painful not to induce forgetfulness.

Such a view of things has persisted throughout Larkin's postwar writings. Indeed, until recently the standard comment on his career was that he had early (i.e., in the late 1940s) determined his characteristic mode and in succeeding decades had merely refined and sharpened it. His supporters seemed content at this, and his detractors came to expect little else from him. The passing of a few years since the publication of *High Windows* has produced some interesting and provocative, if not always insightful revision of this viewpoint, at least among the critics. For one thing, *High Windows* has been seen as at least a partial return to the quasi-Yeatsian manner of the *North Ship* poems written during World War II. Larkin's supposed rejection of Yeats for Hardy as a model, which he discussed in his introduction to the 1966 reissue of *The North Ship,* seems not to have stuck and has caused one doubting critic to ask, "Was ever a professional librarian and dedicated poet so mercilessly pushed about by a number of stray books?"[44] The issue of Larkin's poetic origins has caused some to see Auden as more significant than Hardy, anyway.[45] Certainly the ongoing struggle between the neoromantic Yeats and the more empiricist manner of Hardy that some would see in Larkin resembles what Auden himself went through, especially in the 1930s.

Many poems in *High Windows*—such as "Sad Steps," "The Building," those pieces explicitly concerned with traditions of British life, and, of course, the title poem—demonstrate Larkin's continuing tendency to write empirically. These and many others have direct links, ideological and formal, with poems in earlier collections. Nevertheless, the surrealist "Card-Players," the epigrammatic "This Be the Verse," and the quasi-Symbolist "Solar" suggest his willingness to deal in other styles, as well. Given another ten years and another volume, Larkin might succeed in resisting the category to which most of his readers have consigned him. But even if not, his position among the principal British poets of the century seems secure.

Chapter Four

The Naturalist Response: Hughes and Hill

The empiricist tendency of Fuller and Larkin, as well as other poets associated with the Movement, reflected a distrust of the romanticism that had informed much writing of the late 1930s and the 1940s—most notably that of the Apocalyptics, and of Dylan Thomas and his followers. While acknowledging the need for illusion in human affairs, poets working in this vein sought greater reconciliation with realism than their more romantic contemporaries had sought.

This search obviously carried a measure of optimism, a belief in the possibility of maintaining both hope and honesty without fundamentally compromising either. On the commonsense level there was the feeling that, while neither private nor public utopias were possible, at least an appreciable if sporadic contentment was attainable, depending in part on retaining links with private and collective pasts, in the form of memory and tradition, even as necessary change was accepted and in some instances welcomed.

As the postwar period developed, however, many writers became increasingly impatient with the conservatism of such a stance. They found the posture of "muddling through" intolerably dull, but, more to the point, they found it intolerably dishonest. To them the empiricist response involved the very compromise it sought to avoid, by trying to ignore much of recent European history and by believing that all could be—and had been—escaped. Such writers called for a truthfulness that went beyond empiricism and projected a much more extreme stance, and a more extreme poetry, in dealing with contemporary existence.

Restive Britain

Such extremism no doubt reflected in part a dissatisfaction with the style of life that caution and empiricism had produced for most

Britishers. Whatever relaxation of austerity had been permitted in the modest prosperity of the mid-1950s gave way, by the end of that decade, to the realization that Britain was in serious economic difficulty, which likely would last into the next century. Beyond matters of the economy, however, the Profumo scandal of 1963, the ineffectiveness of British-led sanctions againt Rhodesia after her 1964 withdrawal from the Commonwealth, uncertainty as to how to respond to escalated American involvement in Vietnam, the widening gulf between labor and management and the perilous rise in strikes and work stoppages in the late 1960s, the renewal of violence in Northern Ireland in 1969, and a mounting distrust and even hatred of civil authority generally—all signaled the increasing difficulty of governing equably and effectively what once had seemed a nation of model decorum.

Of course, all such developments had their counterparts in Europe and in the United States. However, taken together, they seemed especially convulsive to a Britain traditionally ill-disposed to radical change and scarcely recovered from World War II.

Restive Poetics and the American Connection

One of the most celebrated expressions of this restiveness as it surfaced in British poetry was the spirited introduction to the Penguin anthology *The New Poetry* (1962) written by the critic and poet A. Alvarez, and regarded by many as a rejoinder to Robert Conquest's Movement manifesto of six years previously. Clearly Conquest himself took it in this spirit, as he replied directly to Alvarez in the introduction to *New Lines II* (1963). Alvarez's essay criticized the Movement as the latest in a chain of developments, beginning with the 1930s reaction against modernism and continuing through the 1940s reaction against Auden, which had taken the life and spirit out of British poetry by removing, first, technical innovation, then intelligence, and now emotion. The result of such evolution Alvarez termed a "unity of flatness" informed by political "gentility": "a belief that life is always more or less orderly, people always more or less polite, their emotions and habits more or less decent and more or less controllable; that God, in short, is more or less good."[1]

Against this gentility formula Alvarez placed the experiences of D. H. Lawrence and George Orwell, each of whom had discovered and acknowledged the horror of life, and the collective experience of two world wars, concentration camps, genocide, and the threat of nuclear war, which, along with the insights of modern psychiatry, should have taught us that individually and collectively we are vulnerable to uncontrollable forces of cruelty both within and outside ourselves. Because for Alvarez the poetry associated with the Movement involved an implicit denial of life's capacity for cruelty and misery, he called for a new seriousness among poets that would go beyond the pretenses of gentility. In the *New Poetry* anthology itself Movement poets and poems were sharply outflanked by more extreme and generally younger writers; for example, Alvarez included twice as many selections by Thom Gunn or Ted Hughes as by Philip Larkin or Donald Davie.

Alvarez's general sentiments were repeated by American critics not long afterward. In a 1965 essay Chad Walsh, admitting that the "breathing period and time of taking stock" afforded by the Movement probably had been a good thing, nevertheless warned that "if it continues too long, English poetry will become a backwater and an eddy,"[2] while in several books and essays of the late 1960s M. L. Rosenthal complained of contemporary British poets' lack of daring and urged them to attend to their more extreme American counterparts as models.[3]

In fact, it was the work of a particular group of Americans that many British writers and critics had seen since the early sixties as the best hope for a British poetry seemingly mired in gentility. Specifically, Alvarez singled out for praise and inclusion in *The New Poetry* the recent writings of Robert Lowell and John Berryman, who, he felt, had managed to free Eliot's principles of poetic craft and intelligence from the dogma of rigid impersonality proffered by Eliot. Reconciling Eliot with D. H. Lawrence, these two Americans, according to Alvarez, had been able to get at "the quick of their experience" and to produce a "new depth poetry,"[4] against which the writing of a Larkin or a Davie seemed lifeless.

In the second edition of *The New Poetry* (1965) Alvarez would augment poems by Lowell and Berryman with those of Anne Sexton and Sylvia Plath, two other so-called "Confessional" poets. In his "Gentility" essay he noted with satisfaction how Lowell had gone beyond the impersonality and rhetorical mannerism of his earlier collections, notably *Lord Weary's Castle* (1946) and *The Mills of the Kavanaughs* (1951), and had become able, in *Life Studies* (1959), to cope with his personal disturbances "nakedly, and without evasion."[5] Certainly poems such as "Skunk Hour" and "Waking in the Blue" confront deep personal problems in a compelling and disturbing manner. Berryman similarly had moved into a more direct confrontation of personal agonies after the publication of *Homage to Mistress Bradstreet* (1956), when he began writing the poems that would make up his various dream-song volumes. Even Sylvia Plath, considerably younger than Lowell or Berryman and much more prone from the beginning to write in the confessional mode, surprised critics in the posthumously published *Ariel* (1965), where she seemed to confirm and extend the suicidal obsessiveness of her two previous volumes, to produce perhaps the most disturbing impact on English readers since Dylan Thomas's *Deaths and Entrances* twenty years previously.[6] Besides Anne Sexton, others sometimes associated with Confessional poetry—though never so centrally as Lowell, Berryman, or Plath—included W. D. Snodgrass, Theodore Roethke, Stanley Kunitz, Randall Jarrell, Delmore Schwartz, and Allen Ginsberg.

In accepting the 1960 National Book Award for *Life Studies,* Lowell invoked what throughout the decade would be a frequently echoed distinction between two competing poetries, which he labeled, respectively, "cooked" and "raw":

The cooked, marvellously expert, often seems laboriously concocted to be tasted and digested by a graduate student. The raw, huge blood-dripping gobbets of unseasoned experience, are dished up for midnight listeners. There is a poetry that can only be studied, and a poetry that can only be declaimed.[7]

His preference for the raw, declamatory variety is clear. As practiced by him and the other Confessionals, it showed little regard for accepted proprieties of subject matter or language and depended on seemingly open poetic forms. Its speakers usually seemed unbalanced and in great emotional pain. Above all, it sought to express a sense of difficulty, of feelings and experience beyond the consolations of rationality.

While British readers and critics proved highly receptive to this kind of poetry, and while it stimulated a healthy reconsideration of contemporary English verse as it had developed since the war, some critics expressed skepticism as to the value and validity of Confessional writing. Anthony Thwaite found Berryman's *Dream Songs* "posturing and written in non-languages" and pronounced his sonnets "the New Apocalpyse nourished on martinis,"[8] while Alan Brownjohn questioned the "authority of personal despair" in a writer such as Berryman, and wondered "Is all this quirky rawness noble, or a bit too much of a good thing?"[9] But that negative pronouncements such as these on even the most lambasted of the Confessionals rarely went unanswered can be seen in the *Spectator* comments of Martin Seymour-Smith, who explained to Berryman's detractors: "This time of the twentieth century, one may say, is not any longer a time for stanzas, or even perhaps, for coherence as it has always (and not wrongly) been understood. The world is not coherent, and the people in it have been exposed as anti-coherent."[10]

Besides the debate over the Confessionals, Britain in the 1960s offered many other signs of restive poetics. Some observers regarded the *Group Anthology* (1963) as a counter to *New Lines*. But, while some of the work of Philip Housbaum, Edward Lucie-Smith, George Macbeth, and their cohorts might be termed Confessional, they exhibited much less homogeneity of attitude and practice than either the Movement poets or the Confessionals. Certainly there was no concerted anti-Movement sentiment common to them, their only principles being a variety of viewpoints and strong clashes of opinion in their frequent meetings.[11] More consciously counter to the spirit of the Movement was the anthology *Mavericks* (1957), where one of its editors, Dannie Abse, complained of the coldness and technical glibness of much Movement writing, and argued that poetic form should reflect more of a struggle by the poet with his materials.

During the sixties poetry in England turned public as never before. Poetry readings and recitals, as well as the combining of poetry with folk, rock, and other varieties of popular music, became an accepted practice in centers throughout the British Isles. Perhaps the most celebrated group of young poets to ride this new wave were the Liverpool group—Brian Patten, Adrian Henri, and Roger McGough—who achieved a considerable popular following with their poems and distinctive reading styles. They illustrate what some critics have seen as a significant decentralizing of poetry during this time, as places like Birmingham, Newcastle, Belfast, and Liverpool challenged London as a center of poetic activity. The "pop" style of the Liverpool poets related, too, to the subversive, iconoclastic quality of much new poetry of this time, as it attracted a variety of orthodoxies, actual and imagined.

Perhaps the climax of all these developments—the point at which, according to one observer, underground poetry really came of age[12]— was the International Poetry Incarnation, staged at London's historic Albert Hall in the spring of 1965, and attended by 7,000 enthusiasts. While its luminaries included Allen Ginsberg, Lawrence Ferlinghetti, Christopher Logue, and Adrian Mitchell, the interest of the evening, as one in attendance put it, "lay not in individuals but in the confrontation of attitudes which took place...."[13] Edward Lucie-Smith gives a brief but evocative description of the occasion:

Everywhere the same faces—the stereotyped looks of young Englishmen and women in the mid-sixties: beards for the men; long, swinging, shining hair for the girls. A girl with a cine camera and with Courrèges sunglasses pushed up on her forehead wandered around the arena taking pictures; a young man in a blue cotton suit from Carnaby Street was toying with a slightly withered iris; here and there people were swigging bottles of whiskey.[14]

Anthony Thwaite links the emergence of "pop" poetry with the Beatles' rise and the general atmosphere of dissent between the Suez crisis and the final years of the Vietnam War.[15] Whether making entertainers of poets has produced much of permanent value is questionable. Certainly it helped create a larger audience open to enjoying poetry, though the lumping of poetry with other modes of popular entertainment was perhaps unfortunate. It made many poets more conscious of the—literally—"spoken" dimension of their writing, though perhaps at the expense of its more strictly literary properties. And the "pop" poetry movement resulted in more serious attention to song lyrics and a further awareness of the exchange possibilities between what had been taken as high and low poetic forms. Where previously no one had bothered to analyze the poetic qualities of a Noel Coward or Ira Gershwin—or, in their times, of a Stephen Foster or a W. S. Gilbert—suddenly it became academically fashionable to consider the relative literary merits of John Lennon or Bob Dylan, particularly in relation to their contemporaries on the poetry circuit. Such developments, along with the practices of more legitimate poets of the time, promised to keep open the question of poetry's relationship to mass culture.

Ted Hughes

Probably the most celebrated, and certainly the best known, of the figures to emerge from the anthology wars of the fifties and early sixties is Ted Hughes. Though most familiar to Americans as the husband of Sylvia Plath, Hughes more than any other of the newer British poets came to be associated with a radical poetic and with a corollary radical stance toward contemporary civilization. In the quarter-century since he first broke into print he has established himself as the strongest English counter to the Movement mentality, and the most viable and most respected British analogue to the American Confessional poets. This is not to label Hughes a Confessional—his poetry generally exhibits a toughness and impersonality markedly different from that found even in his wife's writing, with which his has a great affinity—but to suggest the radically naturalist stance he discovered in his youth and has maintained steadily, though in several differing forms, against the cultivated empiricism of much postwar British poetry. Given the aloofness of recent British poets toward their American contemporaries, the controversy generated by Ted Hughes is scarcely surprising.

Not that such controversy is solely the result of his closeness to American poets, for such closeness has its limits. Indeed, the principal American models at least for his early work included such moderate figures as John Crowe Ransom and Richard Wilbur. What lies mainly behind the furor over Hughes, indeed what separates him most sharply from the poets of empiricism, is his unwillingness to compromise his basically naturalist vision. Such an uncompromising spirit runs throughout his work, from the 1950s to the present, and runs counter to the spirit of accommodation at the heart of the empiricist poetic. Of course, Hughes might argue that his is the more genuinely empiricist outlook in that it faces the ugly truth that optimism and illusion too rarely pay off as legitimate responses to life.

Hughes's output in the last twenty-five years is impressive, in terms of both strength and quantity. It includes seven major collections of verse, an equal number of collections for children, plays, adaptations, translations, editions of other poets, short fiction, dozens of reviews and essays—plus numerous limited editions of his own poems, recordings, and radio talks. Such prolificacy has helped make Hughes a force in recent British literature, as well as the first, and perhaps only, internationally acclaimed superstar among post-war British poets. Whatever one's feelings about him, little of this work can be ignored in accurately determining the nature of his art. The Hughes controversy probably peaked with the publication of his fourth collection, *Crow,* in 1970. Critics already hostile to his writing pointed to the *Crow* pieces as the logical conclusion, or deeper layer, of the degeneracy and inhumaneness they had associated with Hughes for years. Almost as soon as such criticism started, however, admirers began to deny that Hughes necessarily condoned the violence represented in his poems—claiming that, unlike his more romantic detractors, he preferred to face honestly the unpleasantness of life—and argued that *Crow* occupied a necessary and distinguished place in the developmental line of his writings. Whether to regard his career as progressive or as static thus became a much more crucial issue among his readers than among those of the empiricists, who by definition had adopted a fairly fixed attitude.

One of the constants attributed to Hughes's poems, recent as well as early, is a concern with nature. This label of nature-poet accounts in part for his being connected with such figures as Hopkins, Lawrence, and Dylan Thomas. Such labeling is misleading, though, in that in much of his most representative work, particularly those celebrated early poems by which he won his reputation, Hughes is concerned more with man in nature, or surrounded by nature, than merely with nature itself. The title poem of *The Hawk in the Rain* (1957) centers upon a state of mind, common in Hughes's writings, where the speaker explores his feeling of weakness in comparison with the more powerful creatures and forces of nature. Specifically, he laments how he "drown[s] in the drumming ploughland" and "drag[s] up / Heel after heel from the swallowing of the earth's mouth" while the hawk remains poised high above the ground "in a weightless quiet," seemingly without effort. The similarity to Hopkins becomes more obvious as he notes how the wind "Thumbs my eyes, throws my breath, tackles my heart" and characterizes himself as the "bloodily grabbed dazed last-moment-counting / Morsel in the earth's mouth." The last of the poem's three sentences sees Hughes imagining the hawk succumbing to the wind's force in terms ("the round angelic eye / Smashed, mix his heart's blood with the mire of the land") that only intensify our sense of his own helplessness even as the hawk remains unperturbed.

Other even more acclaimed early pieces, notably "Wind" and "October Dawn," show the solitary human terrified, even mesmerized, by observing nature. "Wind" is little more than a chronicle of such accumulated terrors, while "October Dawn" becomes almost comic as its speaker—with an imagination, if not a rigor, worthy of an Aquinas or Calvin—constructs out of a slight formation of ice on some wine left out overnight an image of the return of the ice age:

> ... sound by sight
> Will Mamoth and Sabre-toothed celebrate
>
> Reunion while a fist of cold
> Squeezes the fire at the core of the world.

Two poems written perhaps ten years after these and included in *Wodwo* (1967) record similarly fascinated observings of what Hughes finds as seminal moments emblematic of nature's strength and relentlessness. In "Sugar Loaf" he seeks to insulate himself against the terror inherent in such observations by claiming an advantage in his superior knowledge. Thus the poem moves from his rather impersonal description of a trickle of water cutting through the crown of a hill, through the awareness afforded him by his power to imagine and predict ("I see the whole huge hill in the small pool's stomach"), to the hill's obliviousness: "This will be serious for the hill. / It suspects nothing." However, the personification in these lines, as well as his further characterizing of the hill as not only an unsuspecting but a "dull, trusting giant," implies a fear that by extension he, too, is dull and helpless against unsuspected forces of nature forming his own perhaps dark future. Relatedly, in "Bowled Over" the Hughes speaker more honestly but no less grimly confronts the ominous implications of one's first contact with death, however slight or indirect.

Many of Hughes's most effective poems find him not only observing nature but meditating on his past observings. Repeatedly we see the mature reflector recalling incidents signifying either a breakthrough in his awareness of nature or an unawareness from which he has since progressed. The Yorkshire countryside where Ted Hughes spent his childhood profoundly affected his view of life and poetry. "[M]y interest in animals began when I began," he has admitted, and he has characterized the writing of poems as analogous to the capturing of animals that occupied so much of his time and energy during his first fifteen years.[16] The tracking, capturing, and even pocketing of wild creatures, large and small, as well as years of drawing and of poring over animal pictures, no doubt helped create a fund of experience and imagery to which the older Hughes would return repeatedly in his poetry.

"The Bull Moses," one of Hughes's most anthologized poems and written immediately after *The Hawk in the Rain,* recalls his childhood initiation into nature's otherness, in the form of a bull that frustrated his anthropomorphic expectations. We see the small child noticing first the barn's "blaze of darkness" and the corresponding blankness of the animal's expression. Puzzled by the bull's attending to a troublesome fly while ignoring his own frenzied waving and shouting, the boy then noticed the beast's willingness to be enslaved and led by a brass ring, and inferred from such docility "something / Deliberate in his leisure, some beheld future / Founding in his quiet." The youngster's abruptly bolting the pen door after the bull concluded rather comically a sequence of feelings that could be articulated only many years afterward and that the older narrator-poet regards with amusement but also with appreciation, as the beginning of long pondering over nature's essential distance and mystery. This same process, by which the bull Moses took on emblematic significance, is suggested in "View of a Pig" and "Pike," where Hughes interrupts his grimly effective musings on a dead pig and predatory fish, respectively, to recall an earlier, merrier experience with a greased fairground pig and his first encounter with the cannibalism of pike ("One jammed past its gills down the other's gullet"). In each poem the recalling of a past encounter helps define that of the present.

These poems were written in the late 1950s and collected in *Lupercal* (1960). Their sense of the solitary person confronting nature continues through each of Hughes's later collections. In a way *Crow* might be described as one great discovery of the outside world by its protagonist, though Hughes there blends the solitary and the social, the inside and the outside, and the natural and the artificial as in none of his other books. Nevertheless, certain *Crow* poems— "Crow Alights," "Robin Song," "Crow's Elephant Totem Song," and "Dawn's Rose"—project the same sorts of discovery related in "October Dawn" or "The Bull Moses." The more recent collections,

Season Songs (1975) and *Moortown* (1979), connect even more closely
to the figure of solitary man confronting nature, which so dominated
the first books. One of the *Moortown* poems, "March morning unlike
others," epitomizes such confrontation through Hughes's joyful im-
ages for spring's renewal and the assurance it brings:

> The earth invalid, dropsied, bruised, wheeled
> Out into the sun
> After the frightful operation.
> ....
> While we sit, and smile, and wait, and know
> She is not going to die.

Much of the artistry in these poems consists of Hughes's proj-
ecting a sense of authenticity through such encounters and discov-
eries. For him confrontation with nature seems to operate in much
the same way that jazz music and other exploration into the "natural
noise" of ordinary life ("scattering long-haired grief and scored pity")[17]
operate for Philip Larkin. We know that, despite his Oxford back-
ground and closeness to the formal poetic tradition, Larkin's rela-
tionship to academia has always been somewhat uneasy. Yet, we
know, too—through the view of him in Amis's *Lucky Jim,* as well
as in his own *Jill,* and through his highly esteemed jazz and book
reviews—that he has found within the pale of respectability ways
of accommodating his sometimes considerable distrust of institu-
tional phoniness and inertia. Hughes's reaction against the academic
and the respectable—the trauma of his experience as a student at
Cambridge, for example—has been much more extreme. His po-
etry's fixation with encountering nature can be seen in part as an
attempt to return to what he considers the greater authenticity of
his boyhood. Thus the bittersweet appropriateness of his likening
his chief adult activity, writing poems, to the childhood hunting
of animals, for such a comparison suggests as much the search for
consolation from loss as the conviction that such loss can be
supplanted.

Certainly the differences in outlook between the two poets are
reflected in the differing ways by which their poems are plotted.
As noted earlier, discovery in Larkin's poems generally turns on the
closing of gaps, and the gaps usually are social ones. Most of Hughes's
poems concern the gap between modern man—represented by the

solitary speaker, rather than the variety of characters to be found in Larkin's poems—and the true state of things, to which nature even in its incomprehensibility is the most reliable emblem and guide. The closing of this gap assumes ignoring, or going behind, social concerns. Discovery in Hughes tends to be solitary; indeed, it depends on solitude. Those poems dealing with human relationships only point up the advantages of, and need for, solitude. Certainly the social gaps tend not to get closed, for Hughes sees a basically profound and pre-social problem behind them, a problem that Larkin's empiricism does not acknowledge.

Accordingly, discovery and recognition take on a different cast for Hughes. His discovery-plots rarely start very far from their finish and frequently represent little more than the augmenting or intensifying of an initial feeling or intuition. Thus "The Hawk in the Rain" shows the speaker merely boxing himself in as he tries, halfheartedly and futilely, to deny the inescapability of his dilemma. Similarly, "The Bull Moses," "View of a Pig," and "Pike" all begin with the protagonist's misgivings toward what he is seeing, and move to a darkening of that first impression.

Many Hughes poems concern the search for an appropriate image or metaphor to represent a feeling, usually fear. "October Dawn" seems to operate on such a principle, as do "Gnat Psalm" and "February." In this last poem Hughes considers and discards several types of wolves as emblems for winter's terrifying grip, before settling on a headless breed and noting the folly of putting on wolf-masks as a stay against such terror.

But even so seemingly a finished poem as "February" in the end only begs the qustion with which it begins. Compared with the basic fear and dissatisfaction motivating most Hughes poems, the finding of a suitable image seems a rather minor development. The distinction between a fixed situation or state of mind and a shift of feeling or awareness, which is relatively easy to make in Larkin's poetry, largely breaks down in that of Hughes, where discovery, if it occurs, only highlights a problem without promising solution.

In an early poem, wryly titled "The Man Seeking Experience Enquires His Way of a Drop of Water," Hughes exposes the folly and futility of the entire rationalist-empiricist approach to life by having his central character, steeped in that approach, gain nothing from applying it in a pure, compressed version. Specifically, Hughes's

empiricist argues that a single drop of water, having existed since
the earth's beginning—

> Having studied a journey in the high
> Cathedralled brain, the mole's ear, the fish's ice,
> The abattoir of the tiger's artery,
> The slum of the dog's bowel ...

surely through all that time and all those experiences (and countless
others) must have derived the very essence of existence. "Venerable
elder!" the inquirer pompously addresses the droplet: "Let us learn
of you. / Read us a lesson, a plain lesson how / Experience has worn
or made you anew...."

The result of such logos-centric and egocentric inquiry is, of
course, a total silence. Assuming an affinity, yet a definite supe-
riority, to every element in nature, and priding himself on the
cleverness of condescending to seek wisdom from the seemingly
insignificant droplet, Hughes's empiricist is confounded, as are the
principles of his inquiry. The notion that wisdom consists of "les-
sons" to be drawn systematically from experience and distilled into
a verbal formula—a notion behind most poems in the empiricist
tradition—is undercut by the severe satire of Hughes's parable. Such
satire of overreliance on language is echoed frequently in *Crow* poems
("Crow Communes," "The Battle of Osfrontalis," "Crow Tries the
Media," "Crow Goes Hunting"). Perhaps the key to "The Man
Seeking Experience ..." comes in the observation that "[The droplet]
no more responded than the hour-old child / Does to finger-toy or
coy baby-talk," as it points to a whole complex of false premises
upon which the inquirer is operating.

It points, too, to a somewhat later poem illustrating what Hughes
surely views as sounder principles of inquiry and discovery. Some-
times cited as an astonishing example of his stylistic range, in its
resemblance to "an imagistic piece in the mode of H. D. or Pound
in his Chinese vein,"[18] "Full Moon and Little Frieda" displays a
manner of revelation wholly opposite that sought by the rationalist.
Moreover, the quality of that revelation appears in the poem's im-
agistic form itself, as the fulsome rhetoric, syllogistic progression,
and complex syntax of the other speaker's address to the droplet
here give way to a spareness of detail and connective, a clustering
of simultaneous impressions—

A cool small evening shrunk to a dog bark and the clank of a bucket—
....
A spider's web, tense for the dew's touch,
A pail lifted, still and brimming—mirror
To tempt a first star to a tremor.

and syntactical simplicity. The speaker's attention is totally arrested by these impressions and by the small child's suddenly crying "Moon! ... Moon! Moon!" For the speaker there is no initial awareness of problem or puzzle, no weighing of evidence or alternatives, and no conscious ordering of feelings or impressions—in short, no inquiry.

Yet in the end there is revelation: "The moon has stepped back like an artist gazing amazed at a work / That points at him amazed." The amazement, of course, belongs just as much to the speaker, as he senses the moon's possession of Little Frieda and the directness of her approach to nature, in contrast with the distance and indirectness of his own, as suggested by his metaphors. Hughes depicts a discovery within a discovery, as Frieda's more intense experience — which is less reducible to words — sparks the observer's less intense and more articulable recognition. Each comes rapidly and without warning, and neither is the result of inquiry. For Hughes inquiry belongs to science and empiricism and represents the dead end of civilization.

No poem more vividly articulates his ideas on discovery and revelation than "The Thought-Fox." Indeed, it has been cited as the seminal expression of his epistemological, as well as his poetic, outlook. What it describes, through the carefully and elaborately developed metaphor of the fox, is the way poetic inspiration occurs. It begins with a vague, nameless intuition of something invisible stirring as the hand moves across the blank page, notes the stealthy approach of that something ("Brilliantly, concentratedly / Coming about its own business"), and concludes with the quiet burst of poetic fruition:

... with a sudden sharp hot stink of fox
It enters the dark hole of the head.
The window is starless still; the clock ticks,
The page is printed.

Like a fox, the poem sneaks up on the poet without conscious inquiry or systematic recognition. The foxlike muse speaks mysteriously, and just as the enigmatic ways of nature serve as an analogue to poetic creation, so the realization of finished poetic form suggests the nature of every significant discovery. The pleasure of such experience seems necessarily accompanied by a sense of its depth and distance.

Characteristically, Hughes draws on his fund of nature lore to construct the conceit of poetic musing. Such a conceit is meant to tell us as much about nature as about poetry or discovery. Perhaps as much associated with Hughes as his interest in man surrounded by nature—the discovery of which becomes the emblem for all authentic experience—is his striking and peculiar conception of the natural world. The nature of nature is something Hughes's poetry returns to as a touchstone, and as a constant from which radiate his attitudes toward all other human experiences and concerns.

The tone of the recurring Hughes discovery of nature has led many readers to associate him with D. H. Lawrence. Certainly, as we have seen, there is in such discovery the rejection of "smooth" plotting; insights arrive erratically in Hughes's poetry, as in Lawrence's fiction, and seem tied to the natural world. Also, we find in Hughes the same primitivist and tough-minded strain that makes it difficult to label Lawrence simply a romantic. But Hughes carries this so much farther that, as Calvin Bedient points out, he makes us regard Lawrence's "animal joy" as "a lighter, more fanciful thing" than any attribute he would give nature. [19]

Rather than the meaningful, comprehensible construct of romanticism or science, nature for Hughes is distant, dark, and mysterious. The child in "The Bull Moses" certainly sensed this as he unsuccessfully tried on human explanations for the bull's behavior. Noting the beast's "brow like masonry," he observed that "something come up there onto the brink of the gulf, / Hadn't heard of the world" and that "nothing of our light / Found any reflection in him." Even a partial closing of the gap separating man from nature requires the recognition of that gap and of its ultimate resistance to closure.

What we can know of this mysterious otherworld we call nature is that it is violent, willful, and efficient. Romanticism tends to gloss over such qualities, while science—ironically, like religion—tries to go behind them. The reader of Hughes frequently encounters fierce, predatory creatures; jaguars, vampires, cats, hawks, ghost crabs, and howling wolves populate the skies, forests, and waters of his poems. Often, too, Hughes exposes the fierce life that lies just beneath the surface of a seemingly tranquil natural scene. Thus "To Paint a Water Lily" examines the two worlds in which the lily resides. Hughes magnifies the sights and sounds above the water to reveal the "flies' furious arena," "the air's dragonfly / That eats meat," and "battle-shouts / And death-cries everywhere," while under the water he finds no evidence of evolutionary progress since "prehistoric bedragonned times," but only "Jaws for heads, the set stare, / Ignorant of age as of hour. ..." Such a spectacle makes it difficult to paint the lily in traditional still-life fashion or to understand its seeming calm—unless, of course, one views it as sharing the brutality of its surroundings. Other seeming innocents—ferns, thrushes, even a snowdrop—receive the same scrutiny and awaken the same terror.

For all of its brutality, though, Hughes sees merit in nature's perseverance and relentlessness. If life in its rawest form appears little more than a primitive struggle for survival, Hughes seems to suggest that to underrate the ubiquity of that struggle is to imperil survival itself. However the tiny prehistoric forms of life lurking beneath the peaceful lily pads may offend cultivated sensibilities, they have the antiquity of their species to recommend them to humans, who too often proceed blithely and blindly through a faith in their collective immortality. This is why Hughes insists that "In our time, the heroic struggle is not to become a hero but to remain a living creature."[20] It is why, too, despite his miserable physique, questionable character, and uncertain future, the fact that Crow— and by extension man—is in a position to experience the humiliations of life marks him as at least a temporary victor over death and therefore worthy of acclaim (see "Examination at the Womb-Door" and "Two Legends" in *Crow*). This, Hughes seems to say, may well be our grandest achievement and the ultimate value in existence.

Certainly he takes great pains in his poetry to denigrate other claimed achievements and values. By the time Hughes finishes with us, human self-respect has become a rather sorry thing. Most of his collections surround poems or passages depicting human pride with poems or passages exposing that pride as empty or baseless. In one early poem we meet "Egg Head," confident in the resources of his brain ("walled in translucencies") to protect him from the ravages of his natural state, while in the same collection (*The Hawk in the Rain*) we see another Hughes character smiling confidently at himself in a mirror yet soon being terrified by a mountain goat ("Meeting"). Virtually identical meetings can cut across years of writing, as when Hughes, by combining surrealism and realism, vividly depicts the psychological debilitation brought on by a sunstroke, in a *Lupercal* poem of that title and in a *Wodwo* story titled "The Harvesting." Relatedly, the poem "Strawberry Hill" celebrates the survival of the stoat as a species over the literati of the rationalist age: "Its red unmanageable life / Has licked the stylist out of their skulls, / Has sucked that age like an egg...."

Hughes's poetry further humiliates the human species by suggesting the emptiness of our claims to moral, if not physical, superiority. With a caustic wit worthy of a Swift or a Voltaire, he undercuts the traditional claims of morality and civilization. Thus "Macaw and Little Miss" operates as an analogue to "Full Moon and Little Frieda" by qualifying any impression that Hughes regards children in the manner of Wordsworth. Certainly the Little Miss, like Frieda, establishes an instant affinity with nature—in this case, her grandmother's pet bird—but it is an affinity of frustration and viciousness, as her tantrum at the bird's seeming indifference to sweet-talk ironically parallels that of the macaw itself when she begins striking its cage. More sustained but no more flattering comparisons come in Hughes's describing egregious human behavior in terms of a merciless parasite's actions ("Vampire"), or instant hatred between individuals as a mockery of "human brotherhood" ("Law in the Country of the Cats").

This eternal primitivism among humans, despite their claims of moral advance, is most vividly apparent in Hughes's accounts of modern warfare. Perhaps the tendency of most commentators to ignore the great number of war poems he has written while concentrating on his preoccupation with nature attests to his effectiveness in painting war as but a predictable extension of human nature. Certainly it seems not at all inappropriate that the author of "Pike" or "Vampire" should deal with war.

Hughes presents the paradox of the most advanced of rational and technological constructs serving the most primitive and antirational of impulses, of highly organized societies devoting themselves to destroying the basis of society. Hughes has attributed his will-

ingness to traffic in the ugliness of war at a time when most of his
countrymen, especially the writers of empiricism and the Movement,
were attending to more civilian concerns to his having been born
later than they. Because, he argues, he was not in the war he does
not try to back off from it or from the universal cruelty that he
believes it represents.[21] Having a father, as well as uncles, who
fought in World War I helped set him up to write those several
poems—especially "The Wound," "Bayonet Charge," "Six Young
Men," and "Scapegoats and Rabies"—detailing the horror and suf-
fering of modern war.

It also perhaps set him up to expose the hypocrisy especially
attendant upon recent warfare. If Hughes eschews pacifism, it is
not because he finds war likable or pleasant, but because he pro-
foundly distrusts moral idealism as a base for behavior. Those poems
just mentioned, plus many others, suggest that he finds war suf-
ficiently distasteful. But a poem such as "Griefs for Dead Soldiers"
suggests that he finds even more distasteful the moralistic posturing
and futile emotion that usually accompany the making of war. There
he explores three perspectives on battle casualties. "Mightiest like
some universal cataclysm, / Will be the unveiling of their cenotaph,"
begins his account of the public ceremony honoring the war dead.
Such a viewpoint is soon undercut by his portrayal of the widow
opening the telegram: "She cannot build her sorrow into a monu-
ment / And walk away from it," he observes. But not even her
sorrow is sufficiently reliable for Hughes, who then points to what
he considers the only incontrovertible truth of what has happened:

> Cursing the sun that makes their work long
> Or the black lively flies that bite their wrists,
> The burial party works with a craftsman calm.
> Weighing their grief by the ounce, and burying it.

Because the sun and biting flies—the demands of survival—render
both public ceremony and private grief irrelevant and futile, only
the grave-diggers' response appears both honest and viable. Altruis-
tic principles appear strangely out of place.

They appear out of place partly because they rest on an exhausted
religious and mythical tradition. This is the upshot of those several
Wodwo and *Crow* poems that set the Edenic myths on their heads.
Typically in such inversions God appears tired, asleep, or otherwise

stupid, while issues of mythical proportions are settled by forces outside his awareness or control. With the black humor characteristic of the entire *Crow* volume, "A Childish Prank" depicts human sexuality as a stunt originally designed to awaken man and woman from their soulless torpor, Adam and Eve as wholly unaware of what is being done to them, and the jokester Crow, rather than God, as the inventor and executor of the entire scheme. Repeatedly Hughes satirizes the human tendency, reflected in the Genesis-based legends, to invent and then to petrify speculative explanations for the more troubling aspects of life, instead of facing their ethical and practical implications.

Other *Crow* selections, notably "Crow's First Lesson" and "Crow Tyrannosaurus," deny, by use of the same technique of inversion, the universality of love upon which so much Christian moralizing has been based, and which Hughes regards as foolish and dangerous. Relatedly, in "The Contender"—which forms part of the line, already noted, including Alun Lewis's "Crucifixion" and Stevie Smith's "Was He Married?"—Hughes portrays Christ-like resistance to life as a "senseless trial of strength." Religions of altruism contrast markedly with the spirit of "Crag Jack's Apostasy," where the speaker, toughened by many years' struggle, rejects the theology of the churches and asks instead for a revelation from nature, which he can only approximate with the figure of a wolf's head or of eagles' feet.

Disappointed in his purportedly superior morality and the props afforded by the Western religious tradition, man might turn to the various kinds of progress produced by his rationality, as evidence of his preeminence in nature. Hughes will have none of this. The way in which, according to Hughes, advanced technology aids barbaric warfare has been noted. In one poem ("The Ancient Heroes and the Bomber Pilot") the modern warrior is humbled when he measures his push-button heroism against the hand-to-hand combat of his earlier counterparts, noting that while they may have had "nothing to brag about but the size of their hearts" his own heart is "cold and small."

And, lest war appear but an aberration in an otherwise glorious advance of rationalism, Hughes questions many other results of such an advance. In "Fourth of July" he attacks the New World as an emblem of those domesticating forces that have gradually removed us from nature and nature from itself. "Even the Amazon's taxed and patrolled / To set laws by the few jaws," he jokes, as he attacks "Columbus's huckstering breath" for having reduced the authentic excitement of life so much that now we can only "Wait dully at the traffic crossing, / Or lean over headlines, taking nothing in...." Any progressive view of history Hughes regards merely as humanity's self-serving autobiography, a colossal pack of lies.

In fact, for him the primitivist view of historical man would be not only more honest, but perhaps more pleasing. This is why at numerous points he insists upon the primitive factor behind seeming triumphs of urbanity, such as Beethoven's music ("Ludwig's Death Mask") or Tolstoy's writings ("Kreutzer Sonata"). This is why in praising the "terrifying" efficiency of thrushes, he remarks in the same breath "Mozart's brain had it, and the shark's mouth / That hungers down the blood-smell" ("Thrushes"). This is why he prefers, as do most of us, the story of Odysseus's vengeful fury against the bothersome suitors to that of Telemachus's more patient, civil response.

Because the old myths clearly will not do, Hughes sees a need for new ones. His view of man alone, without viable support from an ethical or religious tradition, resembles that of the empiricists. The difference is that they, especially Larkin, regard with sadness and some resistance the passing of the old props, where Hughes seems to celebrate their demise as an opportunity to repair their damage through his own mythmaking. This element of heroic optimism links him with the modern existentialists,[22] though they might question his self-appointment as shaman or poetic priest to lead contemporary man back into the wilderness.

Hughes's mythmaking rejects the conventionally social or political solutions to the contemporary human dilemma. To remedy that dilemma he posits, in poem after poem, models of immersion in the primitive. Predictably many such models come from nature. "Hawk Roosting" takes us into the consciousness of that wild, proud bird:

> It took the whole of Creation
> To produce my foot, my each feather:
> Now I hold Creation in my foot
>
> Or fly up, and revolve it all slowly—
> I kill where I please because it is all mine.

As much as any of his writings, this single poem has provoked the charge that Hughes favors violence. While "Hawk Roosting" may support that charge, in the context of his many other related poems, it supports even more the notion that he favors an honestly violent outlook over either a dishonestly violent one or one that denies the omnipresence of violence in even the most civilized existence.

Certainly such honesty—by which the recognition of the violence in nature and man constitutes the only solid foundation for constructing a new beginning—informs the whole of *Crow,* and especially its most violent pieces. It informs, too, the confrontation of the otherness in self and surroundings making up such mythlike poems as "Wodwo," "Gog," and "Pibroch," as in each Hughes depicts a creature uncertain of his status ("But what shall I be called am I the first / have I an owner what shape am I ...," wonders Wodwo) but free of the old notions and determined to observe the natural world very carefully.

Two Hughes characters further illustrate his counterproposals for human existence. One, Dick Straightup, survives by quietly defying time ("Past eighty, but never in eighty years / — / Eighty winters on the windy ridge / Of England—has he buttoned his shirt or jacket.") and inspires the premature epitaph: "Now, you are strong as the earth you have entered." This image of blending with nature enters Hughes's affectionate tall tale about Dick, when after a wintry evening of drinking and singing he slept in a gutter and froze there: "He was chipped out at dawn / Warm as a pie and snoring."

"The Martyrdom of Bishop Farrar," inspired by legendary accounts of the sixteenth-century clergyman's defiance of his Catholic tormentors, likewise celebrates a persistence that, despite adversity and seeming defeat, constitutes for Hughes an authentic morality and triumph. With gritty images Hughes describes the burning of the Bishop: "Bloody Mary's venomous flames can curl: / They can shrivel sinew and char bone / Of foot, ankle, knee and thigh, and boil / Bowels." But, by the final stanzas, Hughes employs a more purely metaphorical language to mark the effect of the shrewd clergyman's defiant last words:

> ... they rang and shone
> As good gold as any queen's crown.
> ....

Out of his mouth, fire like a glory broke,
And smoke burned his sermons into the skies.

Like morality, sexual love receives redefinition in many Hughes poems. "Her Husband," with its exposé of working-class marriage reminiscent of *Sons and Lovers,* clearly suggests Hughes's denial of conventional notions of love, as do the anti-Edenic *Crow* pieces already noted. This is why in "Dove-Breeder" and "A Modest Proposal" he characterizes love as violent energy. The first of these compares love striking a gentle man to a hawk invading a dovecote, with the result that "Now he rides the morning mist / With a big-eyed hawk on his fist." In the second Hughes again develops an elaborate metaphor—that of two battling wolves—to suggest an approach to love more appropriate to its reality than the gentler alternatives of the romantic tradition. Because love is most natural, he implies, it must be naturally violent, else it denies its essence.

Through all of these poems—indeed, through all of his volumes—run certain stylistic tendencies more or less central to his writing. Perhaps foremost is a penchant for metaphorical extravagance. To be sure, the extended metaphors of "Dove-Breeder," "A Modest Proposal," and several other *Hawk in the Rain* poems proved ultimately uncharacteristic, as they were generally replaced by smaller systems or isolated images carrying, if anything, a greater power to startle. Thus the vantage from which decomposing leaves are watched became "The furnace door whirling with larvae" ("Mayday on Holderness"), or a frog was addressed as "a boy's prize, / No bigger than a rat—all dumb silence/In your little old woman hands" ("Bullfrog"), while Hughes elsewhere casually noted the "rubber tongues of cows ("Thistles") and the "sleeping eye" of a mountain ("The Bear").

Frequently his metaphors or groups of metaphors became surrealistic, as when he compares a new moon to "a splinter, flicked / Into the wide eyeball" ("New Moon in January") or speaks of an owl's "[sailing] clear of tomorrow's conscience" ("Crow and the Birds"). The effectiveness of this last example depends upon its place within a series of similarly absurdist parallels. The image of the owl appears between that of a swift "[flicking] through the breath of a violet" and that of a sparrow "[preening] himself of yesterday's promise." Many other Hughes poems depend on a similar accretion of parallel, but not necessarily otherwise related, metaphors.

Throughout his career Hughes has seemed intent upon developing a distinctive style to realize his distinctive poetic. Corollary to this intention has been a distrust—indeed, a self-conscious rejection—of sources and influences. Empiricist comfort with literary tradition has no place in his mythmaking scheme. And, but for the few poems based on classical allusion—such as "Phaetons," "Cleopatra to the Asp," and "Lupercalia"—his writing is as free as Larkin's and considerably freer than that of Fuller or the war poets of "learned" reference. More significant, though, has been his endeavor to avoid, and to shake off, the burdens of the recent poetic past, for he has claimed:

The problem of any poet writing at present is how not to be overwhelmed by the influences of the great period now just over. The bequest of that generation is too rich. At the same time, as far as its usefulness to a living poet goes, it is obsolete. The huge poetic account they amassed is somehow—without ever having been really spent—bankrupt. Perhaps the world has changed too quickly. Now among the greater number who go on presenting dud cheques, one sees poets preferring to accept total poverty—as a more honest alternative. [23]

Such independence is hard to achieve. In quest of it Hughes has repeatedly denied many of the models commonly attributed to him—such as Donne, Lawrence, Blake, and Yeats—and ultimately acknowledged an ongoing debt only to Shakespeare. Significantly, the Shakespeare he admires is not the esoteric Shakespeare of the scholars, but the "super-easy" poet whose language Hughes terms "super-crude ... backyard improvisation ... dialect taken to the limit." [24]

The various shifts evident in the succession of his volumes perhaps reflect this flight from what he regards as the corruption of tradition, and may represent what Harold Bloom means in speaking of the "anxiety of influence." Where the volumes of Larkin or Fuller seem to blend imperceptibly into each other, those of Hughes are distinct. Reviewers of his second book, *Lupercal*, noticed its departures from *The Hawk in the Rain*: its toning down of conceit and hyperbole, and its greater emphasis upon animals and nature, rather than wholly human subjects. [25] As for *Wodwo*, the third collection, it seems to some critics to reflect Sylvia Plath's suicide in its more stark confrontation with the demonic in nature and man, and in its greater attention to the quiet suffering of creatures than to their will to survive. [26] It reflects, too, Hughes's movement away from the short, fairly even lines and stanzas of the earlier books, to more experimental versification and to frequently longer poems. The *Selected Poems 1956–67*, published the same year as *Wodwo*, showed a purging of poems deriving from presumably rejected models, and this same insistence on independence from poetic authority.

In retrospect *Crow* seems the direction toward which all of this was moving, for there Hughes synthesized what earlier had seemed striking but only occasional and erratic tendencies, both ideological and stylistic. In *Crow* formal variety and experiment, as well as the cynical urge behind much of Hughes's writing, received wider expression than before. There the will to destroy present and past before embarking on the creation of authentic myth appears, ironically, both totally cynical and totally heroic. As A. Kingsley Weatherhead suggests, "The world vision of the early poems that was akin to tragedy has given way to one closer to comedy or farce."[27] Weatherhead sees, too, a connection between the flatter language of *Crow* and its total abandonment of what in the earlier collections was at least a semblance of comprehensible order—only a "barren scenario of pain" seems to remain.[28]

"Crow's Account of St. George" illustrates the black humor and nihilistic satire pervading the entire collection. Hughes's modern dragon-slayer "sees everything in the universe / Is a track of numbers racing toward an answer," and accordingly "rides those racing tracks." The catalog of such busy research, which "refrigerates an emptiness" and "Decreates all to outer space," results in but a momentary triumph, as the researcher faces a demon that he can neither escape nor destroy. First he tries to outwit his taunting adversary—"bird head, / Bald, lizard-eyed, the size of a football, on two staggering bird-legs,"—by using his statistical tools. Next he resorts to physical attacks on the crowlike monster, which survives in various forms and sizes before being overcome and "bifurcated." In a horrifyingly terse finale Hughes has his computer-age St. George drop his sword and run "dumb-faced" from the house "Where his wife and children lie in their blood." The enormity of his error, the misplaced reliance in the powers of reason and numbers, reduces him to a primitive despair and forms the basis of Crow's absurdist parable.

And yet, despite such darkness, *Crow* is not without its glimmering of optimism. A sort of fortunate fall seems implied in the very choice of the crow as the protagonist or central emblem, in place of the corrupted symbols of conventional poetry and religion.

Also, Crow's awareness and survival, however minimal or unheroic, seem an advance over the hypocrisy Hughes imputes to the Western tradition. If, as Weatherhead contends, *Crow* is arbitrarily structured,[29] such arbitrariness appears appropriately deviant from the Aristotelian logic and poetic Hughes is attempting to refute, and thus more credible in the context of his other writings than the order that an admiring critic might impose on *Crow*.[30] Further, as Faas suggests, *Crow* definitely signals Hughes's embrace of primitive poetry and song, from which a fresh start for Western man may arise.[31] With *Crow* Hughes grooms himself for the role of contemporary mythmaker only implied in the earlier poetry.

Whether *Gaudette* or any of his other later writings realize this role is open to serious question. The poems making up *Cave Birds* (1978) seem but a continuation of *Crow,* which Hughes regards as unfinished,[32] while the pieces in *Moortown,* with the exception of the "Prometheus" and "Earth-Numb" groups, are so gentle as to suggest a Hughes-before-Hughes, a step back into a Wordsworthian existence stripped of romantic rhetoric.

Only in *Gaudette* does Hughes extend the radical vision established with *Crow.* The bizarre sequence presents the final day of a changeling sent by "elemental spirits" to supplant an Anglican clergyman, Nicholas Lumb, who has been abducted to the netherworld. Having made love to all the women of Lumb's parish, in a sort of missionary effort, the changeling-Lumb desires independence from the constraints of his status, and therefore is punished by the parish husbands' discovering him in an orgy with their wives.

Technically *Gaudette* shows Hughes at his most striking: deftly mixing experimental verse and prose, and combining depth of feeling with cosmic (and sometimes comic) irony in his delineation of central and peripheral characters. The language of *Gaudette* is said to be Hughes's most Shakespearean, while the entire poem reflects his doppelgänger conception of himself and his quarter-century fascination with the earth-mother notion of Robert Graves's *White Goddess*.[33] Certainly the idea of a quasi-divine ambassador bringing the "good news" of erotic love to a love-starved Christian community corrects the harsh tone and antifemale bias of *Crow.* And a lyric such as "Churches topple" helps locate Hughes's hope for man in a naturalistic universe, as its address to the female principle in nature concludes: "In all that time / The river / Has deepened its defile / Has been its own purification / Between your breasts / Between your thighs." Clearly this seems a new kind of poetry for Hughes, and perhaps a new kind of beginning on the rubble of the civilized hypocrisy exploded in his earlier collections.

But *Gaudete* is not a collection ultimately concerned with triumph. Nor can one be certain of the hope Hughes seems to articulate in "Churches topple" and the other evocative lyrics making up the book's "Epilogue." Because of the uncertainty of *Gaudete's* status— an uncertainty compounded by the somewhat regressive collections appearing after it—for most readers the essential Hughes will continue to be several poems written before *Crow* appeared. While Hughes has succeeded in making such poems impressive fixtures in the British poetry of this century, whether he will realize the more profound ambition of liberating mythmaker for his time is yet uncertain.

Geoffrey Hill

To class Geoffrey Hill with Ted Hughes may seem odd, as Hill's poetry differs from Hughes's in many ways. For one thing, Hill's writing makes for difficult reading. He rarely exhibits the accessibility of a Hughes or even a Larkin. Ever since Hill began to catch the attention of reviewers, they have tended to combine admonition and consolation in reassuring readers that a Geoffrey Hill passage or poem, however incomprehensible even after four or five readings, nevertheless rewards by its rhetorical force, its beauty, and its tantalizing promise that just one more reading might get to the heart of its meaning. Where the poetry of Hughes or of the empiricists begins to pay off on a first attempt at understanding, Hill's only promises to pay off eventually. But, where modernist obscurity annoys the admirer of Hughes's cold clarity or Larkin's more warm-blooded variety, that same reader is likely to be merely embarrassed at his own inability to handle the uncanny obscurity of Hill's writing, which often demands increasing attention with each element of meaning it yields. To be caught up in Hill's poetry—and this is quite easy—is to feel trapped: unable to dismiss the poem as absurd or pretentious, yet equally unable to feel secure in it without giving considerably more attention to the text.

Certainly this penchant toward difficulty develops out of Hill's earliest writing. *For the Unfallen* (1959), most of which he wrote in his early twenties, offers many lines, passages, and even entire poems illustrating it. Typically syntax, more than diction, accounts for much of this difficulty. Thus the "Requiem for the Plantagenet Kings" opens with an elaborately complex sentence fragment growing out of the title, and moves through an equally elaborate sentence, with an almost-hidden grammatical subject, before giving way to more orderly syntax in its completion. Here syntactical obscurity reinforces the tension and destructiveness Hill would describe, as it does in the first of the "Two Formal Elegies," a sonnet celebrating the toughness of Jewish survival. There Hill establishes syntactical uncertainty by delaying the subject of the first sentence for more than four lines, and continues that uncertainty through the grammatically complex sentences that follow. The group of short poems titled "Metamorphoses" similarly illustrates the uncanny combination of disarmingly simple diction with tortuous syntax reminiscent of Donne or Hopkins that creates Hill's peculiar brand of difficulty.

This same difficulty has continued to mark his writing even as he has disclaimed many of those first poems. Indeed, in the "Three Baroque Meditations," written sometime in the mid-1960s, he explicitly turns the parallel between the reader's difficulties and the writer's into an emblem of life's difficulty. He begins by noting how, despite the majesty afforded life by language and philosophy, as a poet he feels hounded by the jungle law of nature ("shadowed" by the "lithe / Paradigm Sleep-and-Kill"). In the second meditation he moves this *realpoetik* a step further. Beginning with a characteristically packed and powerful line, "Anguish bloated by the replete scream," Hill develops his ongoing realization as poet: the intimation that producing true poetry only compounds the agony of reality by revealing further agonies. Rather than release or escape, the finished poem ("perfect / In its impalpable bitterness") gives the poet only a "Scent of a further country where worse / Furies promenade and bask their claws." Finally, in "The Dead Bride" he turns to allegory by having the virgin ideality ("So white") recount her union with reality through her husband the poet, whose daily "disciplines of language" she matches with a daily cleansing of her "pink tongue / From its nightly prowl...." As the poet gradually realizes the impossibility of the union he has attempted to foster, his poetry, originally intended to celebrate that marriage, becomes a means of "solemnizing" his ultimate loss of ideality.

Hill thus sees the poem mourning the price of its own fruition, and its density and complexity—the poem's hard beauty—as emblematic of the poet's hard-earned awareness. A key component of this hardness is a frequent reliance upon rhyme and a line of measured stress, which marks even many of Hill's most recent poems. Rather than revolting against or bowing to the pressure of prosodic tradition, he appears to have absorbed that tradition into his peculiar viewpoint.

Relatedly, the greater elusiveness of his poetry is accompanied by a greater allusiveness than found in the writing of Ted Hughes, the empiricists, or most other British poets emerging since 1939. Instead of the timeless present of Hughes, the historicity of Larkin or John Betjeman, or the studied contemporaneousness in much remaining postwar poetry, Hill offers a sense of time-as-continuum, almost Augustinian in its starkness. Neither progressive nor retrogressive, his view and use of history suggest immediacy without motion, perspective without distance.

His poems can deal with the Versailles Conference in 1919 or with King Solomon's mines, with Nazi Germany and the holocaust or with Wordsworth, with the Plantagenet kings or with Jewish legends. One sequence concerns poets of different eras and nationalities martyred by repressive regimes. Another explores the muddle of commerce and society in the twentieth century. An entire collection, *Mercian Hymns* (1971), is devoted to the resonances between eighth-century Mercia under King Offa and the modern England in which Hill has grown up. Such historical allusion and cultural cross-reference are constants in these and most of Hill's other poems. As with prosody, where Hughes rejects history and culture, Hill appears to have absorbed such traditional materials into his vision of poetry and human existence.

One of his most impressive achievements in this line is "Funeral Music," published in his second book, *King Log* (1968). Concerned with three soldier-poets beheaded in the War of the Roses, this set of eight quasi-sonnets has won comparison with Robert Lowell's *History* (1973) as a thoughtful exploration of the poet and society's relationship to time and to the historical past.[34] Hill claims to be attempting a "florid grim music broken by grunts and shrieks";[35] certainly the entire sequence illustrates the "maximal, directed ambiguity" attributed to all of his writing.[36]

Such play between foreground and background begins with the
first poem's mix of barbarism and refined ceremony, as the vaguely
Platonic "Processionals in the exemplary cave, / Benediction of shad-
ows" give way to the "meaty conduit of blood" by which the three
heads are struck down. The poem ends with a dazzling pile-up of
sharply paradoxical images, to reinforce the doubleness of vision
with which we are to view these men, their lives, their deaths, and
the human history of which they are a part.

Just as Hill has disclaimed any narrative or dramatic order in
"Funeral Music,"[37] critics have commended his avoidance of realistic
unity in creating a more radical structure.[38] Such structure emerges
in the tightening of the paradoxical riddling with which the se-
quence begins. The feeling generated by these poems is uncertainty
reinforced by shifting and indeterminate point of view. While some-
times, but not always, Hill writes in the first person, the viewpoint
of such writing seems only vaguely that of an insider. Thus the
second poem introduces the indeterminate "we" to examine the self-
sacrifice that might be attributed to the three dead warriors. But,
the poem suggests, even if they are to be seen as martyrs, the
principle behind their altruism can only be described as "fat Caritas."
For what sort of charity demands such senselessness as the Battle of
Towton or the deaths of cultured gentlemen? That battle Hill else-
where likens to the holocaust, while he finds the dead soldier-poets
"vulnerable alike to admiration and skepticism."[39] Certainly key
phrases, such as "fastidious trumpet / Spilling into the ruck," pro-
vide a measure of each.

The succeeding poems manage to peck away at both admiration
and skepticism without destroying either. The third depicts re-
pentance as probably the result of battle fatigue. In the next, faith
in the soul's immortality appears only negative, developing out of
a sense of the intellect's inadequacy. Even in the sixth poem, the
most poignant of the sequence—where a soldier sees in his little
son the sign of his own fall from innocence—the speaker asserts an
ambiguous belief in "my / Abandonment, since it is what I have."
Is this abandonment of him, or by him? Does his belief mark him
as a penitent seeking peace with his conscience, or a worldling
rationalizing further cruelties? Hill, like his reader, cannot tell.

In fact, the final poem, which Merle Brown has compared to
Matthew Arnold's "Dover Beach" and T. S. Eliot's *Four Quartets*,[40]
collects the uncertainties of the preceding seven. Just as Hill has

been taunted by the seeming inconsistencies of character and be-
havior of the three warrior-poets, so he is torn by the frustration
not only of not knowing what they were, but of not knowing how
others will regard him, and by an awful sense of our inadequacy,
individually and collectively, to do or be what we would. As Brown
points out, Hill accomplishes this through a "we" encompassing
the dead poets, the contemporary historian trying to fathom them,
and all humankind. "Contractual ghosts of pity," Hill calls us:
"bear[ing] witness, / Despite ourselves, to what is beyond us, / Each
distant sphere of harmony forever / Poised, unanswerable." He sees
in the lives and deaths of the three men, and in his indeterminate
riddling over them, an emblem of the inconsequentiality of indi-
vidual effort, for good or evil. Whatever scorn he might have for
them turns to pity for all people, himself included, "Dragged half-
unnerved out of this worldly place, / Crying to the end 'I have not
finished.' "

As quietly elegant as any of Larkin's ruminations on death, "Fu-
neral Music" illustrates powerfully the humane academicism in-
forming all of Hill's writing. It illustrates his notion of "history as
poetry": "Poetry unearths from among the speechless dead / Lazarus
mystified, common man / Of death" ("History as Poetry"). The
poet's search for "Fortunate auguries; whirrings; tarred golden dung"
through his "knack of tongues" thus puts poetry at the head of
meaningful human activities.

No doubt the assertiveness of this position, and the scholarliness
it assumes, has helped Geoffrey Hill to win a following among
academic critics and to transcend critical wars, even in the United
States. Readers for whom Larkin is too stuffy or Hughes too strident
and immature have agreed on Hill amidst little else they might
agree on. Thus Harold Bloom has admitted Hill to his phalanx of
"strong" poets—indeed, he has praised Hill as "the strongest British
poet now alive" and "the most Blakean of modern poets"[41]—while
another American, the poet Donald Hall, for whom Bloom's poetics
are anathema, has lauded Hill with equal enthusiasm. Complaining
only of the Bloom introduction included in the American gathering
of Hill's first three collections, Hall has urged readers: "Buy the
book, read Hill, and ignore Bloom. Better still, tear the introduction
out of the book and return it to Houghton Mifflin."[42]

As suggested earlier, many things about Hill—not the least of
which is the reception just described—should, and to a great extent

do, set him apart from Ted Hughes. In this context Hill's penchant for meditative writing and his general avoidance of flamboyance ought to be noted. Many of his poems, particularly his early ones, are explicitly religious in concern and devotional in tone. One of the earliest, "The Bidden Guest," expresses the frustration at the confessional of the would-be penitent unable to turn from his errancy. Reminiscent of pieces by Hopkins and Eliot, this poem illustrates not only Hill's deeply religious bent, but the craftsmanship marking all of his writings. And if his later books open up to wider subjects and concerns—if, for example, *Mercian Hymns* is as lively and daring in conception as Hughes's *Gaudette*—the viewpoint remains broadly religious, and in his latest collection, *Tenebrae* (1978), he has returned to explicitly religious writing.

Nevertheless, Hill's insistently harsh portrayal of the world links him to Hughes. It colors all the poems of his first collection, *For the Unfallen;* indeed, as its title suggests, a sense of life's savagery is probably the central intended attitude here. Certainly it marked Hill's teenage rewriting of the Creation, where six days of God's work led to the conclusion that "By blood we live, the hot, the cold, / To ravage and redeem the world: / There is no bloodless myth will hold" ("Genesis")—a conclusion not unlike that informing *Crow*. Hill's reinterpretations of New Testament myths are founded on this same naturalistic skepticism. In one he responds to traditional nativity portrayals by characterizing Jesus as a "dumb child-king," his admirers as a gathering of "bestial and common hardship," and the adoring angels as "[frozen] into an attitude / Recalling the dead" ("Picture of a Nativity"). Such eerie destylization occurs, too, in his "Canticle for Good Friday," which begins with the cold assertion that "The Cross staggered him," moves quickly through the ascent to Calvary, and ends with the surrealistic view of the death as "Creation's issue congealing (and one woman's)." Though such poems may remind us of Yeats's "The Magi" and Eliot's "Journey of the Magi"—or of the more recent ironic responses to the crucifixion by Lewis, Amis, and Smith noted earlier—Hill's intent seems not so much to lend dramatic or historical irony to the Christian myths as to focus on the starkness of their natural and human settings.

The starkness of human love is especially evident in Hill's early poetry. Style and attitude reinforce each other in the ironically titled "Turtle Dove," where syntactic density—not so much obscurity as a sense of weightedness—matches the complexity of motives in a troubled marriage. Hill reveals an exhausted—and exhausting—relationship, where each principal is driven, rather than attracted, toward the other, and where each "[forges] passion upon speech." The poem deals mostly with the wife, with how she "modelled her real distress" and endured frustration to "affront" her husband, who was fully aware of the mix of grief and "formed surface of habit" in her outward behavior. Her eyes are said to have been "starved," and his, "devouring"; with neither was healthy giving possible. Her response, like his, to their problematic relationship, is characteristically circular: "as one self-dared, / She went to him, plied there; like a furious dove / Bore down with visitations of such love / As his lithe, fathoming heart absorbed and buried." The effect of such an account, and the terms in which it is rendered, is not so much sympathy as horror, and not so much distaste as wonder. A similar tension arises in the companion piece "The Troublesome Reign"—where the man's rising passion initially wins "concession to desire" in the woman but ultimately produces only an uneasy afterward—as in all of Hill's other poems concerned with love, most notably the later *Songbook of Sebastian Arrurruz*.

On occasion Hill's admiration for survival can match that of Hughes. It is most strikingly shown in "Four Poems Regarding the Endurance of Poets." There Hill plays on the ambiguity of his title's key term, as each lyric reveals "endurance" in the sense of what the particular poet put up with, the fact that he endured, and the means by which he managed. The method of Robert Desnos, the poet-resister who died in Terezin Camp in 1945, illustrates those of the others. Hill has Desnos speak of the merit of willing oneself into a mental state akin to death and burial, punctuated by periodic "resurrection," as a stay against pain and despair. Analogous tactics by the others—Tommaso Campanella, imprisoned by the Inquisition; Miguel Herandez, another resistance fighter; and Osip Mandelstam—likewise suggest the value Hill places on survival in a world assumed to be harsh and unsparing.

Nevertheless, mere survival does not hold for Hill the ultimate value it holds for Hughes. "Four Poems ..." illustrates his admiration only for survivors who either are victims or who possess special virtues. In fact, usually the survivors in Hill's world are predators or exploiters, and for these he has no use. Thus he goes beyond Hughes in not only portraying life as harsh and pitiless, but in

registering a complaint against its harshness. In this is what Harold
Bloom terms his "desperate humanism,"[43] for it is with an infini-
tesimal chance of success or satisfaction that he shows a quiet rage
against the naturalistic universe he portrays. However tough-minded
his view of things, in almost every poem he finds it impossible
merely to acquiesce or to avoid a plaintive strain. Perhaps more than
anything else in those poems, this ongoing struggle against cynical
complacency, in the face of a reality within and without himself
that justifies scarcely any other response, accounts for the dignified
austerity, the heroism, of his writing.

While it is true that for Hill there is no discovery of life's moral
terror, but only an assumption of it—and that his early poetry
concentrates in laying out that assumption, rather than commenting
on it—even his most detached pieces contain at least an element
of complaint against a state of affairs that he knows should not
surprise him. Perhaps the most celebrated of these, "In Memory of
Jane Fraser," depicts the disparity between natural and human needs.
When the bitter winter forced the snow itself to "like sheep [lie]
in the fold" and the winds to "[beg] at each door," when it made
the hills "blue" and the moor shrouded, Jane Fraser held on. The
hyperbole of this opening picture leads to more somber irony, as
her "siege" is characterized as a "brooding over death / Like a strong
bird above its prey." The poem ends with an added sense of a cosmos
askew to the character implicit in the dead woman's tenacity. "She
died before the world could stir," Hill remarks, as he notes nature's
belated self-awakening. Though the regret is understated, it clearly
emerges from Hill's intense and wishful personifications. The nat-
uralism of the poem thus lies closer to Hardy than to Hughes.

Such a strain of clear if understated regret likewise marks the
three *King Log* poems dealing with Nazi Germany. "Ovid in the
Third Reich" begins with the simple assertions by its respectable
protagonist that "I love my work and my children" and that "God
/ Is distant, difficult," and takes as its epigraph a passage from the
Amores claiming that innocence is wholly contingent upon the denial
of guilt, and guilt upon confession. Such speciousness colors the
dignified explanation by Hill's character that to look down on the
"damned" is unwise, as he celebrates the harmony of the damned
with divine love. The power of the human mind to rationalize
barbarity lies at the heart of the resonant horror produced by this
poem's eight lines, for here we see not merely the indifference often

attributed to the civilian mentality in a totalitarian state, but the even more terrifying ability to absorb the Reich's cruelties into a personal theology and ethic. The chilling compactness of this poem, by which Hill creates a "symbolic" feeling without symbols, is matched in the four lines of "I Had Hope When Violence Was Ceas't," where a concentration camp victim expresses the hopeless sense of "flesh oozing toward its last outrage."

"September Song," the third poem about the Nazi terror, exhibits a freer but no less efficient form. As in Auden's "To an Unknown Citizen," Hill's speaker catalogs the way in which a dead Jewish child ("born 19.6.32–deported 24.9.42") fulfilled the state's expectations:

> As estimated, you died. Things marched,
> sufficient, to that end.
> Just so much Zyklon and leather, patented
> terror, so many routine cries.

Audenesque wryness, however, gives way to the deep personal feelings of the speaker, who contrasts his own relative security—permitting him to observe "The smoke / of harmless fires" on a September day—with the destruction of the young victim and the smoke that it released.

Perhaps the precursor, at least among modern poets, of the austere, oblique humanism informing Hill's writing is Eliot. Certainly Hill's most striking exposition of that humanism, *Mercian Hymns*, resembles *The Waste Land* in its attitude toward secular society, its use of a wide variety of materials and references, its seeming impersonality, and its inclusion of notes to the central text itself, which appear almost a parody of Eliot.

Ostensibly the thirty sections of this sequence concern the life and reign of Offa, the eighth-century king of the West Midland, whose dominion the poet sees reaching to the mid–twentieth century or beyond. Hill characterizes Offa's reign as materially and politically impressive, yet as morally bankrupt. His most notable achievements—the unification of practically all of southern England, and the establishment of a reliable form of coinage for the English—Hill casts as emblematic of the values dominating English culture to the present. In a section titled "The Crowning of Offa" the king dismisses his seizure of power through the murder of a cousin and civil war by saying "So much for the elves' wergild," and ironically alludes to the fisher-king myth by describing himself as a child as "a prodigal, a maimed one." Offa's ruthlessness in suppressing resistance is seen throughout the book, but especially in the catalog of official duties, which include forgiving "the death-howls of his rival" (X, "King Offa's Laws"), and in the account of an ordinary day for the king, when he "threatened malefactors with ash from his noon cigar" (XIV, "Offa's Laws"). Like the respectable citizen of "Ovid in the Third Reich," Offa is capable of routinely detaching himself from the cruelties he condones, but his domestic virtue falls far short of the German's, as we learn that "At dinner he relished the mockery of drinking his / family's health" (XIV, "Offa's Laws").

As for the coinage business, Hill's accounts are equally disparaging. Crediting Offa with "Coins handsome as Nero's" is a dubious compliment, as is the account of his system's ingenuity concluding: "Value from a sparse people, scrapers of salt-pans and byres" (XI, "Offa's Coins"). The idea of decay runs through *Mercian Hymns,* but especially in Hill's outrageously satiric depiction of a modern-day unearthing of Offa's coins, when the workers ("paid to caulk water-pipes") "brewed / and pissed amid splendour," and when the forces of autumn—"telluric / cultures enriched with shards, corms, nodules, the / sunk solids of gravity"—cause the bewildered Offa to conclude, "I have accrued a golden / and stinking blaze" (XII, "Offa's Coins").

Central to the effectiveness of *Mercian Hymns* is the mixing of ancient and contemporary materials, by which Hill suggests the continuing influence of the egregious Offa. The first "hymn" mocks both epic beginnings and religious invocations by addressing Offa as "King of the perennial holly-groves, the river sand- / stone; overlord of the M5 ... guardian of / the Welsh Bridge and Iron Bridge: contractor / to the desirable new estates ..." and by having the invoked spirit reply: "I liked that ... sing it again." Such anachronistic juxtaposition abounds in the succeeding hymns, as carparks, phonographs, pubs, and solicitors fill the picture of Offa's ongoing reign. We even find Offa driving a maroon GT to Rome to see the Pope. This king's spirit, which stresses property and power, survives the centuries, as Hill joins Hughes in protesting the progressive view of Western history. The prose poems making up this protest constitute Hill's most extreme venture into technical experiment, just as their studied casualness of diction and tone depart sharply from his usual practice. And in his end-notes Hill vacillates between offering useful background information and anticipating pedantic objections by parodying historical method. Despite such boldness of form, however, *Mercian Hymns* confirms Hill's disparagement of a people and a civilization largely indifferent to metaphysical or humane values.

Such disparagement continues to be a significant element in his most recent collection, *Tenebrae* (1978). The central tendency of his work through *Mercian Hymns* was away from discrete lyrics and toward unified sequences, and away from the metaphysical tautness of his first poems and toward more relaxed and experimental forms. Certainly *Tenebrae* reflects a continuing attraction for sequences; all but a few of its poems are contained in fairly tight groupings. Style is another matter, however, as Hill turns again to what an earlier reviewer termed "a line packed tight to the buckling point."[44]

The character of most of this latest writing is explicitly religious, recalling Donne, Crashaw, Hopkins, and even Emily Dickinson in its intensity. Thus the sonnet sequence *Lacrimae* consists of seven devotions modeled partly on the meditations of the sixteenth-century Catholic poet Robert Southwell. Hill gives his own naturalistic twist to Southwell's devotions, however, by shifting the order, by questioning the division between sacred and profane love so central to those earlier meditations, and by infusing a general tone of contemporary skepticism regarding the purity of devotional practice.[45] The result is not so much the scorn of a Hughes toward religious piety, or even the sympathetic irony of a Larkin; nor is it precisely parody of traditional devotional form. Rather, Hill seems to turn the screws further on himself, the would-be modern penitent, by updating the psychological tortures undergone by Donne and Hopkins in their search for tranquillity. Given the grim view of the human order offered in his earlier poetry, Hill can only see the sincere believer as partly self-deluded, as wincingly trapped between "harsh grace and hurtful scorn" ("Lacrimae Coactae").

Whether the poems in *Tenebrae* merit the attention or praise given the best pieces of his earlier books is open to question. Even if crafted with the same care, they seem generally less exciting. Certainly, though, their religious tenor explains much of the energy generated by those earlier writings. Hill's perspective remains distinct from that of those poets out of whose tradition he works in that it is insistently naturalistic. However, it separates him from

Hughes in that it is ultimately metaphysical and religious in tone and technique. Because *Tenebrae* seems to consolidate the attitudes and practices of his poetry thus far, a combination of interest and suspense must attend his next book.

Chapter Five
The Meditative Response: Smith and Jennings

Postwar Britain has shared in the growth of secularism and indifference to religion that has marked virtually all Western nations. And, like the other British arts and institutions, literature has largely accepted such a situation, so much so that the earlier, much-publicized conversion of key writers—notably Eliot, Greene, and Waugh—to High Anglicanism or Catholicism, rather than signaling a new Oxford Movement among intellectuals, has seemed more an aberration amid the scurrying for purely secular peace and prosperity.

Despite the paucity of literature professing religious concern, however, a strain of fervent and distinguished religious poetry has survived in Britain. Illustrative of this type of writing is the work of R. S. Thomas, an Anglican priest who has been turning out poetry collections since the 1940s. Thomas's verse illustrates, too, a broader pattern among some poets, a tendency toward the kind of writing that in English poetry stretches all the way back to the early seventeenth century and that Louis Martz has called "meditative."[1] As described by Martz, the meditative poem as a type, while at its height among the so-called metaphysicals, survived the nineteenth century through some of Wordsworth's writing, and especially through Hopkins and Dickinson, and has continued in the twentieth century with such disparate work as that of Yeats and the later Wallace Stevens.[2] In terms of recent British poetry, the meditative poem has dominated the work of certain writers as a means of coping with an irreligious age through an essentially religious perspective. More than the poems of Thomas, much work of two others, Stevie Smith and Elizabeth Jennings, especially suggests a link with Donne and the other Renaissance writers of meditative poetry. While this recent meditative poetry reflects a religious insider's viewpoint, it recalls the perils of maintaining faith in a faithless time, most dramatically recorded in Hopkins's writings.

The strongest poems of Smith and Jennings suggest, too, the extent
to which the century of secularization since Hopkins has com-
pounded such perils.

Stevie Smith

When she died in 1971, Florence Margaret Smith, nicknamed
"Stevie" after a famous jockey, had for some time been known as a
minor poet of eccentric style and outlook, and had more recently
achieved greater celebrity for her platform rendering of poems during
poetry festivals popular in the 1960s; "the laughing, singing poet,"
an *Observer* writer called her in 1967, to describe her unpredictable
way of singing poems before adoring audiences of mixed generations.
"One of the most original poets of her time," claimed the author
of her *TLS* obituary.[3] And, with an eye to the full range of her
talent and tone, A. Alvarez, reviewing her *Collected Poems* upon its
1975 publication, pronounced Stevie Smith "deadly funny."[4] The
later success of Hugh Whitebread's play *Stevie* and the resulting
film, both starring Glenda Jackson and both based largely on Smith's
own writings, have led to a considerable rise in popular and critical
interest in her. Besides the *Collected Poems,* the last few years have
seen the reprinting of her three novels[5] and the appearance of a
volume of previously uncollected verse and prose titled *Me Again.*[6]
All have won praise, and all have focused attention on the authorial
personality suggested, and obscured, by the wryly sad, childishly
profound tone of her central writings. Even the standard college
anthologies, the Oxford and the American-based Norton, have be-
gun to include poems by Stevie Smith, the latter proclaiming her
"one of the absolute originals of English literature."[7]

Even as they defied classification, Stevie Smith's poems proved
disarmingly seductive to a limited but loyal audience throughout
her lifetime, including many writers of much wider reputation than
she herself enjoyed. Disparate critical voices such as Desmond
McCarthy, Ogden Nash, Robert Lowell, and Philip Larkin wrote
admiringly of her verse. In a 1962 letter to Stevie Smith another
American, Sylvia Plath, described herself as "an addict of your
poetry, a desperate Smith-addict."[8] To such loyalists the public
recognition finally given Stevie Smith in the 1960s, especially her
receiving the Queen's Gold Medal for Poetry in 1969, no doubt
seemed inexplicably belated honor for a talent they had known and

loved for a long time. The singularity of that talent led one reviewer to characterize her career as "a moving record of dedication, faithful to no fashion, astute and quirky perhaps, but unflinchingly honest."⁹

Of what does such singularity consist, and how does it convey honesty? Almost all of Stevie Smith's critics have spoken of the childlike qualities of her verse and have compared her with Edward Lear and Lewis Carroll. The world of her poetry includes various fairy-tale creatures and characters from legend and myth. Some are largely her inventions, such as the aristocratic family of the Earl of Egremont ("The Castle"), the Princess Anemone, or the Knight Fafair. Others represent Smith's peculiar reading of traditional materials, as in "Persephone," "The Frog Prince," or "The Frozen Lake"—the last a treatment of the Excalibur legend. Almost always such pieces at least begin on a disarmingly informal, even flippant note: "I am Persephone / Who played with her darlings in Sicily / Against a background of social security" ("Persephone").

A significant number of Stevie Smith poems deal with pets and other animals, but in a manner distinctly different from that of Hughes, Lawrence, or even a more conventionally romantic writer. Most concern dogs and cats—the latter being favored in her later collections—but occasional poems deal with apes, birds, and unspecified beasts. Almost without exception she writes affectionately of these animals, often addressing them directly:

> O Pug, some people do not like you
> But I like you,
> Some people say you do not breathe, you snore,
> I don't mind,
> One person says he is always conscious of your behind,
> Is that your fault?
>
> ("O Pug!")

The directness of such address lends support to the image of Stevie Smith as a grown-up child cast in the role of poet.

Certainly her prosodic practices do little to dispel that image. Like Emily Dickinson, she makes frequent use of the stanza forms of hymns, even specifying particular hymn-tunes to which her poems are to be sung. More striking is her conscious use of the meters and formulas of nursery rhymes:

> I love little Heber
> His coat is so warm
> And if I don't speak to him
> He'll do me no harm
> ("Heber")

> It was the mighty Engine Drain, the Engine Drain, the Engine
> drain,
> Down which the water went, the water went, the mighty waters
> of the inland sea.
> ("The Engine Drain")

Despite its frequency, such surface simplicity usually proves misleading. Indeed, simplistic surface occupies a key place in the strategy of surprise behind many of Stevie Smith's most effective poems. Sometimes she can move through extended lines and complex sentences to a nursery-rhyme conclusion epigrammatic in its starkness: "I put it to my head / And now I'm dead" ("Death Came to Me"). Often, too, she develops serious philosophical implications from an initially childlike perspective. "Our Bog is dood, our Bog is dood," begins one poem, ultimately reinforcing a sense of distance from theological squabbles and from the proud insistence of religious believer and skeptic alike. Another ("The Bereaved Swan") is reminiscent of both a children's television show and a concretist poem in the way it works through monosyllabic words and lines

> Wan
> Swan
> On the lake
> Like a cake
> Of soap

ultimately to encompass entire sentences and to project a deeply felt longing for death. Such lines illustrate, too, her penchant for enjambment, found especially in poems of surface simplicity:

> In the wood of Wallow
> Mash, walked Eugenia, a callow
> Girl, they said she was,
> An Ass.
> ("The Ass")

Such disparity between the poem's measured line and its syntactical units undermines simple meaning and helps produce a sense of seriousness behind apparent playfulness. In other poems enjambment is accompanied by radical shifts in line length and punctuation—with sometimes the sudden elimination of the latter—to reinforce intended meaning and tone.

Such techniques suggest a craftiness, as well as a sense of poetic craft, that far exceeds childish self-indulgence. Likewise, the whimsical and even nonsensical element most often associated with Stevie Smith belies a profound seriousness. Where Ted Hughes depends on hyperbole or extreme irreverence for his most characteristic effects, Smith learns more on absurdism, non sequitur, and flippancy—which is not the same as irreverence—for hers. The result is an upsetting of romantic elegance, which has its prosodic dimension in some of the techniques just mentioned.

The majority of Stevie Smith's *Collected Poems* exhibit elements of nonsense. In some, such elements inhabit the entire poem. Relatedly, many poems seem especially aimed at foiling romantic conventions. Specifically Smith satirizes graveyard poetry (see "To the Dog Belvoir" or "Death of the Dog Belvoir," which begins: "Belvoir thy coat was not more golden than thy heart"); the charms of village life ("Brickenden, Hertfordshire" and "The Lads of the Village"); sentimental views of children ("To Carry the Child") and orphans ("The Orphan Reformed"); self-pity ("Dear Female Heart"); courtship ("The After-thought" and "Correspondence between Mr. Harrison in Newcastle and Mr. Sholto Peach Harrison in Hull"); and even Gothic murder mysteries ("The Grange"). Much of her poetry features gratuitous violence and black humor, as in "Who Shot Eugenie" or "Bag-Snatching in Dublin," which closes its account of the young heroine's fate with the unsentimental observation that "A bruiser in a fix / Murdered her for 6/6."

Such writing challenges the limits of what many readers will tolerate as poetry. Indeed, a special fascination of Stevie Smith's poems lies in their indeterminateness of intention. Many keep us guessing at her seriousness or artlessness. They raise the issue of how "childish" a perspective or poetic practice can be considered adult, or where eccentricity ends and drivel begins. Thus the much-anthologized piece "Tenuous and Precarious" opens intriguingly— "Tenuous and Precarious / Were my guardians / Precarious and Tenuous / Two Romans"—and hints at social and historical satire, and even allegory, with increasingly witty stanzas on the speaker's father, Hazardous; her brother, Spurious; her husband, Perfidious; and her son, Surreptitious. Suddenly, however, the poem moves off to her cat, Tedious ("Count not Tedious / Yet," she insists with typically artful enjambment), and concludes with an exasperatingly clever revelation:

> My name is Finis,
> Finis, Finis,
> I am Finis,
> Six, five, four, three, two,
> One Roman,
> Finis.

Taken literally, the poem may point to Stevie Smith's preoccupation with death and suicide. However, no doubt to many readers it has seemed ultimately nonsense but skillfully crafted nonsense—or skillfully crafted but nonsense, depending on one's priorities. And no doubt it and others like it help account for her vogue in the 1960s, when high art was especially under attack from the "pop" camp. It reminds us, too, of the difficulty of placing Stevie Smith, as the "pop" Stevie so often interrupts the profound Stevie, and as she seems to have labored throughout her career—as in "Tenuous and Precarious"—to confound the distinction between the two. Indeed, wit and nonsense seem to operate as strategies of psychic survival in her poetry, as stays against the despair at which much of her writing more than hints. Because meditation seems always to have been dangerous to her, the *Collected Poems* is punctuated by groups of poems, isolated pieces, and even single lines in which she backs away from her meditative struggle.

Much of that struggle explicitly concerned religion. Like Hopkins, Stevie Smith engaged in a perpetual wrestling match with what she perceived as her own godlessness. This is why she praised Hopkins for the "wonderful suffering time he had" and complained of H. G. Wells: "He has no conception of spiritual strife or the importance of spiritual things at all."[10] An Anglican clergyman who knew Stevie Smith well describes her as "ambivalent: neither a believer, an unbeliever nor agnostic, but oddly all three at once," and further insists, "One could say that she did not like the God of Christian orthodoxy, but she could not disregard Him or ever quite bring herself to disbelieve in Him."[11] Her published lecture on "Some Impediments to Christian Commitment," like the complaint against Wells, suggests a writer profoundly plagued, on the one hand, by a need to believe totally and, on the other, by a sensibility and conscience bent on scrutinizing all professions of such belief.

Two poems from her first published collection, *A Good Time Was Had by All* (1937), set the terms and range of tones for that struggle. Both start from a base of orthodox belief. One ("Egocentric") explores the puzzle of personal unhappiness amid the plenitude of creation. In it Smith catalogs the wonders of nature, suggesting a masterful and even caring First Cause, yet finds nature "my glory and my bane" next to her private sufferings. "What care I if Skies are blue, / If God created Gnat and Gnu," she asks, to end with the couplet that began the poem: "What care I if good God be / If he be not good to me?" While this poem's title suggests self-reproach, its text suggests a person understandably troubled by conflicting doubts and by an inability finally to be consoled by either the abstractions of theology or the evidences of nature.

The other poem ("Mrs. Simpkins") offers a more secure faith in such abstractions—or at least in the Trinity—for there Smith describes satirically the results of another woman's slide from orthodoxy into spiritualism. With outrageous rhymes, which alone would please an Ogden Nash, she has a spirit speak to Mrs. Simpkins at a seance:

> We spirits can come back to you if your seance is orthodox
> But you can't come over to us till your body's shut in a box

Twisting Thomas Hardy's "The Going," she has Mr. Simpkins, upon discovering that ultimately "there's no rest / From one's uncles and brothers and sisters nor even the wife of one's breast," shoot himself to gain at least temporary repose. In this instance Stevie Smith's orthodox sensibility, which accepts religious mystery, rejects unorthodox behavior as mindless, much as in the other poem her unorthodox sensibility found conventional belief unsatisfying.

Dozens of later poems continue this vacillation. In a few, simple religious faith offers undoubted comfort. Much more frequent, however, are those explicitly unflattering portrayals of religion, ranging from a state of mild skepticism to what William James termed "the sick soul."[12] In fact, this is precisely how Stevie Smith characterizes her own soul in "The Blood Flows Back," where neurotic guilt and religion feed on each other. This distrust of religion becomes cold distance in such short pieces as "The Children of the Cross," "Tableau de 'Inconstance des Mauvais Anges,' " and "The Violent Hand"—all of which attribute cruelty to spiritual forces traditionally considered benign.

More often Stevie Smith contented herself with exposing the paradoxes of Christian theology. Reminiscent of "The Tiger" by Blake, whom Smith resembled in many ways and in many poems, is "The Zoo," which explores the riddle of a supposedly kind God creating the bestial lion ("God gave him lovely teeth and claws / So that he might eat little boys"), while "Ah, will the Savior ... ?" examines the same idea of God's creatures' basic helplessness—and blamelessness—this time with the Emily Dickinson device of the dead person awaiting salvation. And again, in "Dear Child of God" Stevie Smith dumps original sin on its true originator, the God who "put this poison in us."

Such adeptness at wittily manipulating the terms of conventional religion is nowhere more evident, however, than in the ironically titled "One of Many." This brief but biting narrative traces the results of a child's being cautioned that he is but one of many and ought to think more of others. Such urging to humility, and resulting loss of self-regard, leads to his murdering another child. The final scene finds him at the gallows waiting to be hanged, and produces this sharp conclusion:

Christ died for sinners, intoned the Prison Chaplain from his miscellany. Weeping bitterly the little child cries: I die one of many.

Here Stevie Smith records her pragmatic objection to a certain theologically based view of humanity and to the ethical system it engenders. In barely a dozen lines she exposes the tensions between self-regard and selflessness, between instinct and will, and between nature and nurture complicating Christian ethics. In other, later poems she continued this ironic manner, though more gently, by satirizing the cloistered virtue often encouraged by religion ("The Weak Monk"), the enmity among religious groups over ritual observances ("A Jew Is Angry with his Friend who does not Believe in Circumcision"), the strange power of humanity to see through religious barriers ("An Agnostic" and "A Religious Man"), and many other aspects of Christian religion and religiosity.

Of course, even at her most caustic Stevie Smith retains an essentially inside perspective on Christianity. Always her poetry at least implies a return to the religious fold, a return confirmed by particular poems scattered throughout her career. While one rarely finds an easy or simplistic faith in her writing—while the wrestling match goes on—the decision to remain in that match appears to be her own. Perhaps this is why on occasion she can go behind the gloom and complexity created by theology and ethics to proclaim exuberantly a god intent only on the joy of creation. In "No Categories!" she distinguishes between such a god of "gutsy creation" and his plodding angels of "scholarly grimaces" and "do this and that," urging him: "Scatter / Their pride; laugh them away." Such projection onto the deity succeeds equally in "Away, Melancholy," where in quasi-liturgical fashion she finds joy in the fact of persistent human aspiration. No less optimistic, and more interesting, is the poem, reminiscent of Yeats's Crazy Jane writings, beginning "Mother, among the dustbins and the manure / I feel the measure of my humanity, an allure / As of the presence of God" ("Mother, among the Dustbins"). A similar insistence on the wedding of humanity and divinity is found in "Distractions and the Human Crowd," which advances an essentially religious argument for secular study.

Typically, however, Stevie Smith's determination to separate healthy religiosity from the unhealthy involves the vacillation mentioned earlier. Several of her best poems derive from religious uncertainty. In one she admits, "There is a god in whom I do not believe / Yet to this god my love stretches" ("God the Eater"). In another she depicts her belief asking her skepticism, "Why do you rage so much against Christ" and exhorting wonder at the incarnation—only to have skepticism concede nothing by replying, "Oh I would if I thought it were so, / Oh I know that you think it is so" ("Why do you rage?"). On a more personal level does she express this vacillation between belief and doubt in "Edmonton, thy cemetery ...," as she recounts first the comfort religion gives her in the face of death—"while I hold to this belief / I walk, oh cemetery, / Thy footpaths happily"—and then the intrusive return of Doubt, "[When] I begin to sing with him / As if belief had never been."

Sometimes habitual uncertainty takes the form of riddling the paradoxes of Christian theology itself. "Can Perfection be less than Perfection?" she asks, as she wrestles with the seeming inconsistency of a being born both humble and divine, and with the contradictions-in-terms in the concept of a "Perfect Man," in the puzzle of an unchanging deity who temporarily "changed" states, and in the ultimate unfairness of a God-Man: "If He was God He was not like us, / He could not lose" ("Oh Christianity, Christianity"). Such remarks suggest the perspective of one painfully aware of herself as one of life's losers yet determined to win a viable religion through admittedly limited intellectual and moral capacities.

The most profound among Stevie Smith's many rehearsals of her religious dilemma comes in a poem largely lacking the humor and verbal tricks of her central style. Anthologized perhaps more often than any other single Smith piece, "Was He Married?" moves through the paradoxes of Christianity and Smith's personal difficulties with such a faith to expound the central problem attending religion itself, particularly in modern times. The poem's basic structure turns on a quasi-Socratic dialogue between two voices—not necessarily characters as such, but sufficiently individualized not to be merely opposing parts of the same personality.

"Was he married, did he try / To support as he grew less fond of them / Wife and family?" begins the first voice, to open a series of questions about Jesus as a man, which gradually reduce him to an abstraction of little use to "mixed" and erring mortals. Each concession made by the second voice adds paradoxically to the image of Jesus as perfect and as perfectly meaningless; the strengths ascribed to him thus develop as weaknesses. Never subject to confusion, to guilt, or to a sense of inferiority—never subject to any demonstrably human feelings—such a being emerges by the end of the poem as a fabrication—and an inappropriate one at that—of human idealism. "All human beings should have a medal / A god cannot carry it," the first speaker concludes, as the two viewpoints gradually blend into agreement at the ethical inadequacy of theology. The poem concludes by acknowledging the human need to "love love and hate hate" without deifying either, though the likelihood of such an advance remains in doubt. More than any of Stevie Smith's more flamboyant poems, this quietly sad piece places her religious posture in clear perspective.

While religion certainly centers her meditative process—and while it recurs as the subject in dozens of poems—it is by no means the only principal concern of her writing. Death and love seem to have interested her with equal frequency and intensity. "I love death, I think it's the most exciting thing," she once told an interviewer.[13] Such excited love surfaces periodically throughout the *Collected Poems*, but especially in her second collection, *Tender Only to One*, and its title poem, where, in the guise of a young girl picking petals off a flower ("Is it you, or you, or you?"), she gradually reveals that she is in love with Death. The restraint with which Stevie Smith here controls the emergence of death-as-beloved provides another link with Emily Dickinson. It relates, too, to many of her other poems, notably the two titled "Come Death" and "Why do I ...," a posthumously published piece where she praises death as a good and loyal friend.

More frequently, and especially as she grew older, her poems revealed an attraction to suicide. Often she merely observed sympathetically the suicidal bent of a poem's central character; in this respect "Lot's Wife," first published in 1942, and "The Hostage," which came out much later, are representative. The understatement with which she praises a man who died recklessly climbing rocks near the seaside—"I would not say that he was wrong, / Although he succeeded in doing nothing but die" ("Harold's Leap")—hints at a sense of killing oneself as a commendable achievement. Such a sense becomes explicit in those many death-wish poems, where she expresses her desire to die or her envy of the dying.

Stevie Smith's fascination with death and dying has often been noticed; she herself commented on it as a constant in her writing. Although the suicidal tendency of her poetry probably peaked in the early 1950s—when she attempted suicide at the publisher's office where she had worked for many years, and retired to care for her aunt and to write—it continued until her death. At the same time, in certain poems scattered throughout her career one finds a skepticism about suicide balancing her profound skepticism about life itself. The desire for exactness in such matters parallels her desire for a proper proportion of belief and disbelief in questions of religion, a proportion she seems always to have sought but never found.

"Study to deserve Death," begins one of her more memorable meditations on the question of how to die, as she develops the image of death as a proud veteran of many battles, whose endurance ought to be emulated even, ironically, as one wishes to be dead. "Prate not to me of suicide," she warns us, "that such end denied / Makes welcomer yet the death that's to be deserved" ("Study to Deserve Death"). Such reassessment of the initially attractive path of suicide appears again in several poems depicting despair, such as "I Am," where the character pathetically allows society's judgment of him as abnormal to force him to shoot himself. Seen in this light, such a death appears decidedly unheroic.

In "Exeat," which Smith included in the final collection published in her lifetime, she meditates on her own moral and intellectual problems with suicide. Citing the cruel Roman emperor who routinely refused the death-wishes of prisoners by saying "We are not friends enough yet," she envisions her muse and her conscience each replying to her own urge to die, "We are not friends enough yet." She asks how a poet can commit suicide before he has learned to listen "properly" to his muse, or how a lover of virtue can kill himself before he has become truly virtuous. Ironically the very challenges of life that seem to compel suicide at the same time forestall it. In a moving conclusion Smith imagines a state of readiness, presumably far into her future, when Life may come to her "with love" and say, "We are friends enough now for me to give you death." Only under such admittedly hypothetical circumstances could she judge suicide good or beautiful. Just as her religious skepticism drove her to a measure of belief, her despair of living compelled her to reject the most certain way out of life's difficulties.

The affront to human dignity represented by suicide seemed to Stevie Smith to overshadow the numerous indignities heaped on her by life. Death emerged as a principal concern of her writing with her second collection, *Tender Only to One*. But not until her third, *Mother, What is Man?* (1942), did she begin to concentrate on love and human relations, which, like religion and death, are informed for her by this same issue of human dignity. Of course, the dignity question tends not to operate so explicitly here as in her poems dealing with the natural and institutional forces surrounding us. Nor, it must be admitted, did she write proportionally so many successful or striking poems as when she concentrated on religion or death. Nevertheless, those she did write, and their connection with her other writings, merit comment.

"All things pass / Love and mankind is grass," she wrote in a 1930s epigram, the ungrammaticality of which suggests her insistent linking of love with life. Every one of her collections contains poems depicting love affairs that have deteriorated or ended. Every one shows speakers and characters lamenting such relationships and on occasion lapsing into either suicidal despair or violence. "The Murderer" recalls Browning's "Porphyria's Lover" in the macabre way its speaker calmly and indirectly recounts "how we had an accident" and how "my love went away." While this is an extreme even in the world of Stevie Smith, the great majority of her poems treating love do little to dispel an essentially negative image of love and its possibilities.

Corollary to such an image are a decidedly poor self-image of the disappointed lover and a distrust of marriage. Illustrative of such weak self-conception is the prison of passion shown in an early poem titled "I Hate This Girl." There the male speaker acknowledges his girlfriend's coldness and his hatred for her, but fondly asks "[W]hat do I do?" to conclude: "Kiss her, kiss her, / And wish that she would kiss me." Equally pathetic is "Love Me!," where the speaker, having given up trying to gain the affection of people, dares to seek out only the rocks and trees, and even there feels hesitant.

Perhaps the most moving of Stevie Smith's anti-love poems, though, is the one beginning "Do take Muriel out / She is looking so glum" and continuing in this manner for several stanzas, noting her loss of friends and her need to be "taken out," before the shocking final quatrain:

> Do take Muriel out
> Although your name is Death
> She will not complain
> When you dance her over the blasted heath.
> ("Do Take Muriel Out")

This ending not only answers the question of the addressee's identity, implicit from the beginning, but confirms the entire poem as a projection of a person who, if not Muriel, might as well be. The hopelessness and loneliness of love thus merge with the suicidal impulse of so many of the other poems.

As for marriage and family life, even when achieved they are said to offer little hope. In "Portrait" the groom-to-be attempts, with uncertain success, to dispel his doubts about the girl he is to marry ("She was not always so unkind I swear") by determining to marry her to a "fair false thought." In "The Wedding Photograph," written many years later, we see a bride's thoughts, which combine a Hardyesque view of marriage with Stevie Smith's characteristic wackiness. Specifically we see a girl about to marry a man who will soon take off for some sort of jungle mission. Black comedy quickly emerges as she admits to Harry's photograph: "It is the death which lights my beautiful eyes / But people think you are lucky to go off with such a pretty prize" ("The Wedding Photograph"). Only the thought of his imminent death allows her to contemplate marrying him. Other, lesser poems continue this mood as they picture failures of communication and feeling between parents and children. Clearly such a poet put little faith in human relationships.

Even so, she occasionally achieved a quieter if still uneasy perspective on such matters. She seems never to have lost sight of the ideal of friendship, however short of it actual relationships might fall. "The pleasures of friendship are exquisite," she remarks in one poem ("The Pleasures of Friendship"). In another ("Autumn") she describes the cryptic courtship of a middle-aged man and a widow, where he tells her, "I am no longer passionate, / But we can have some conversation before it is too late." Such acknowledgment of life's—and love's—imperfection, and an accompanying insistence that a realizable best under the circumstances be sought, seem to color the poem "Valuable," where Stevie Smith describes the way promiscuous young girls undervalue themselves. Though she might be accused of being overly judgmental and of offering simplistic solutions to complex social problems, the advice above all to retain self-respect—something she is sure society will not give—appears not unperceptive.

It is such perceptiveness that kept Stevie Smith from becoming very optimistic in matters of human relations. While she can caution against despair, she generally projects a quiet disappointment that people cannot live together more happily. Such disappointment she expressed movingly in her best-known single poem, "Not Waving But Drowning," the power of which depends not only on the appropriateness of the central metaphor—a drowning man mistakenly thought by his friends to have been waving—or on such prosodic matters as controlled line length and rhythmic balance, which the poem's mere dozen lines exhibit remarkably, but on the profound human dilemma to which it points: the want of understanding, the misleading (and misinterpreted) signs decorating social intercourse, and the varieties of distance and gaps between individuals and groups, especially in modern times. Through her development of the poem's dominant image Stevie Smith seems to recognize both the urgency with which citizens of "advanced" societies attempt to communicate feelings and needs, and the proportionally—and ironically—high degree of failure produced by such attempts.

Never in all her hundreds of meditations on religion, death, and love does she achieve a very fixed or satisfying solution to the problems her poems explore. Even so, one gets the impression that for her the act of poetic meditation itself—especially when accompanied by the equally self-expressive drawings she loved to include with her poems—satisfied an important need in her, relieved at least a small measure of her discontent, and permitted her to face the rest of it with courage. While despair threatened to overtake her poetry—as it threatened to overtake her life—she apparently found in the act of projecting discontent into lines, stanzas, speakers, and situations a way of surviving. In this she transcended confessionalism and became a true lyricist, much like Hopkins, whose struggle and poetry she so much admired. In this, too, she achieved to a great degree the "religion of healthy-mindedness" recommended by William James.[14] The combination of disarming wit and prosodic grace marking her best poems have won her belated but solid recognition; certainly she is part of an ongoing British tradition. But, as D. J. Enright suggests, while "[a]t moments she is like a lot of other poets ... finally, in the totality of her work, she is simply like herself."[15] This poetic and personal gift of finding, and being, oneself constitutes Stevie Smith's richest contribution to her readers' lives.

Elizabeth Jennings

In Elizabeth Jennings we find a writer at once more and less problematic than Stevie Smith. While Smith's eccentricity made her difficult to place even at the beginning of her career, Jennings won immediate placement as she began to publish—through the subjects, stance, and style of her early poetry, and through the social and educational background out of which such poetry had emerged. Since that beginning, in the early 1950s, she has published almost twenty volumes of verse. This might be regarded as a most distinguished postwar output except that, as even her admirers are forced

to admit, Elizabeth Jennings has published—and probably writ-
ten—much more than she should have. A proper evaluation and
placement of her work demands the culling out of those truly pow-
erful poems from the hundreds of others.

Jennings's early placement was among the Movement writers.
The only woman whose work appeared in Robert Conquest's *New
Lines* anthology, she was also the only woman imported to the United
States by Donald Hall, Robert Pack, and Louis Simpson in their
influential 1957 collection, *New Poetry of England and America*. Dur-
ing the quarter-century since, she has remained insistently loyal to
the Movement in terms of the modest dimensions and fixed forms
of her writing. The great majority of her poems are rhymed; virtually
all fall within the compass of thirty lines, with most contained well
within that limit. While she can vary line length and rhyme scheme
between and even within single poems, usually the rhyming is
regular and individual lines no more than ten syllables long.

Even more than their superficial forms do the concerns and at-
titudes developed in Jennings's poems reflect their roots in the
Movement. An early piece, "Identity," begins with the typically
Movement ploy of self-correction—"When I decide I shall assemble
you / Or, more precisely, when I decide which thoughts / Of mine
about you fit most easily together"—before its speaker goes on to
describe the relationship they can enjoy. Here Jennings stresses
honesty and mutual tolerance, rather than passion, and illusion and
exploitation, rather than selfless idealism, as she concludes: "That
you love what is truthful to your will / Is all that ever can be
answered for / And, what is more, / Is all we make each other when
we love." The quiet tone, the modest expectations, and the com-
monsense self-awareness tie in with the antiromanticism informing
most Larkin and Fuller poems, particularly those dealing with love.

Another link with Larkin, and one especially prominent in Jen-
nings's early writing, is a fascination with time and disillusionment.
Like Larkin, she can remind the reader of Hardy when she explores
adult nostalgia for childhood ("Song at the Beginning of Autumn")
or recalls parting from a lover ("The Parting"). But in this second
instance she goes beyond Hardy in analyzing the strangeness of that
moment of parting: she recognizes that its strangeness signaled a
concluding, yet suspects it served (and serves) as a stay against
ephemerality—and therefore wishes it back. Such sophisticated self-
analysis locates this poem nearer Larkin than Hardy. Jennings's

observation, in "Resemblances," that our search for likenesses stems from our desire to restore "the dear enchanted moment"—and that such desire, while erroneous, futile, and even stupid, is irresistible— links her directly to Larkin's "Triple Time." In the most moving of her poems dealing with time she assembles quietly powerful images to praise "[a]n old man tranquil in his silences," who enjoys a triumph of age by being "himself, abundant and assured" ("Old Man"). Such triumph, while necessarily impermanent, depends on the Movement virtues of clear-sightedness and self-awareness.

Significantly, most of Elizabeth Jennings's poems in this bent came early. Even then one could find her deviating from the fairly circumscribed set of concerns, attitudes, and techniques dominating the work of other writers with whom she was grouped. Of such grouping she has said, "I think it was positively unhelpful, because I tended to be grouped and criticized rather than be grouped and praised."[16] Certainly her early deviation from strictly empiricist tendencies suggests that disappointment among admirers of the Movement rested on dubious premises, and that empiricism was an orthodoxy to which she never aspired.

For one thing, many of her poems, both early and more recent, show an insistent skepticism toward empirical reality itself. With gentle wit she explores the paradox of individual perspective, by which the seemingly most tangible elements of life become much less than tangible. Two brief early poems, "Italian Light" and "Afternoon in Florence," develop an almost Platonic denial of phys- ical objects. "It is not quite a house without the sun," begins the first, as Jennings attributes to the houses she sees a certain "rec- iprocity" to light, so that they "contrive / To be designed of sun." Such personification, while literally absurd, reflects the trickiness of perspective, which becomes the poem's real subject. Likewise, "Afternoon in Florence" establishes the afternoon light itself, rather than what it illuminates, as the reality to which she finds herself responding. Later, in "In the Night" she puzzles on the distinction between me and not-me, finding the relationship shifting and elusive:

> How much am I then what I think, how much what I feel?
> How much the eye that seems to keep stars straight?
> Do I control what I can contemplate
> Or is it my vision that's amenable?

And, in at least one poem, the power of subjectivity seems not merely puzzling but terrifying, as the takeover of the mind by neurotic guilt is likened to the haunting of a house by ghosts: "It is our helplessness they choose / And our refusals that they haunt" ("Ghosts").

Elsewhere Jennings criticizes subjectivity, which for her too often becomes the excuse for selfishness. But, while acknowledging the ethical need to get beyond the self, she wrestles with the problem of what, if anything, lies "out there" or of how one can tell. In one particularly eloquent piece ("An Education") she blends Thomas Traherne and Wordsworth to recall a significant incident from childhood which has remained among her "intellectual bric-a-brac." Specifically, she tells of walking outdoors one night when she was ten years old, and being "elevated into wonder / Unknown before" by the sight of "a sky surely spawning stars." "My ten years fell away / As I was caught up in an education / Sublime and starry," she notes. Having kept the memory of "this strange illumination," she confesses, "I am a wanderer still among those stars." The wonder of that moment, which defies rational analysis, marks for Jennings the beginning of her meditative mode and of her fascination with the possibility of reality beyond the empirically verifiable.

Given her ongoing search for a transcendent that refuses to be circumscribed by empiricism, it is scarcely surprising that a religious viewpoint informs much of Jennings's writing. Repeatedly she has insisted that "My Roman Catholic religion and my poems are the most important things in my life."[17] Though she obviously lacks the humor of a Stevie Smith, the intensity with which she projects her religious outlook often compensates for that lack.

One poem especially exhibiting such intensity is "In This Time," which comes from the 1950s. It occupies a place among her writings comparable to that of "Church Going" among Larkin's, and represents Jennings's characteristic response to the secularism out of which sprang the humanism of a Larkin, as well as the satirical thrusts at traditional religion offered up by Amis and other Movement figures. In many respects this is, at least superficially, a Movement poem: its lines and stanzas appear highly organized, and it largely lacks the romantic imagery found in much of her other verse. She even adopts the stance of the rational agnostic, to expose what she sees as the ultimately unsatisfactory nature of secularism, no matter how well intentioned.

The first of the poem's two stanzas suggests the folly of maintaining an appreciation for religious myth and legend in the absence of belief. Even a child, Jennings insists, can see through the sham of such gesturings. In this she denies the ending of "Church Going," since for her a religious state of mind without a particular religious creed represents, at best, self-delusion. Where Larkin's speaker can thus delude himself, hers cannot.

With the second stanza, though, she moves a step further, to expose secular humanism as a contradiction in terms. Larkin's churchgoer ultimately insisted that despite institutional religion's demise the religious impulse would continue. Besides her uncertainty about this, Jennings states that without the church, and without the ritual and public religiosity that it fosters, more than religion itself is in danger. Indeed, she suggests that modern society's rationalistic dismissal of received religion constitutes an abandonment of the basis for all ethical behavior:

> We have retreated inwards to our minds
>   Too much, have made rooms there with all doors closed,
> All windows shuttered....
>   ....
> We only know a way to love ourselves,
> Have lost the power that made us lose ourselves.

Society's collective neurosis is thus connected with its secular outlook. How but in religion, she asks, is ethics effectively sanctioned? Where but in Judeo-Christian legend does unselfishness receive its ultimate imperative? By the poem's end so desperate is the speaker— so in need of escape from the trap into which she has fallen—that she asks, "Let anything that is not us return."

Return it does in a number of explicitly religious poems. In probably the most interesting of these Jennings explores the states of mind of figures from the New Testament and from church history. In "The Annunciation" Mary's predicament is described with great sympathy, as she is seen trying to sort out the human from the superhuman element. Her need to return to the familiarly human aspects of her life is countered by the knowledge that she bears a god. But her ecstasy at what she has been told is balanced by her sense of lacking control over her life and over her giving of life, and of the ostracism she may suffer. Several other steps in the life of Jesus are treated by Jennings in separate poems, concluding with "The Resurrection," where one of the hopeful mourners tells of coming to belief through negatives, and of having his sense of personal failure in not grasping immediately what had happened overcome by a full, if belated, awareness of that happening: "Despair returned but now it danced, it danced," he concludes. A similar sense of epiphany appears in "Teresa of Avila," where Jennings abandons traditional verse form in favor of the prose poem, to depict St. Teresa's quiet but powerfully mystical discovery of a religious vocation. Perhaps the warmest of these portrayals shows the "dancing metaphysical thought" of Thomas Aquinas, who "patterned and explained the world" and "stayed the child of great questions, saint but like an angel," and "whose sole wish was for the pure gold of continual inquiry" ("Thomas Aquinas").

Recent collections have increasingly concentrated on religious subjects, especially as they have dealt with Jennings's recurring breakdowns and stints in mental hospitals. Two of these, *Consequently I Rejoice* (1977) and *Moments of Grace* (1979), are particularly reminiscent of John Donne's *Devotions* in combining the chronicle of illness and recovery with religious meditation. While the result sometimes is liturgical in nature, it rarely fails to remind the reader of the personal suffering out of which Jennings is writing. Thus one of the *Moments of Grace* begins with a psalmlike catalog of God's ubiquity, but turns finally on the divine presence in emotional distress: "But most he is the need that shows in hunger / And in the tears shed in the lonely fastness. And in sorrow after anger" ("A Chorus").

Such fusing of the relationship with God and the relationship with other humans seems a natural outgrowth of those many earlier poems in which Jennings considered various people in her life and her feelings about them. Her first collections contain a number of vaguely plaintive lyrics on love and its problems; in most we find a persona unsure of herself, afraid of a relationship yet equally fearful of breaking it off prematurely.

The largely trite situations and muddy imagery of these pieces gives way, in *Moments of Grace,* to at least three genuinely strong poems on romantic love. In the first, Jennings confesses her inability to "keep the anger up" and relishes "[m]oments when every anger comes to grief / And we are rich in right apologies" ("Forgiveness"). The second ("Never Such Peace") represents, in a sense, her answer to Keats, as she recalls not postcoital depression, but a profound tranquillity following sex. Indeed, she remembers her and her lover's being transported together by "an epic sunset," "as if the acts which we had done / Were flared out in the west," and of being awed as the room was gradually filled by "outer star-paced air." Despite its admitted rarity, such a triumph seems credible as Jennings renders it, as it does in another poem, "A New Patience," uncommon among her writings for being a third-person narrative. With equally uncommon fictionality she quickly but movingly reveals her central character as a released convict who, after lovemaking, discovers in himself the ability to dismiss imprisonment and to follow a new sense of resolve—presumably steeled by the love he has found.

Even more powerful than these, and more characteristically meditative, are those poems where Jennings writes of the family. Family life is scarcely blissful in the world of her poetry; she views it with mistrust, fear, and deep sadness. In "Family Affairs" she begins by distinguishing anger from the even more insidious pettiness coloring family disputes: "We pick at quarrels now / As fussy women stitch at cotton." Her sense of helplessness and involvement despite her awareness carries over to "My Grandmother," where, with intense concrete detail, she somewhat guiltily recalls once refusing to accompany her grandmother on some expedition and feeling no grief when the old lady died. The speaker's state of mind seems troubled yet curiously untroubled; while sensing the pathos of the grandmother's lot, she knows that belated grief or guilt are futile. Darker than this poem are the soliloquy of the father lamenting the wide gulf between him and his son ("Father") and the "Warning to Parents," where Jennings urges parents to discourage sensitivity among their children and to nurture, instead, an imperviousness to suffering that will allow them to survive the sadism characterizing the human species.

Because such Swiftian bitterness clearly represents an extreme for Jennings, one senses a backdrop of regret even in "Warning to Parents." Regret becomes explicit in her most powerful family poem, "One Flesh." Although this piece nominally concerns a middle-aged married couple grown indifferent toward each other, its central character is their adult daughter, who muses on the mystery of how the intimate passion to which she owes her being has given way to such separateness. She begins by imagining her father and mother in separate beds, he half-reading a book and she "like a girl dreaming of childhood, / All men elsewhere." "They hardly ever touch, / Or if they do it is like a confession / Of having little feeling—or too much," the daughter comments, and concludes by wondering if they even know what has happened or that they're old.

Clearly *she* knows, and she is awed by such knowledge. The poem develops feeling more for the daughter in her helpless awareness than for the parents, perhaps insulated by their indifference—though, the daughter hints, perhaps not. By showing her speaker both knowing and painfully ignorant—and both unable and afraid to find the truth—Jennings pictures the child helplessly hovering over her parents, and thus creates an emblem not merely of failed passion but of the ultimate separateness of our lives despite our desire to be joined. By the end of the poem we share the daughter's wonder that people can be so "[s]trangely apart, yet strangely close together."

Such wonder differs in tone from the empiricist coolness that Amis and Fuller, and even Larkin, would probably generate toward such a situation. There is in their writing a determination not to be surprised by such things. Elizabeth Jennings's capacity for surprise connects with the religious sense she exhibits so explicitly in other poems, and with the mellowness found in some of her more recent writing on human relationships. "To My Mother at 73" repeats the daughter's sense of distance from her parent found in "One Flesh." Yet, we see, too, in the daughter's painful questioning—"Must we both fumble not to show our fears / Of holding back our pain, our kindness too?"—the faith that such distance can be narrowed. Such faith seems vindicated in "Losing and Finding," where Jennings recalls befriending a lost child. She describes taking him to a nearby park and being caught up in protective tenderness. Biblical paradox and religious overtones combine in her final meditation on the child and the event:

> And it was you who rescued me, you know.
> Among the swings, the meadow and the river,
> You took me out of time, rubbed off on me
> What it feels like to care without restriction,
> To trust and never think of a betrayal.

In this and perhaps a dozen other poems Elizabeth Jennings has won a fixed if modest place in contemporary British literature. The persistent element of realism in her writing links her to the Movement; in this she continues to be the postwar Oxford M.A. and professional librarian. Where she goes beyond such bounds, though, is in the unabashed emotion and religiosity that color even her most secular poems. Besides disobeying the Movement stricture against writing about art—a surprising number of her poems concern art and the artistic process—she goes back to the centuries-old meditative tradition in her expressed faith in a reality beyond empiricism. It is her peculiar stance, and the eloquence and control with which she exhibits it in her best poetry, that merit and should continue to merit a measure of critical respect.

Chapter Six

The Neoromantic Response: Tomlinson and Heaney

The principal directions of British poetry since 1939 have been, on the one hand, toward realism and empirical fact as the center of concern and, on the other, away from empiricism. Just as the leading wartime poets refined their impatience with the rhetoric and vague imagery produced by the Apocalytics and their like, and thus helped prepare the way for the postwar Movement in fiction and poetry— and perhaps for the outburst of dramatic realism in the early 1950s— so many of the other postwar responses to the felt crisis in British poetry represented a loss of faith in rationality and an abandonment of the empiricist base. There is an element of irony in this, of course, since for all their distrust of extreme emotion, the empirical poets themselves tended to be equally distrustful of extreme rationality.

One way of responding to the problems facing British poetry in midcentury has been to explore certain offshoots of nineteenth-century romanticism. However, the writings of Ted Hughes and Geoffrey Hill suggest that such exploration could never result in any total return to the old ways; their brands of naturalism are decidedly distinct from those fostered in the 1890s. Other viable responses might include an emphasis upon subjectivity and the discontinuity of experience, or upon extreme continuity and linkage with the prehistoric past. Each transcends empiricism by ascribing limitations to discernible facts. Each has its roots in later nineteenth-century romanticism. But, as the poetry of the contemporary neo-romantics Charles Tomlinson and Seamus Heaney shows, such responses in the late twentieth century take on a different cast from that of their progenitors.

Charles Tomlinson

The singularity of Charles Tomlinson's writing, especially in comparison with that of his contemporary countrymen, has fascinated readers for over a quarter-century. Indeed, Calvin Bedient views Tomlinson as "the most considerable British poet to have made his way since the Second World War."[1] Such respect, which others have echoed, stems in part from the challenge of Tomlinson—offered in all of his poetry collections from the very first, and in numerous essays scattered throughout his career—to the principal tendencies of British poetry since the war. In particular he has attacked, through precept and practice, what he deplores as the "self-congratulatory parochialism"[2] of most recent British poets. His 1957 review of *New Lines*[3] dismissed Movement poetry as dull and unambitious, while of the polemics and poetics put forth by Amis and Larkin he has complained, "Instead of the conscious formulation of a position, one has a provincial laziness of mind adopted as a public attitude and as the framework for an equally provincial verse."[4] The asperity of this viewpoint is further suggested by Tomlinson's using as the epigraph to a poem titled "More Foreign Cities" a statement ("From a recent disquisition on poetics" but, in fact, from an essay by Kingsley Amis) to the effect that nobody wishes "any more poems about foreign cities." For Tomlinson such an attitude and the poems resulting from it compromise the very curiosity basic to all art.

Certainly his poems challenge the reader. However, their challenge is not so much to comprehend them as expressions or statements as it is to observe the concrete world with which they deal. The reward for grasping the Tomlinson poem exceeds the boundaries of the poem, as it consists of sharing a process, of seeing life in a manner foreign to most people's experience and even to most "descriptive" poetry. Coming to the Tomlinson poem for the first time usually involves straining to see externals ordinarily ignored or only half-seen. Tomlinson writes to confound our sense of the existence surrounding us, because his own attempts to see and render have proven at once confounding and exhilarating. Because his poems insist that we look hard at what we have learned too often to dismiss lazily as "nature" or "reality," at their best they are disturbing, and even at their worst they usually command attention.

The aspect probably most responsible for this command is what might be termed the "painterly" quality of Tomlinson's writing. So "visual" are his poems, and yet so beyond the ordinary piling up of external detail in the literary sense, that reading them quickly becomes a sort of spying exercise, of looking through the poet's eyes as he tries to see out. Thus it seems no coincidence—indeed,

it seems essential to what goes on in such poems—that Tomlinson
has been a painter, as well as a poet, virtually all of his adult life.
This is why most of his poems demand that we attend carefully to
what we are seeing before reaching for meanings or conclusions,
and certainly before looking elsewhere.

For Tomlinson, to look carefully means principally to ferret out
relationships. As he says in an early poem, "Reality is to be sought
not in concrete, / But in space made articulate" ("Aesthetic"). Such
articulateness stems from relationships—"Facets of copiousness" he
terms them ("Observation of Facts")—that the artist must "sur-
prise." This, in turn, requires a silencing of the self:

> The particular, rather than existing in its own isolate intensity, means
> first of all the demands of a relationship—you are forced to look, feel,
> find words for something not yourself—and it means, like all relationships,
> a certain forgetfulness of self, so that in contemplating something you are
> drawn out of yourself toward that and towards other people....5

Such abandonment of self-concern contrasts sharply with the in-
tensely personal quality of much recent British poetry, especially
that spawned by the Movement. Absorption into the self and its
"everyday" problems Tomlinson necessarily regards as narrow and
unworthy of art. All of this has its stylistic dimension, for, as he
explains: "Style speaks what was seen, / Or it conceals the observation
/ Behind the observer: a voice / Wearing a ruff" ("Observation of
Facts").

Tomlinson's emphasis on exteriority and particularity, and on
intense observation of what lies outside the self, links him directly
with the aesthetic presented over a century ago by John Ruskin and
his followers. Indeed, Tomlinson has cited Ruskin as one of the
seminal influences on his development as painter and poet.6 Cer-
tainly the terms by which he rejects the Movement-Empiricist agenda
for British poetry recall those by which Ruskin rejected the neo-
classical principles of Joshua Reynolds. Because he would agree with
Ruskin that "The first great mistake that people make.... is the
supposition that they must *see* a thing if it be before their eyes,"7
his writing, like Ruskin's, seems designed principally to develop
his reader's powers of observation. Likewise, he appears to have
absorbed Ruskin's dictum that nature affords the best opportunity
for training such powers: "nature is never distinct and never vacant,

she is always mysterious, but always abundant; you always see something but you never see all."[8] Tomlinson's stress on selflessness as both a requisite and a result of genuine observation echoes Ruskin's belief that "true poetry" and the "acuteness of bodily sense" upon which it depends relate to "love": "love I mean in its infiniteness and holy functions, as it embraces divine and human and brutal intelligences, and hallows the physical perceptions of external objects by association, gratitude, veneration, and other pure feelings of our moral nature."[9]

Much of Tomlinson's poetry celebrates the fecundity of nature, since, as one of his admirers has noted, "he is out to save the world for the curious and caring mind."[10] His most obvious forerunners in such an enterprise, at least among British poets, are Hopkins and Dylan Thomas. Dozens of Tomlinson pieces recall such Hopkins classics as "Spring," "The Windover," and "Pied Beauty" in their veneration of nature's variety, but they do so without the guilt lying just beneath the surface even of the Jesuit poet's most exuberant writing. Where Hopkins's nature poems remind us of the attitude taken by his Oxford tutor, Walter Pater, in their stress on the flux of experience—but alternate with expressions of guilt over delighting in purely physical beauty—Tomlinson's exhibit neither the guilt and stylistic frenzy of Hopkins nor Pater's sense of futility in trying to capture experience. Instead we find him quietly confident in his own ability to see and render what he can of the wonderful world outside himself, and undismayed that he can never capture entirely any part of it. In fact, his failure seems to reinforce his sense of wonder.

As for Dylan Thomas, with whose celebratory sense he might identify, Tomlinson long ago came to view the Welshman's preoccupation with the self as unfortunate and the Apocalyptics, whom he inspired, as a dead end. Eschewing Dylanism as much as those Movement writers with whom he has so little else in common, Tomlinson sought his technical models among decidedly non-British sources. The distinctly American modernism of William Carlos Williams, Marianne Moore, and Wallace Stevens proved instructive, as Tomlinson found in them an apparatus for dealing with the external world, "a clear way of going to work, so that you could cut through [the] Freudian swamp and say something clearly."[11] Critics who early detected a French Symbolist strain in Tomlinson's writing[12] were not entirely off the mark, especially given Tomlinson's ambition to integrate English poetry into the larger European tradition. But the French influence for the most part came more indirectly, through his acquaintance with Ezra Pound's work and that of the three Americans just mentioned. He found further inspiration in the Objectivism proposed by Williams and carried on first by the New Yorkers George Oppen and Charles Zukovsky, and later by the Black Mountain School of Charles Olson, Robert Duncan, and Robert Creeley. Their work confirmed the subjugation of personality in his writing and reinforced his interest in the tension between inner and outer experience.

Tomlinson has recalled how unpropitious a time the 1950s were for writing the kind of verse that interested him.[13] His first full-scale collection, *Seeing is Believing,* made the rounds of British publishers for four years before finally appearing in New York in 1961. He felt encouraged during this long wait by a correspondence with Williams, who hailed him as a kindred spirit, and by a trip to America in late 1959, when he first met Williams and Moore. Zukovsky and Oppen he was to meet some time later. The effect on him of all such meetings was a sense of belonging such as he had never felt among British poets, a liberation from any need to be "English" in the narrow sense, and a hearty confirmation of his internationalist tendencies.

The aesthetic principles upon which Tomlinson's poetry rests are revealed most explicitly in his writing about other artists. His familiarity with painters, as well as his penchant for remarks about particular painters and paintings, which resonate into the other arts, shows clearly in "A Garland for Thomas Eakins." In describing Eakins's "Concert Singer," he praises the painter's care for composition, for the relation between space in the scene and space on the canvas. He also praises Eakins's trust in his eye, regardless of what academic knowledge or "right appearances" might dictate. Recalling Walt Whitman's affection for Eakins's portrait of himself ("in correct style / without feathers"), Tomlinson credits Eakins with "figures of perception," as opposed to "figures of elocution." The challenge of reality "only to be recorded" proved sufficient for the American painter's genius:

> *Only*
> to be recorded!
> and his stare

in the self-portrait
calculates the abyss
in the proposition.
                    ("A Garland for Thomas Eakins")

In an equally powerful tribute to Arnold Schoenberg, Tomlinson
goes even farther afield, to develop an analogous aesthetic out of
serial music. Just as the wind "disrupts, effaces / and then restores,"
Schoenberg's music is said to have "redefined" beauty. Tomlinson
credits the composer with liberating music from confining, stale
notions of order, and thus with "[redeeming] both the idiom and
the instrument" ("Ode to Arnold Schoenberg"). Schoenberg's bril-
liance, according to Tomlinson, lay in his ability to effect a higher
order through disordering: "through discontinuities / to the whole
in which discontinuities are held / ... enriched / by the tones'
impurity." Atonality and dissonance, which in Hopkins-like fashion
Tomlinson likens to variously colored quartz, thus led to newer
harmonies. Such hinting at Plato and Coleridge becomes explicit
near the end of the poem, when "sound made intelligible" is de-
scribed as "the unfolded word" and the composer's imagination
compared to the divine in ordering the seemingly unorderable.

Such work of genius as Schoenberg's or Eakins's, Tomlinson con-
trasts with that of Courbet. In "Composition" Tomlinson muses on
the details of a scene that he imagines the French realist would have
ignored, and thus directs us to a strikingly different way of seeing.
This poem illustrates handily Tomlinson's notion of authentic "com-
posing"—in whatever medium—as it attends increasingly to spatial
and geometric aspects—at the expense of the obvious and organic,
which Courbet might have preferred. According to Tomlinson,
Courbet's painting would probably concentrate on the flower in a
vase ("with petals / as solid as meat that press back the sky"), with
minimal attention to perspective. Tomlinson's eye, on the other
hand, zooms in on the space "triangled" between stalk, curtain,
and window frame, and even notices how that space contains a car
parked outside the window. In this he acknowledges and emulates
nature's power to fill space. For Tomlinson the true seer is never
"glutted" with foreground or any single perspective. Rather, he
recognizes the infinite multiplicity of attitudes available at any point
in space or time.

Such a response to the problems of life and art, and to the situation
of contemporary poetry, relates to several earlier epochs in art his-
tory. Despite his fixation on nature and its possibilities, Tomlinson
clearly is no naive romantic. One critic notes how his "taut, re-
sponsive detachment" distinguishes his writing from Wordsworth
and provides a link to classicism.[14] And Tomlinson's frequently
expressed concern with ritual and tradition bespeaks a concern with
decorum relatable to neoclassicism.[15]

Clearly Tomlinson believes in a reality ouside the self. In this
regard he transcends the confines of Paterian sensibility. His em-
phasis on accurate perception and de-emphasis of the ego—what P.
R. King terms Tomlinson's "humility" toward the external world
that provides his subject matter[16]—rejects any facile subjectivism.
Yet in poem after poem he appears equally suspicious of empirical
"facts." In "Face and Image" he speaks of the "unchartable country,
/ variable, virgin / terror and territory" between an object and the
image forming in the viewer's mind. Tomlinson's insistence on this
gap, and his acceptance of it as the province in which the artist
must operate, perhaps account for the terms by which he praises
another painter-hero, John Constable. Citing Constable's concept
of painting as an experimental science, he describes the Englishman's
pursuit of clouds in his painting and praises the persuasively "human
image" by which he represented them on canvas. For art to persuade,
it must include both the subjective passion of the observer and the
objective reality of whatever is observed. In words that recall Hop-
kins's "God's Grandeur," Tomlinson surveys Constable's rendering
of the sun and "remnant clouds": "It shrinks to a crescent / Crushed
out, a still lengthening ooze / As the mass thickens" ("A Meditation
on John Constable"). Because such art is true to what is experienced
as experienced, it yields a knowledge of nature more credible than
the abstractions of philosophy or conventional science.

Often Tomlinson revels in the gap between an object and subject,
and thus denies the distinction. In "Fiascherino," an early poem,
he first describes the play of the sea against a beach, but then moves
his perspective to a cliff-top, where he observes how "the shore / Is
diminished but concentrated, jewelled / With the clarity of warm
colours / That, seen more nearly, would / dissipate / Into masses."
Proximity and distance each reveal differing views and differing
wonders. So does the play of light and shadow on the ceiling through
muslin curtains, as Tomlinson ends his poem indoors, watching the

sea while it "unrolls and rolls itself into the low room." Through this sense of seemingly endless noticings, which is neither subjective nor objective, he offers a true romanticism which, ironically, is a true classicism, as well.

In a much later poem "(Swimming Chenango Lake")—sometimes said to signal a shift in Tomlinson's views, but actually a concentrated statement of the viewpoint extending back to "Fiascherino" and even earlier—he offers a remarkable emblem of the artist's, and perhaps everyman's, ideal encountering of outer life. Specifically, he draws on the American Indian initiation ritual of swimming a lake, to suggest the benefits of openly engaging external reality. Such engagement requires an acknowledging of that reality's separateness from human consciousness. Because moving through water requires grasping, the swimmer must understand that the water exists independent of himself. And, as the poem suggests, the coldness of the water grasps the swimmer every bit as much as he grasps it. Or, to translate the metaphor, one senses the alien quality of the outer world even as one appropriates its meaning for oneself, and thus becomes ("between grasp and grasping") free. Even as the water asserts its alien aspect—its coldness and its potential to kill—it sustains and teaches. What external phenomena teach, according to Tomlinson in his discussion of the poem, is a heightened awareness of "that which we are not, yet of relationship with it."[17] He speaks, too, of the poem, and presumably any work of true art, as an initiation into such awareness, a valuable venture dependent upon equal respect for both the limitations and the powers one brings to the outside world. Through such open confrontation does a full humanness arise.

Lest Tomlinson appear to be constantly engaged in theorizing about the nature of poetry or art, it should be noted that the majority of his poems find him observing the concrete world about him. That such observation proves no simple matter merely provides grounds for the aesthetic position he develops elsewhere. Certainly for him practice in such matters necessarily precedes theorizing.

Tomlinson's observational poems cover a range of scenes and settings. Natural phenomena have dominated his writing at all stages, but especially during the 1950s and 1960s. One such favored phenomenon is the sea, which—appropriately, and perhaps predictably—he finds difficult to define. Indeed, in "Sea Change" the definition of something so fluid and so dependent upon fluctuating play of light and color becomes momentary in the most literal sense. Elsewhere he finds the riddle of time and consciousness vividly illustrated in the flux of water: "That which we were, / Confronted by all that we are not, / Grasp[ing] in subservience of replenishment" ("The Atlantic"). Other sights in nature—such things as fire, sunset, and clouds—inspire other poems showing the mutually reinforcing mysteries of nature and the perceiving mind. Tomlinson has moved gradually toward observing broader landscapes—the season, especially winter, or desert scenes. Nevertheless, all such observings continue this same fascination with the meld of subject and object, the same sense of being overwhelmed by the flux and detail of the world, and the same quiet satisfaction at the way experience replenishes itself.

Besides observing natural scenes (which for Tomlinson can never be "still life") many of his poems move off in different directions. One of the earliest, "The Mediterranean," shifts from describing that region as a "country of grapes" to remarking on another, coexisting country "of trains, planes and gasworks," and to noticing how railroad tracks help define the sea by which they run. Even more extreme in this respect, at least for Tomlinson, is "The Crane," which describes the large machine ("that paternal / Constructive insect, without antennae") in a manner reminiscent of Auden and Spender. On other occasions Tomlinson celebrates not so much the continuity of the natural and artificial as that of the organic and inorganic—some of his Arizona poems (see "Arizona Desert" and "A Death in the Desert") are especially notable in this regard. And, in his poem titled "Crow"—one of his few writings on specific creatures in nature, rather than elements of landscape—he characteristically admires the bird's balance ("all black assumption, / mounting litheness") without moralizing, as Ted Hughes might. Like Tomlinson's swimmer on Lake Chenango or his rower (in a poem of that title), his crow confronts the forces around him with a respect and a confidence that reinforce each other.

Given his bent for scrutinizing the outside world, a quiet intensity is almost inevitable in Tomlinson's writing. This has its technical dimension in the tautness of his line and phrase, and in the spareness by which externals and the perceiving of externals are rendered. In this he is admittedly indebted to Pound, Williams, and the Black Mountain poets. Indeed, he has praised the "dependence" between words and syllables that Williams brings about by "slowing down" the flow of his poetry, chiefly through controlled line length. [18] Thus Thomlinson's own "Oxen: Ploughing at Fiesole"—which develops an emblem of man's harnessing nature yet also of nature's resistant "otherness"—partly depends for its effectiveness on the slow, plodding movement from line to line. The attitude wittily attributed to the oxen becomes:

> We will be useful
> But we will not be swift: now
> Follow us for your improvement
> And at our pace.

The reader feels as "paced" as the ploughman by an other—in this instance the functional placement of line division.

Most of Tomlinson's other poems illustrate the same concern for visual appearance and flow on the page, though none more strikingly than "Before the Dance." There the sense of hovering, of time stopping for the moment just before a Navajo ritual, is rendered by the varying of lines from one to nine syllables in length, and by special care in spotting the longest and shortest lines. Similarly effective is "Canal," where line length underscores the stream's misleading quietness. Tomlinson forces his reader to attend to each word, and ultimately to get so caught up in the wealth of sights and tones to be seen from the canal that the poem's final—and longest—line ("concludes then without conclusion") fittingly suggests the scene's infinite possibilities.

Even in poems where variance of line length seems not so crucial, Tomlinson relies heavily on enjambment as a controlling device:

> The horse is white. Or it
> appears to be under this
> November light that could
> well be October.
>
>   ("Saving the Appearance")

And less frequent but no less striking are those instances where multiple indentation compounds the potential of line division:

> Ranges
>   of clinker heaps

            go orange now:
        through cooler air
          an acrid drift
          seeps upwards
        from the valley mills.
        ("John Maydew, *or* The Allotment")

In this particular case Tomlinson later expands the third line of each
group, then shortens it as the poem approaches its close. Such an
arrangement does for our sense of the "dispossessed / and half-tamed
Englishman" surveying his plot of ground what a periodic unfolding
of syntax and scene does in Tomlinson's more standard poems; it
works against hasty reading or premature conclusion, and thus con-
tributes to a more intense response by the reader.

All of Tomlinson's concern and all his technique converge most
fruitfully in perhaps twenty poems, from among his earliest to some
of his latest. Several of these—such as "Through Binoculars," "Grass
Grain," "Tramontana at Lerici," and "A Sense of Distance"—go at
basic aesthetic principles, though from strikingly varied concrete
bases. As with most of his other writings, we have in such pieces
a peculiar melding of particular and abstract, a sense of philoso-
phizing that scarcely abandons its very earthy roots.

More stark, and more indirect, in approaching related concerns
is the most anthologized Tomlinson poem, the justly celebrated
"Paring the Apple." It offers an alternative to both the human-
interest approach to life and that which reduces existence to a useless
state of inanimateness; "portraits and still-lives," Tomlinson terms
such ventures, respectively. His alternative preserves the multidi-
mensionality and solidity of felt existence without yielding to sub-
jectivity. Characteristically Tomlinson insists on deliberateness and
perspective as requisites for knowing and for living: "The cool blade
/ Severs between coolness, apple-rind / Compelling a recognition."

The human implications of such a method become clear in a
somewhat later poem, "Up at La Serra," which nominally concerns
election day in a rural Italian town. Specifically we see a young
political idealist about to write in celebration of a communist vic-
tory. Despite its (for Tomlinson) unusual subject matter, and despite
its basically narrative form, "Up at La Serra" resembles the typical
Tomlinson lyric in its highly periodic structure: the poem's rather
slight "action" is suspended over almost two hundred lines, which

spin out concretely the physical and emotional landscape out of which the young poet's response emerges. Here Tomlinson again makes careful use of line length and multiple indentation, to control the poem's pace—and to make its conclusion credible and, in its own way, moving. More interesting, however, is the manner in which he begins, by observing the play of sea and light—"The shadow / ran before it lengthening / and a wave went over"—and by remarking how "you could watch it / squander and recompose itself / all day...."

Significantly, Paolo Bertolani, the young poet, resolves in the end to begin his own poem in Tomlinson fashion, *"here with the cliff and with the sea / following its morning shadow in."* The authenticity of this, probably the longest of Tomlinson's poems, is owing not to the development of character and motive in any fictional sense— or the sense in which they develop, say, in a Larkin poem—but to the accretion of nuance and concrete fact in which Paolo and his resolve are embedded. Reflecting the same principles as the poem in which it occurs, Paolo's resolution seems likely to produce neither a political tract nor the kind of poem abjured by Tomlinson himself, but an authentic reflection of experienced life. In this "Up at La Serra," for all of its unusual features, nicely confirms the central aesthetic informing all of Tomlinson's writings.

The title poem of *Written on Water* (1972) blends style and ideology to give a heightened appreciation of the perspective Tomlinson brings to life and to poetry. It explores the paradoxes of its title by asking in what sense anything can be written on water. Tomlinson begins by noting the difficulty of reading the "life lines of erratic waters," particularly at the meeting of two streams "[r]efusing to be one without resistance." The riddle posed by "moving calligraphy," the problem of interpreting the signs before they disappear into the wider stream, recalls those several earlier poems in which Tomlinson struggled to see water clearly; such struggle is emblematic in his poetic vocabulary of the struggle to make sense of the wider life around us.

In "Written on Water" he considers a possible solution to his perpetual problem with existence by recalling momentarily a still pool where he once sought—and found—clarity: "We lived / In a visible church, where everything / Seemed to be at pause, yet nothing was." Almost as soon as he begins considering this pool, it begins to resemble the stream now perplexing him. He remembers how the pool's seemingly smooth surface in fact "puckered and drew away / Over the central depth." He remembers, too, the friction between foliage and the water, "A speech behind speech, continuing revelation / Of itself, never to be revealed." As the poem approaches its conclusion, he sees the link between his present experience of water and his past: he acknowledges that to speak of water at all is "to entertain the image / Of its seamless momentum." Such momentum he sees as emblematic of "each day's flux and lapse."

"Written on Water" displays a deepened recognition of the nature and challenge of life. It displays, too, a remarkable technical parallel, as Tomlinson's style exhibits the seamlessness of water—and of the time and experience for which water operates as so powerful a symbol. Strictly speaking, the poem contains but one sentence. Tomlinson punctuates internally with a series of colons, to narrow the focus and thus to lend "seamless momentum" to the poem. In the end he characteristically takes satisfaction in the tension afforded by "promiscuity of acquaintance" on the one hand—the disturbing flux of particulars washing over his consciousness—and the "music of constancy" on the other, the universality and eternity of water and of what it signifies. This more profound, if less definite, reading ultimately consoles in a way that the particular messages sought initially could not.

Such reading returns Tomlinson to the posture he takes in so many observational poems. That he persists in this posture, which has its roots in his earliest writing, is not to say that his poetry lacks development. On the contrary, the various progressions represented in his successive books suggest the power and potential of his basic approach to existence and human perception. The first principal collection, *Seeing is Believing* (1960), represented an advance on his two earlier, minor books—*Relations and Contraries* (1951) and *The Necklace* (1955)—in that Tomlinson moved away from broad-sweeping theoretical statements to the application and physical illustration of his aesthetic, mostly through observings of nature. The very title of his next collection, *A Peopled Landscape* (1963), signaled his willingness to traffic in more human subjects than before. In addition, these poems displayed more extremes of tone and imagery, as well as a generally greater degree of experimentation, than the reader of the previous books might expect.

With *American Scenes* (1966) Tomlinson confirmed the internationalist tendencies that had been building up in his poetry: he took his scenes and subjects not only from the American Southwest or Mexico, but from New England, New York, and even downtown San Francisco. *The Way of a World* (1969) showed a more aggressive Tomlinson; interestingly, he offered the most concentrated rehearsal of his basic aesthetic since his earliest writing, but with much more assertiveness—perhaps owing to the perspective of several years and collections of concrete experimentation. And with *Written on Water* (1972) came confirmation of time as a key issue in Tomlinson's moral universe, as well as some of his very best poems.

The strong composition in each of these succeeding collections was paralleled by Tomlinson's increased interest in translation. Comparison of his rendering of key poems by the Sicilian lyricist Lucio Piccolo (1903–60) with translations contained in the standard Piccolo collection[19] reveals a continuing fascination with the problems of perception and a commitment to an honest representation of those problems. Whether Tomlinson's own poetry of the last ten years—collected in *The Way In* (1974) and *The Shaft* (1978)—matches in intensity and ambitiousness either his translations or the poems of earlier decades is open to serious question. Indeed, Calvin Bedient finds *The Shaft* "more comfortable ... [but] less exciting" than the earlier books[20]—a judgment difficult to dispute, given the more conservative material and style of the recent poems. Perhaps Tomlinson will never regain the brilliance of his major collections. Even so, his place among the foremost poets writing in English—on either side of the Atlantic—is indisputable. More than any of his fellow Englishmen he has succeeded in making peace with the modernist tradition, particularly the American strain, and in absorbing it into a contemporary poetic and contemporary poetry of permanent value.

Seamus Heaney

Behind the writing of practically every recent British poet has been the question of how he or she might deal with contemporary history. For some the experience of the Auden group proved persuasive, in inspiring either a wholesale examination of contemporary culture and events or an avoidance of the contemporary in favor of more personal or more transcendental concerns. For others, perhaps too young to have been influenced by the literature of the 1930s or perhaps eschewing literary influences altogether, a more idiosyncratic posture toward recent history has seemed appropriate. However, for Seamus Heaney, born in 1939 a Catholic in Ulster, the postwar era has afforded little respite from larger events. His coming of age as a poet has so coincided with the most recent "troubles" in his native land that the public world presses on his writing to a degree perhaps unfelt by any other poet of such prominence writing in English since Auden.

For the Irish, or at least Eire, the years of World War II represented a lull in an otherwise explosive twentieth-century history. The Irish Free State, hammered out after the 1922–23 Civil War through years of crises and negotiations—to the consternation of an IRA bent on total separation from England and union with the northern counties—proclaimed and maintained its neutrality in the war against Hitler, thanks largely to the spirited resistance of Prime Minister Eamon de Valera to pressures from both England and the United States. While most of Ireland's citizens certainly wished no German victory, neutrality did much to bolster their spirit of national sovereignty. And, while the British used land and sea bases in the north, even Ulster was exempted from wartime conscription.[21] Certainly the Irish of both North and South enjoyed a measure of prosperity once the Germans had been defeated.

For the next twenty years, and especially after the Republic of Ireland was proclaimed in 1949, Northern Ireland remained a relatively quiet part of the United Kingdom, while its southern neighbor developed independently. Even a concerted IRA campaign against Ulster in the late 1950s had little effect there or in England, and southern support for that once-powerful terrorist organization dropped precipitously.

In the mid-1960s, however, there began a civil-rights movement within the Catholic minority of Ulster—determined to reverse a half-century of officially sanctioned discrimination in parliamentary districting, housing, and employment, and wholly divorced from the IRA and its violent ways. The resulting promise of reforms by a mildly sympathetic government made many of the Protestant majority, jealous of their advantages and ever fearful of being swallowed up by the Republic, suddenly very uneasy. It also made them vulnerable to the mob psychology of Ian Paisley, who spoke to their needs and fears as no official leader in Belfast or London could. And just as Paisley appeared the only public figure whom many Protestants felt they could trust, and as mob violence and police brutality against civil-rights demonstrators and Catholic citizens increased—as demonstration increasingly meant riot—the IRA gradually emerged as the only credible source of solace and protection to many terrified Catholics living in Belfast and Londonderry.[22] Gradually, too, the cause of civil rights merged into the cause of Irish nationalism long championed by the IRA.

In August 1969 British troops were sent in to restore legal order. However, violence and terror only increased, as the IRA and counterpart Protestant groups exchanged atrocities. By early 1971 the first British soldier had been killed in Belfast. That summer the British government began its policy of internment, under which suspects, mostly Catholic, would be jailed without trial or other ordinary civil rights. Terrorist bombings, vigilante raids, serious injury or death to thousands of citizens (mostly innocent), hunger strikes, oratory of hatred, children playing at war—the horrible pattern of events that has since continued to plague Northern Ireland was thus set in place, with little prospect of long-range reversal.

Most of Seamus Heaney's poems reflect at least indirectly the political tensions of Ulster. Indeed, his whole career as a poet can be seen centering on the question of how he ought to respond to his homeland's troubles. Overt references to the political scene are confined to the three collections published since the 1960s: *Wintering Out* (1972), *North* (1975), and *Field Work* (1979). There entire poems concern such matters as a curfew violator's death ("Casualty"), police helicopter surveillance ("At the Water's Edge"), the treatment of Irish girls who fall in love with British soldiers ("Punishment"), and the eerie presence of armored cars in the formerly peaceful Northern Irish countryside ("The Toombe Road"). In moving detail Heaney examines the burial following a "neighborly murder" ("Funeral Rites"), the wartime atmosphere gripping the cities ("A Northern Hoard"), and the meaninglessness of "liberal" formulas in the face of his homeland's "little destiny" toward self-destruction ("Whatever You Say Say Nothing"). So powerful is the fatalism of such poems that Heaney finds himself having to go back two hundred years to imagine a prelapsarian Belfast, free of sectarian hatred ("Linen Town"). Even then his imagining is colored by the ominous sense of a fall about to occur in the ill-conceived rebellion of 1798, the last time Irish Catholics and Protestants could unite against their English oppressors.

Elsewhere he views Northern Ireland's recent difficulties more obliquely or allusively. "Requiem for the Croppies" celebrates the 1798 rebels' transcendent closeness to the soil and to each other, as symbolized by the barley that after their burial grew out of seeds in their pockets. Another poem gently satirizes a Presbyterian neighbor's harshness—"his fabulous, biblical dismissal / that tongue of chosen people" ("The Other Side")—while recognizing the social and emotional needs that bind him and the poet in neighborliness. In other poems ostensibly concerned with nonpolitical matters Heaney can refer momentarily to old Irish Catholic grievances, as when he alludes to the terrible potato famine of 1845–49 ("At a Potato Digging"), regrets the first stage Irishman's popularizing the stereotype of the Irish as drunken and boorish ("Traditions"), or suddenly urges the Roman historian Tacitus to observe "how we slaughter / for the common good / and shave the heads / of the notorious" ("Kinship"). Heaney's extended identification of the aggressive, male principle with England and the submissive, female with Ireland— especially in a cluster of poems contained in *North*—represents another means of rehearsing Irish complaints and of at least alluding to the current problems of Northern Ireland.

Given this preoccupation with Ireland and her long-standing problems, as well as such expressions of sympathy with an Irish viewpoint, one might question the appropriateness of including Seamus Heaney in a study of recent *British* poetry. Or, one might ask whether such inclusion does not imply a stance regarding the basic issue of Northern Ireland itself. The answers to such questions, as well as at least some justification for placing Heaney among recent British poets, lie in certain aspects of his background, the peculiarities of his literary upbringing, and the posture that he has taken toward such questions.

Born and raised on a farm in rural County Derry, Heaney regards his early contact with the sights and sounds near his home as even now the most powerful influences on his sensibilities.[23] Though aware of religious differences among his neighbors, he and his family felt close to a number of Protestants.[24] The harmony between Catholics and Protestants in this rural community translated for Heaney into a later determination to avoid religious distinctions in choosing his associates, particularly the young fellow poets whose friendship meant so much to him as a student at Queen's University, Belfast. Again, though knowing as a matter of course who was Catholic or

Protestant, the young members of this Ulster Group—which, besides Heaney, included Michael Langley, Derek Mahon, and Seamus Deane—felt spurred more by shared interests, one of which Heaney describes as "exhilaration ... that we were moving an inch or two past the old pieties, and rigidities, and the old divisions."[25]

His celebrated move, in 1972, from Belfast and a teaching post at Queen's to a farm in County Wicklow in the South provoked criticism reminiscent of that inspired by Auden's move to America. But, like Auden's move, Heaney's reflected more the vocational strategies of the poet than any political or otherwise ideological commitment. Certainly neither religion nor politics lay at the heart of Heaney's decision to go south. Although allowing that "I had never considered myself British" and though admitting to "a fair hoard of resentment against the Unionist crowd,"[26] Heaney felt uncomfortable at being viewed—and interviewed—as some sort of spokesman for the Catholic minority in the North. As he says, "I wanted to be alone with myself,"[27] something that public events and his growing celebrity were not permitting. Despite a keen interest in Irish history and culture and a belief in the legitimacy of Catholic grievances in the North, his behavior suggests a man hoping to escape the limitations of political and religious labels.

Surely his not considering himself a Britisher need not disqualify him from being considered in some real sense a British poet. In fact, the hybrid manner by which he came to poetry almost demands it. Recently he has spoken of the "business" of being an Irish poet as "a literary game almost" and something he doesn't worry about.[28] While a Philip Larkin might "worry" about his own credentials as a bona fide British poet, many of the writers among whom Heaney is being placed here—Hughes and Tomlinson come to mind immediately—probably would not. To label Heaney's poetry as definitively Irish or British is to ignore what he recognizes as principal factors in his developing literary sensibility.

"I began as a poet when my roots crossed with my reading," Heaney has recalled.[29] The place of his birth and the surrounding countryside, which he knows intimately, account principally for his sense of rootedness. To these were gradually added friendships, language and speech patterns, and other cultural associations that he considers broadly Irish. His schooling, of course, and in particular his formal introduction to poetry, he readily labels English, and

considers them an equally strong influence on his way of viewing
poetry:

> I suppose the feminine element for me involves the matter of Ireland, and
> the masculine strain is drawn from the involvement with English literature.
> I speak and write in English, but do not altogether share the preoccupations
> and perspectives of an Englishman. I teach English literature, I publish
> in London, but the English tradition is not ultimately home. I live off
> another hump as well.[30]

Even since his move south he has continued to speak of the two
"humps" off which he lives, and which contribute equally to his
writing, and to caution other writers in the same situation not to
go to an extreme by denying either the English or the Irish element.
In a recent interview he has observed that "the melodies of the
English line" constitute an important part of the Northern Irish-
man's sense of language, and that to be true to the language as he
knows and speaks it requires fidelity to those melodies, rather than
wholesale rejection or artificial replacement with Irish melodies.[31]
   Certainly the poets who are important to Heaney, as well as those
to whom he has been compared, reflect as much English as Irish
factors. Robert Frost and Ted Hughes seem to have awakened the
young poet's realization that he could center his writing on his own
feelings and experiences.[32] Hopkins, Wordsworth, and, of course,
Yeats—whose complex relationship to the Irish Heaney has con-
sidered at length[33]—represent other strong forces in the making of
the poet. Much as he concerned himself with Ireland as a youth and
a university student, much as his participation in the so-called Ulster
Revival of the late 1950s and early 1960s convinced him that good
poetry could be written there, and much as he has praised the
authentic Irish writers of modern times—especially Patrick Kavan-
augh and James Joyce—Heaney has never hesitated to acknowledge,
not disparagingly, his own relationship to the English poetic
tradition.
   Indeed, his very manner of discussing some of the figures in that
tradition most important to him suggests the central tension in-
forming the poetry Heaney has written since his university days.
In a 1974 lecture he observed a stylistic difference between Hopkins
and Keats, by which consonants in the former's writing "alliterate
to maintain a design," while those of the latter "release a flow":

"Keats woos us to receive, Hopkins alerts us to perceive."[34] More recently Heaney has offered a similar distinction between Yeats and Wordsworth in asserting that where Wordsworth strives to hear his inner voice, Yeats is much more intent on controlling his.[35]

Control and perception both figure prominently in the title poem of Heaney's fourth collection. "North" distills the discovery process of several years of writing and of considering his proper role as a poet. The opening lines find him on the west coast of Ireland and allude to his long-standing fascination with Northern European legends and exploits as a way of understanding the hatred and violence plaguing his homeland in modern times. After reflecting on the "unmagical" quality of Icelandic and Danish models, he suddenly remembers "fabulous raiders" closer to home, namely those lying in Orkney and Dublin: "those in the solid / belly of stone ships / those hacked and glinting / in the gravel of thawed streams." Imagining their voices "lifted again / in violence and epiphany," he receives from them an elaborate program for responding to Ireland's contemporary crisis. Specifically, they advise him to "lie down / in the word-hoard," that is, to cultivate the centuries of linguistic treasure at his command. He is advised, too, to cultivate the darkness and to expect, rather than any dazzling enlightenment, at most a sort of midnight sun. Finally, the spirits urge him to keep his eye "clear / as the bleb of an icicle" and to "trust the feel of what nubbed treasure / Your hands have known." Such earthy advice corresponds nicely to certain developments central to Heaney's writing up to, and including, *North*. It expresses his felt need to embrace the darkness—the "North" in himself, in his people, and in Western civilization generally. It suggests a route to the heart of contemporary terror through the more remote.

Because such a vocation satisfies the public poet's responsibility to perceive and grasp what is happening to his people, the tone of "North" is ultimately one of triumph. Heaney thus acknowledges the bardic obligations of the ancient scop, as several forces in his poetic merge. More unsettling, because more uncertain, is the final poem in the *North* collection, titled "Exposure." Actually the last of six lyrics organized under the rubric "Singing School"—an ironic allusion to Yeats's "Sailing to Byzantium"—"Exposure" captures a moment of meditation in which the poet weighs, with considerable regret, the price he has paid for the vocation described in "North." Significantly Heaney sets his meditation at Wicklow. While the bulk of his other *North* poems were written there, they reflected the momentum of his desire to do justice to the situation of Northern Ireland. Here, though, it is that very desire that he scrutinizes while awaiting the sight of a comet on a December evening. "How did I end up like this?" he asks, before going on to recall friends, foes, and accusations against himself—presumably for his decision to go south—as well as the "[b]eautiful prismatic counselling" of well-wishers. Such counsel he painfully recalled in the next-to-last "Singing School" lyric, "Fosterage," by describing a scene several years earlier when he was told, "Go your own way. / Do your own work" and when the example of "Poor Hopkins" ("his buckled self") loomed central in his artistic conscience. This was in 1962, however, before the loomings described in the four previous lyrics had taken form. This first of these movingly reveals the problems of being an aspiring poet in a culture torn by petty prejudice and prone to judge by something so superficial as the religious connotations of one's name. "A Constable Calls" and "Orange Drums, Tyrone, 1969" remember an earlier official sanctioning of anti-Catholic prejudice and a more recent one, respectively. And "Summer 1969" finds Heaney at the Prado in Madrid, where the events of Goya's *Shootings of the Third of May* and an Ulster torn by civil strife and police riots blend surrealistically in his consciousness.

The first five "Singing School" poems thus rehearse the problems that give way to the painful self-scrutiny of "Exposure." The ironies of these rehearsals, as well as of such self-scrutiny, Heaney foreshadowed by epigraphs from *The Prelude* and Yeats's *Autobiographies:* the Wordsworth passage refers to the poet's childhood relocation from his birthplace to Hawkshead, and the Yeats to his boyhood sympathy with the Orangemen and detestation of the Fenians. The difficulties of relocation and of confused sympathies inform the entire "Singing School" sequence, particularly "Exposure." Heaney concludes his self-questioning with a denial ("I am neither internee nor informer") and a corresponding claim that he is an "inner émigré, grown long-haired / And thoughtful," which he completes with the telling image of a "wood-kerne":

> Escaped from the massacre,
> Taking protective colouring
> From bole and bark, feeling
> Every wind that blows.

He further concludes that in probing the past for the key to Ireland's present dilemma ("blowing up these sparks / For their meagre heat") he may have missed something more fundamental, if more personal. To miss this "once-in-a-lifetime portent"—here represented by the comet—may constitute a poetic failure more profound and inexcusable than any of his failings on a more public or political level.

Heaney's earlier, extended search for the appropriate way to write on that public level has been described by several commentators, including Heaney himself. The turning point, according to each of these accounts, was his reading the English translation of P. V. Glob's *The Bog People: Iron Age Man Preserved* shortly after its publication in 1969. Jon Stallworthy compares the impact of this discovery to that of the young T. S. Eliot's reading Jessie L. Weston's *From Ritual to Romance* a half-century earlier.[36] Just as Weston suggested to Eliot the central images of *The Waste Land,* so Glob's accounts of the Danish bogland excavations of the early 1950s gave Heaney the "befitting emblems of adversity"[37] with which to regard contemporary Irish history. Glob argued that some of the bodies found in Northern Denmark were of men strangled or otherwise murdered as ritual sacrifice to the Earth Goddess, to guarantee the surrounding land's fertility.[38] Such ritual murder suggested to Heaney a "field of force"[39] in which to comprehend the seemingly senseless brutality of modern Ireland. For him the contemporary sectarian barbarism thus attained an archetypal significance, as photographs of the almost perfectly preserved bog victims from the Iron Age blended in his mind with Irish atrocity photographs in daily newspapers.[40] *The Bog People* confirmed his vow to turn his poetry into a pilgrimage by which Irish culture might be restored to itself.[41]

It confirmed, too, an interest in bogs dating from his childhood. "To this day," he admits, "green, wet corners, flooded wastes, soft rushy bottoms, any place with the invitation of watery ground and tundra, vegetation, even glimpsed from a car or a train, possess an immediate and deeply peaceful attraction."[42] Indeed, to the young Seamus growing up at Mossbawn, life's most vivid experiences involved encounters with the boggy world around him.

Remembrances of such encounters dominate his first collection, *Death of a Naturalist* (1966). The title poem renders, in quasi-comic fashion, his terrifying discovery of the sheer organic force held in the "slobber / Of frogspawn" observed at a local flax-dam. Taking samples home to watch the tadpoles develop, he adopted a most pastoral, domesticated view of such processes until one hot day he found hundreds of frogs croaking around the flax-dam:

> Some hopped:
> The slap and plop were obscene threats. Some sat
> Poised like mud grenades, their blunt heads farting.
> I sickened, turned, and ran....
>   ("Death of a Naturalist")

So much for the quiet beauty and dignity of nature. Such was his terror that he feared dipping his hand into the slime, lest the spawn "clutch" it.

Likewise "An Advancement of Learning" concerns another milestone in Heaney's youthful demythologizing of nature. Walking beside a river, he came upon a rat, causing him his usual terror. This time, though, he learned to face the enemy—"I stared him out / Forgetting how I used to panic"—with the result that "This terror, cold, wet-furred, small-clawed, / Retreated up a pipe for sewage."

Both poems take their effectiveness in part from the adult perspective of their narrator. Often in *Death of a Naturalist* that perspective becomes more explicit, as Heaney—in such poems as "The Early Purges," "Follower," and "Turkeys Observed"—compares his more recent feelings with what he felt as a child. Despite any disillusionment reflected in such comparison, in such pieces as "Cow in Calf" or "Trout"—which provides a sharp contrast with Ted Hughes's "Pike"—Heaney retains an affection for nature. And he begins in some of these early poems to connect his experience of nature with wider concerns: the extended reference to the potato famine in the middle of "At a Potato Digging" illustrates this possibility in his writing. The brief lyric titled "Waterfall" illustrates, too, Heaney's assumption that what is observed can be pinned down with some finality, an assumption rather at odds with Charles Tomlinson's views.

The *Death of a Naturalist* poems won recognition for their toughness of diction, with one critic describing Heaney's early poetry as "carefully guarded against the curse of lilt."[43] They achieved notice, also, for their intentness. In "Digging" Heaney offered the seeds of the vocational self-consciousness later to be reinforced by *The Bog People* and expressed most extremely in "North." Digging, the occupation of his father and grandfather, both skilled farmers, emerges here as the metaphor for what Heaney would do as a poet. "I've no spade to follow men like them," he allows, as he vows to "dig" with his pen.

Surely the next collection, *Door into the Dark* (1969), better satisfied that urge to dig. Generally its poems are less emotional and less sentimental than many in the earlier book, and more exploratory of the human psyche. Generally, too, they display greater metaphorical experimentation. One of these newer poems renders the nightmarish vision of a man furiously cutting a stalk "[w]ith a billhook, / Whose head was hand-forged," only to find another man's head under the hook, and then to awaken—but not before hearing the steel of the hook "stop / In the bone of the brow" ("Dream"). The narrator's continuing horror refers not so much to the dream itself as to the fact that he could harbor such a vision. The dream of the poem thus operates as an intimation of a perhaps even more horrifying darkness just beneath the surface of a seemingly benign consciousness.

Another discovery narrative from the same collection, "The Outlaw," brings to mind Ted Hughes's "The Bull Moses." Here, though, the discoverer is an adult, and the discovery concerns more the protagonist's similarity to the beast than any difference between them. Specifically, the narrator, a farmer, tells of once enlisting the services of an unlicensed bull, kept "well away / From the road." His recalling that occasion in detail relates to the highly comic way in which he responded—and still responds—to the bull's behavior. The very terms by which he characterizes the animal in the various stages of stud

> Unhurried as an old steam engine shunting.
> ... No hectic panting,
> Just the unbusy ease of a good tradesman:
> ... impassive as a tank,
> Dropping off like a tipped-up load of sand

register the shock of a disappointed romantic. They help register, too, the narrator's increasing uneasiness as he emerges in his own mind a coconspirator, along with the bull and its owner, against the law, against morality, and perhaps against nature itself. After recalling the need to drag his nervous Friesian to the bull's shed, he remembers giving the owner the "clammy silver, though why / I could not guess"—clearly an attempt to repress awareness of participating in an illicit deed. Guilt shows, too, in his account of the two owners' parting: "I walked ahead of her, the rope now slack / While Kelly whooped and prodded his outlaw." Understanding too well the cow's now-docile behavior, he fails to transfer his share of blame onto Kelly and the "outlaw."

Such poems represent necessary forays into the darkness Heaney wished to fathom. Others celebrate occupations typically demanding the same patience, poise, and courage as his projected digging. Thus the salmon fisherman, who recognizes that he and his prey share the same fate—"We're both annihilated on the fly" ("The Salmon Fisher to the Salmon")—emerges as a hero, as do the blacksmith, in "The Forge," and the independent workman described in "Thatcher." The skilled smith presents a parable for "working" the dark, for forging a reality out of imaginings. Likewise the thatcher, with his magical power to mend and make a roof, seems a model at "pinning down his world, handful by handful" ("Thatcher"). And in "A Lough Neagh Sequence" Heaney celebrates the eel-fishers' adeptness at bringing in their "furling, slippy / Haul" ("Lilting"). Eels—"[p]hosphorescent, sinewed slime" ("Vision")—serve as an emblem of all that Heaney fears, and of all that he must confront as a poet. Hence his admiration for those who have survived such confrontation.

Wintering Out (1972) continued the confrontational digging already advanced by *Door into the Dark*. Obviously put together in the context of the renewed troubles in Northern Ireland, Heaney's third collection is even more given to the purposeful exploration of the darkness, and especially civilization's dark past. Several poems extend the occupational celebrations already noted to connect with Irish history. Thus a servant boy ("jobber among shadows") is praised for his stoic perserverance in "wintering out / the back-end of a bad year" ("Servant Boy"). Gradually his figure becomes an emblem for the proud, downtrodden laboring class ("resentful / and impenitent") in their psychic struggle against the wealthy and powerful—and presumably for the native Irish against their British conquerors—while his characteristic activity, "carrying the warm eggs," represents a hopeful portent for the future. Likewise "The Last Mummer" examines a figure rooted in a largely irrecoverable past; his treatment by a contemporary society intent on television and other ephemera produces a profound sense of loss. At the same time his survival, as well as his continuing defiance of the new order, holds out some hope of Ireland's reunion with her deepest cultural traditions. It is in this book that Heaney first made explicit use of Glob's bogland researches. In fact, the emblem of the bog as an "information retrieval system" and "memory bank"[44] had first appeared in the final poem of *Door into the Dark,* where, noting the absence from Ireland of "prairies" in the American sense, Heaney sought a more profound frontier in the "bog that keeps crusting / Beneath the sights of the sun" ("Bogland"). Fascinated by the preservative qualities of the bog water, he went on in this poem to explore the wonders yielded by the Irish bogs—notably the skeleton of the Great Irish Elk and "Butter sunk under / More than a hundred years"; to remark how "Our pioneers keep striking / Inwards and downwards"; and to conclude, "The wet centre is bottomless." Written quickly, after Heaney visited the National Museum in Dublin,[45] "Bogland" clearly reflected a watershed in his search for "befitting emblems of adversity."

His next bog poem, the one included in *Wintering Out,* served as a further step in realizing the bog people's symbolic potential. Here Heaney reflects on one of the most extraordinary bog discoveries, the so-called Tolland Man, who two thousand years ago was strangled with a rope. He begins by vowing to visit the Tolland Man and do homage to the corpse and its accoutrements, including the gruel miraculously preserved in the stomach: "Bridegroom to the goddess, / She tightened her torc on him" ("The Tollund Man"). Next, he considers consecrating the Irish bog, presumably filled with centuries of "scattered, ambushed / Flesh of labourers," and, finally, he imagines feeling "lost, / Unhappy and at home" reviewing this and other corpses given up by "the old man-killing parishes." As a citizen of a comparatively new "man-killing" society, he senses a powerful attraction to the Tolland Man as an emblem of the present misery's rootedness in a dark past.

Wintering Out introduced another strand of continuity between new and old, as in several poems Heaney explored language itself as a door into the distant past. The striking sequence "Gifts of Rain," though ostensibly describing a fierce storm, develops the parallel between language and landscape as further evidence of rootedness. Through powerful images and hard words—

> nimble snout of flood ...
> like a cat swaying
> its red spoors through a basin
> ... the race
> slabbering past the gable

the poem conveys the force of the "tawny gutteral water ... breathing its mists / through vowels and history," and thus shows the way in which language accompanies—and perhaps precedes—our most remote awareness of the natural elements surrounding us.

Similarly, in "Toombe" Heaney delights in language as raw sound; he becomes "naturalized" in the process of rolling over in his mouth, ear, and mind that place name of his childhood. With "Broagh" he further extends the analogy of language and landscape to include the inhabitants, as that name's sound and pronunciation become a sure and appropriate way of separating the true Irish from pretenders or outsiders. And, while in "The Backward Look" he remarks the ephemerality of language and the irrecoverability of the original Irish tongue—which he compares to a snipe—nevertheless in "A New Song" he can assert the "vowelling embrace" of Irish folk, land, and speech. Even the obsolete, in language or other behavior, retains value for Heaney because of its indirect bearing on the present and future, and because of its link with the landscape and thus with the past.[46]

All such poems, as well as the entire project of digging into the impersonal past, relate to the Yeatsian principles of perception and self-control noted earlier. Despite its strong spots, *Wintering Out* is Heaney's most uneven collection. A measure of its unevenness may be due to Heaney's ambivalence between Yeatsian self-control and Wordsworthian self-indulgence, an ambivalence reflected in the book's organization. Where the majority of its poems, those comprising part 1, concern the bogs, the Irish people and language, or some other aspect of Heaney's search for a historical and cultural key to the contemporary political crisis, another, smaller group, dealing with more personal or domestic matters, make up part 2. While hardly so ambitious or strong as those in the first part, some of these other poems have a decided beauty of their own and constitute a direct link to the largely autobiographical writing in *Death of a Naturalist*. And of course they have their analogue in those few poems of *Door into the Dark* that do not quite fit Heaney's digging scheme but nevertheless possess poise and dignity in relation to their quieter subjects. With *North* (1975) Heaney managed better to unify his vision. Virtually every selection reflects the vocational intention of the title poem. Even the division into two parts here underscores his ambition, as the second section is reserved for those more openly realistic poems dealing with contemporary politics. In the first section Heaney's strands of myth, bog, lore, language, and landscape come together in dazzling fashion. Poem after poem confirms the wisdom and strength of his vision of Ireland and of himself as a visionary poet who can lead his people back to themselves. The very titles— "Antaeus," "Belderg," "The Digging Skeleton," "Bog Queen"— suggest a tough, integrated attack on the troubles confronting modern society, and especially modern Ireland.

Perhaps most notable is "Viking Dublin: Trial Pieces," which brings to mind Hughes's "Thought Fox" in its sharp delineation of the creative process. With increasingly bold metaphors, suggested by Viking remains, Heaney tries on terms for what he does when he digs. These terms become tighter and more definite as the poem progresses—as he digs in on digging and renders his poetic poetically. First he considers some small skeletal remain ("It could be a jaw-bone / or a rib ..."), which on closer inspection proves marvelously elusive: "like an eel swallowed in a basket of eels ... a bill in flight, / a swimming nostril." Admitting that such notions are but "trial pieces, / the craft's mystery improvised on bone," he next characterizes the "nostril" as a "migrant prow" and then as a "buoyant / migrant line" back into the Irish past. Such metaphorical tightening continues as the poet's "worm of thought" leads him to invite his reader to "fly" with him, to join with Viking expertise in becoming "neighborly, scoretaking / killers, haggers / and hagglers, gombeen-men, / hoarders of grudges and gain." Combining Old Norse poetry and Joyce's *Portrait,* he invokes: "Old fathers, be with us, / old cunning assessors / of feuds and of sites / for ambush or town." The poet as hunter, the poetic process as hunting, the completed poem as triumph over a tough adversary—such images suggest the excitement and confidence of Heaney's will to dig.

Other poems, especially "Bone Dreams," exhibit the same metaphorical extravagance and high wit in their digging. But, as noted earlier, *North* does not end on nearly so triumphant a note. Retrospectively the entire collection appears an attempt to repress the

uncertainty and self-recrimination that come out in "Exposure."
This is why in *Field Work* (1979) Heaney tries to recover the op-
portunities increasingly neglected in the poetry of the four earlier
collections. This is not to say that he now turns his back on politics
or the larger social dimension of things. He still can write of murder
and the murdered, of uneasy truces enforced by the British military
presence in Ulster, and of the confusion of being Irish in a divided
Ireland. But even those poems most concerned with such matters
treat them in more modest tones than before, and more from the
viewpoint of the victims to whom sympathy is offered than from
that of the probing, would-be omniscient poet. It is almost as if
Heaney finally recognizes the ultimately bottomless depth of all he
has sought to understand.

The majority of pieces in this latest book constitute a respite from
the public role Heaney took earlier. Here, as Jon Stallworthy has
it, "Heaney's green is primarily the green of the vegetable kingdom
and only secondarily that of the Irish flag."[47] Thus the opening
poem rehearses his decision to savor his own experience, to be
"quickened" into "verb, pure verb" ("Oysters"). Those poems trac-
ing his rediscovery of nature—"The Badgers," "The Otter," "Polder,"
and the beautiful sequence of "Glanmore Sonnets"—all meld his
power to observe and his power to love. He can write amusingly of
his wife's jealousy of his poetry: "She would plunge all poets in the
ninth circle" ("An Afterwards"). He can write elegiacally of an
Irishman *not* killed in the troubles ("In Memoriam Sean O'Riada").
He can write movingly of his wife's harvest bow as an emblem of
his poetry: *"The end of art is peace* / Could be the motto of this frail
device" ("The Harvest Bow"). Peace, rather than perception or con-
quest, governs this most recent writing.

All of this has its prosodic dimension. The capacity for tough
language, of course, persists—"not pretty or grand but a squatting
farmer's feel for the richest mold," one reviewer terms it.[48] However,
one finds here a willingness to utilize a longer, and sometimes looser,
poetic line, thus reversing the trend of Heaney's earlier books. As
he recently told an interviewer, "the line and the life are intimately
related": "that narrow line, that tight line, came out of time when
I was very tight myself."[49] Certainly *Field Work* exhibits a variety
of forms unmatched in his poetry since its very beginning. And
yet, while viewing the shift between his latest collections as "a shift
in trust"—"a learning to trust melody, to trust art as reality, to

trust artfulness as an affirmation and not to go into the self-punishment so much"—he maintains, "Those two volumes are negotiating with each other."[50]

What will come of such negotiation only his next poems, or his next collection, can tell. Even so, Seamus Heaney has established himself as a poet of major stature—and for many readers *the* principal poet writing in English to have emerged since the death of Yeats. Such is his stature and so much is he at the height of his power as a craftsman that, in the view of more than one observer, not since Yeats or the young Eliot has an English-writing poet's next book been so eagerly awaited.

The suspense, as well as the stature, is surely owing to the ongoing struggle in his writing between the two principles he has related to Yeats and Wordsworth, respectively. In all of this the figure of Robert Lowell, whose memory inspired the beautiful "Elegy" in *Field Work*, has been especially important.[51] If Heaney has confronted the political realities of his time as no major British poet since Auden, he has demonstrated the personal risk of such confrontation. And if, as the latest phase of his career suggests, he has come to grips with that risk, he has demonstrated an integrity and maturity that can be a model not only for poets, but for all thoughtful citizens of the contemporary world.

Chapter Seven

Conclusion: British Poetry into the Twenty-First Century

To conclude any discussion in literary history is problematic and, in a sense, absurd, since literary history, or at least the literature it chronicles, is seamless. This is especially true in the case of a contemporary literature. If, as was argued at the beginning of this study, 1939 as a point at which to begin examining recent British poetry is not entirely arbitrary, certainly any time since as a point for cutting off that examination *is* arbitrary. And because, as Philip Larkin observes in "Triple Time," the present is always receding immediately into the past, strictly speaking no literature is contemporary. Even if the dead war poets and Stevie Smith can give us no new poems, or although Larkin expects to write no more, [1] the others, from Fuller to Heaney, are still going at it even as these words are being written and read.

The resulting diachronic incompleteness in the foregoing study is compounded by a certain synchronic incompleteness. The absence of commanding figures in British poetry of the last forty years comparable to Yeats and Eliot—or, for that matter, to Harold Pinter in drama—makes the selection of poets examined in detail difficult, and the exclusion of others risky and to a degree unfair. To discuss Fuller and Larkin as illustrative of an ongoing empirical strain in British poetry is, to be sure, permissible and even legitimate. But, would replacing either with a Donald Davie, a D. J. Enright or a Kingsley Amis be less acceptable or less valid? And, could not Brian Patten be equally useful in describing the naturalist strain as Geoffrey Hill or even Hughes himself? Or, might not that brief noting of R. S. Thomas at the beginning of chapter 5 be extended to a discussion equal in depth—and value—to that accorded Stevie Smith or Elizabeth Jennings as a meditative poet? The list of potential replacements in any of the chapters is seemingly endless—George

Barker, George Macbeth, Charles Causley, Thom Gunn and Vernon Scannell also come to mind immediately—as is that of poets whose oblique relationship to the strands giving rise to these chapters suggest the possibility—indeed, the likelihood—of other categories equally deserving of attention in such a study. The writings of Dannie Abse, Gavin Ewart, Douglas Dunn, Jon Silkin and W. S. Graham, just for starters, complicate the vision of recent British poetry in vital and interesting ways.

Even so, the strands and specific poets studied here account for most of the British poetry since 1939 likely to survive into the twenty-first century or beyond. Additionally, they permit valid observations about recent British poetry as a whole and about the likely directions of British poetry as recent and current poets and movements give way to newer ones.

Principally these poets and their poems reveal motion first toward realism and empiricism—culminating with the Movement and its various offshoots in the late 1950s and early 1960s—then off in a variety of other directions, each differing in some central respect from the empiricist mode. These later directions—here labelled naturalist, meditative and neoromantic—to a degree represent not only a reaction against empiricism, but a continuation of strands in British verse reaching back into the nineteenth century and even earlier.

As noted before, Philip Larkin's latest collection suggests a partial return to his youthful Yeatsian mode of writing. In this we have something of a paradigm for British poetry as a whole since Yeats's death, as the modest, controlled dimension of most empiricist writing has gradually given way to the possibility of a poetry broader not only in its technique and tone, but in the issues it confronts. Relatedly, Seamus Heaney's career reflects a tension between impersonal and personal views of poetry not unlike that marking the work of Stephen Spender and C. Day Lewis in the later 1930s. And Heaney's latest book may reflect a permanent shift to the kind of personal writing ultimately favored by each member of the original Auden group.

However, despite this measure of resemblance among some poets to writers of the 1930s, recent British poetry has faced with differing consequences some other problems confronting those earlier writers. For all of the caution inspired by the postwar British experience, the acceptance and appropriation of mass culture ventured by Auden has been confirmed in the subsequent decades. As a consequence mass culture and its adherents have come to accept poetry and poets more readily than before. Certainly the 1960s readings and festivals further helped put poetry into an easier relationship with the general reading public, though they had never grown so estranged as in the United States. While amid all the distractions of contemporary life poetry now represents no great preoccupation for most Britishers, it has secured a fixed if modest place in the cultural spectrum.

British poetry's relationship to the culture and poetry of other nations also has been more nearly settled, at least by the work of certain key figures emerging in the last forty years. To be sure, the insularity of Larkin continues to have its proponents. But, at the same time a healthy strain of internationalism—championed by Charles Tomlinson, Ted Hughes, George Macbeth and Michael Hamburger, among others, and further signaled by the enthusiasm for translation among practicing poets—has developed and promises to grow stronger. In no respect is this strain more evident than in many contemporary poets' fascination with modern American po-etry, a fascination free of the patronage and cynicism toward Amer-ican literature shown by Britishers before World War I, and of the self-consciousness and even inferiority often felt in the time since. A further sign of appreciation, on both sides of the Atlantic, for the distinctive values of each of the two literatures, as well as their connections, are those fairly recent attempts to examine Anglo-American literary relations objectively—notably Martin Green's *Transatlantic Patterns* (1977) and Stephen Spender's *Love-Hate Relations* (1974).

Having spent much time in the United States, Spender is sin-gularly qualified to undertake such an examination. His career since World War II illustrates another facet of internationalism in British poetry, the frequent and fruitful exchange of poets as readers and lecturers. Among recent writers Thom Gunn, Donald Davie, Charles Tomlinson and Seamus Heaney have been prominent as touring lecturers and writers-in-residence at American universities.

Of course, the opening up of British poetry to influences from abroad—indeed, the expansion into varying directions evident since the Movement and the 1950s—has been paralleled, and presumably encouraged, by similar developments in drama and fiction. The explosion of British drama, signaled by the emergence of Pinter and Osborne roughly a decade after World War II, has made London the theater capital of the world and its playwrights the advance guard of contemporary drama. Of course, however stodgy British drama might have gotten during the war, there was always the example of the self-exiled Samuel Beckett. Certainly the recognition given *Waiting for Godot* in the early 1950s inspired experimentation among younger British dramatists. The flowering of the theater in the decades since—the rise to prominence of such figures as Tom Stoppard, Peter Shaffer, and Arnold Wesker—no doubt has reinforced rebelliousness among the younger poets of the time.

And while for a time British fiction essentially meant novels and stories in the Movement vein—or the work of more established traditionalists such as Graham Greene, Elizabeth Bowen, and Evelyn Waugh—since the 1950s it, too, has moved out in a variety of directions encouraging similar efforts among poets. The novels of Anthony Burgess, Lawrence Durrell, Doris Lessing, David Lodge, and John Fowles—just to name a few, and by no means the same few who might strike anyone else as equally representative of the period—suggest by themselves the play with genre and style that has characterized so much British fiction in the last quarter-century. As with poetry, the traditional mode continues in fiction as a sort of underpinning or point of departure for the experimentalists, but even this has encouraged experimentation. If at any time in the last forty years the British novel seemed consigned to inescapable stodginess—and this may have been an illusion—surely the writings of the above-named authors, as well as dozens of others who might as readily be mentioned, justify a measure of the excitement accorded recent British drama and represent a useful parallel to developments in British poetry of the same period.

While fiction and drama suggest developments similar to those in poetry, the economics of writing and publishing during this time certainly have much to do with the kinds of poetry available to the reading public. The gravitation of the principal poets, and not only the empiricists, toward broadly academic occupations should be evident. Relatedly, since World War II contemporary poetry has become a subject of academic study even on pre-university levels. Young people have come not so much to discover or even read poems as to "study" them, largely in school. This trend has resulted in a primarily academic market for poets. Such hovering under the academic wing—so much so that some critics have complained that "No new poet is safely established until he is on the syllabus"[2]—

has its roots in the New Criticism and analogous educational developments in postwar America, and in the recent opening up of university education in the British Isles. It connects, too, with the growth of government support for culture in postwar Britain, notably the Arts Council with its funding of readings, workshops, publications, and poetry centers.

The attitudes of poets toward such institutionalizing of their craft range from enthusiastic support to open disgust. The latter position was clearly expressed when Philip Larkin snapped at one interviewer—"Oh, for Christ's sake, one doesn't *study* poets! You *read* them and think, 'That's marvellous, how is it done, could I do it?' and that's how you learn"[3]—or when he told another:

I think we got much better poetry when it was all regarded as sinful or subversive and you had to hide it under the cushion when somebody came in. What I don't like about subsidies and official support is that they destroy the essential nexus between the writer and the reader. If the writer is being paid to write and the reader is being paid to read, the element of impulsive contact vanishes.[4]

Whether so pristine a relationship as Larkin envisions could exist in an age of mass media and mass education, or whether it ever existed except on a very limited scale, is questionable. That he supports his writing with a university librarianship ironically illustrates one aspect of the situation he deplores. Clearly institutional support for poetry has meant publication of some poets and books that would go unpublished in a freer literary marketplace. Clearly, too, it has meant the threat of conformity, of feeling bound to write for a narrowly "academic" audience—by adopting either a preconceived academic style, or an artifically antiacademic one.

Perhaps equally determinant of whatever freedom British poets have enjoyed in recent times is the nature of the publishing industry. Despite occasional rumblings from the provinces, London remains dominant, the one place where poets want to be published. This necessarily makes for a degree of homogeneity, as does the uncertain status of poetry among major publishers. Because some of the principal publishers of poetry have become attached to the educational market, small presses continue as a major means by which unknown poets and poems of merit find readers.[5]

Any concern over homogeneity or conformity among British poets might be partly relieved by two fairly recent events—not of major literary significance but perhaps representative of a lively and varied climate of opinion regarding poetry and its possibilities. The first, the critical response to D. J. Enright's *Oxford Book of Contemporary Verse*, suggests a return not only to the anthology wars of the 1950s, but to even earlier spirited debates over what British poetry might be. The polemics of Enright's introduction to his anthology have been suggested. Equally fierce were the rejoinders of certain critics, accusing Enright of wanting self-effacement[6] and finding his defense of Movement formulas "remote from the actualities of our time."[7]

The second representative event occurred at the 1981 Cambridge Poetry Festival. There, in a symposium titled "While Rome Burns: What use has poetry in a world in jeopardy?," several writers argued over poetry's place in contemporary Western culture. Most memorable were those exchanges between Adrian Mitchell, a well-established poet and playwright, and George Steiner, the Cambridge literary scholar and theorist. Mitchell insisted, with much vocal support from the audience, that in the face of threatened nuclear destruction, poetry must take a political stance, and that contemporary political poetry therefore has considerable merit. Steiner countered by observing the lack of "inner necessity" characterizing most contemporary writing in the West, whether political or not. This situation he contrasted with that of the poet in a repressive society, where poetry by definition operates as the "idiom of the counter-state." Or, as he has asked in one of his essays, "What Western regime flinches at a poem?"[8] Despite Steiner's scoffing at the "vacuum of urbane freedom" available to the poet in the West, Mitchell objected that the writer's freedom to speak out and the possibility of being heard in sufficient time were not illusory and must be pursued. In support of this viewpoint another poet and small-press publisher, Anthony Rudolf, chimed in that his press had conciously changed direction to embrace the political imperative described by Mitchell.

Like the controversy over the Enright anthology, the Cambridge debate recalled an earlier period in British literary history. Specifically its terms, as well as the spirit in which it was conducted, recalled the disagreement over poetry's place during those last uneasy years before World War II. To be sure, no consensus was reached at Cambridge that May afternoon. If this suggests a failure to answer an important question that poets had chosen to put off with the war's beginning, it also suggests a recognition of that question's difficulty, and its probable unanswerability.

Such events as these, as well as poems actually written by British poets since 1939, are evidence that British poetry can and will cross-examine itself periodically and will resist settling into any single mold. In the meantime new poets and new poems will appear. Larkin's joyous remark about the British propensity to sea-bathing— "Still going on, all of it, still going on!" ("To the Sea")—applies equally to British poetry. Who the prominent British poets of the next century will be—or whether a principal figure will finally emerge to take Yeats's place—there is no sense conjecturing. What seems certain, though, is that arguably the greatest poetic tradition in human history has not given out, but will continue to replenish itself in surprising and significant ways.

Notes and References

Preface

1. John Matthias, Foreword to *23 Modern British Poets* (Chicago, 1971), xiii.
2. Alan Brownjohn, "A View of English Poets in the Early 'Seventies,' " in *British Poetry Since 1960, A Critical Survey*, ed. Michael Schmidt and Grevel Lindop (Oxford, 1972), 240.

Chapter One

1. Noel Coward, "Twentieth Century Blues," in *The Noel Coward Songbook* (New York: Simon & Schuster, 1953), 89–91.
2. Noel Coward, *Songbook*, 72.
3. A. J. P. Taylor, *English History 1914–1945* (Oxford: Clarendon Press, 1965), 311.
4. Monroe Spears, *The Poetry of W. H. Auden* (New York: Oxford University Press, 1963), 59.
5. Roy Fuller, "Poetic Memories of the Thirties," *Michigan Quarterly Review* 12 (1973):218.
6. A. K. Weatherhead, "British Leftist Poetry of the Nineteen Thirties," *Michigan Quarterly Review* 10 (1971):20.
7. D. E. S. Maxwell, *Poets of the Thirties* (New York: Barnes & Noble, 1969), 42.
8. Bernard Bergonzi, *Reading the Thirties* (Pittsburgh: University of Pittsburgh Press, 1978), 39–54.
9. Maxwell, *Poets of the Thirties*, 159.
10. See Wendall Johnson, "Auden, Hopkins and the Poetry of Reticence," *Twentieth-Century Literature* 20 (1974): 165–71.
11. Preface to *The English Auden*, ed. Edward Mendelson (New York: Random House, 1977), xv.
12. George Orwell, "Inside the Whale," in *Collected Essays, Journalism and Letters of George Orwell* (New York: Harcourt, 1968) I, 515.
13. Stephen Spender, "Background to the Thirties," in *The Thirties and After* (New York: Random House, 1978), 4.
14. Bergonzi, *Reading the Thirties*, 10–37.
15. Mendelson, *The English Auden*, xiv.
16. Ibid., xviii.
17. Spender, "Background to the Thirties," 12.

18. Stephen Spender, "Poetry and Revolution," in *The Thirties and After*, 32–35. Originally published in *New Country* in 1933.

19. Maxwell, *Poets of the Thirties*, 175.

20. See Rowland Smith, "The Spanish Civil War and the British Literary Right," *Dalhousie Review* 51 (1971–72): 60–76.

21. Christopher Caudwell, *Illusion and Reality* (New York: International Publishers, 1937), 285.

22. Stephen Spender, "W. B. Yeats as a Realist," *Criterion* 14 (1934): 25.

Chapter Two

1. Keith Douglas, "Poets in This War," *Times Literary Supplement* (hereinafter cited as *TLS*), 23 April 1971, 478.

2. See Robert Graves and Alan Hodge, *The Long Week-End: A Social History of Great Britain 1918–1939* (London: Faber, 1940).

3. Alfred F. Havighurst, *Britain in Transition* (Chicago: University of Chicago, 1979), 309, 315.

4. Robert Hewison, *Under Siege: Literary Life in London 1939–1945* (New York: Oxford University Press, 1977), 80.

5. Angus Calder, *The People's War* (New York: Pantheon, 1969), 511.

6. Hewison, *Under Siege*, 16–18.

7. George Orwell in *Collected Essays*, II, 305.

8. Calder, *People's War*, 511.

9. Cyril Connolly, "Comment," *Horizon*, no. 60 (December 1944), 367.

10. Hewison, *Under Siege*, 97.

11. Quoted from Henry Treece's Preface to *The Crown and The Sickle* (1944) by John Press in *A Map of Modern English Verse* (London: Oxford University Press, 1969), 230.

12. John Lehmann, *I Am My Brother* (New York: Reynal, 1960), 231.

13. Douglas, "Poets in This War," 478.

14. See Paul Fussell, *The Great War and Modern Memory* (New York and London: Oxford University Press, 1975), 318 and passim.

15. Douglas, "Poets in This War," 478.

16. Desmond Graham, *Keith Douglas* (London, 1974), 11–18.

17. Ibid., 53.

18. Ibid., 100.

19. Ibid., 204.

20. Edmund Blunden, Foreword to Keith Douglas, *Collected Poems*, ed. Sir John Waller, G. S. Fraser, and J. C. Hall (London, 1966), 17.

21. Graham, *Douglas*, ix.

22. Keith Douglas, *Complete Poems*, ed. Desmond Graham (Oxford, 1978), 127.

23. See Graham, *Douglas*, 24, 27.

24. Douglas, *Complete Poems*, 124.

25. Vernon Scannell, *Not Without Glory: Poets of the Second World War* (London, 1976), 38.

26. Graham, *Douglas*, 132.

27. Olivia Manning, "Poets in Exile," *Horizon* 10 (1944): 278.

28. Graham, *Douglas*, 225.

29. A. Banerjee, *Spirit Above Wars* (London: Macmillan, 1976), 20–22.

30. Ted Hughes, "The Poetry of Keith Douglas," *Critical Quarterly* 5 (1963): 47.

31. Roy Fuller, "The Warrior Bard," *Encounter* 43 (September 1974): 76.

32. Keith Douglas, *Alamein to Zem Zem* (London: Oxford University Press, 1979), 16.

33. Douglas, *Alamein to Zem Zem*, 72.

34. Alun Lewis, *Selected Poetry and Prose*, ed. Ian Hamilton (London, 1966), 27.

35. Alun Lewis, *In the Green Tree* (London, 1948), 23.

36. Ibid., 56.

37. Ibid., 39.

38. Banerjee, *Spirit Above Wars*, 165.

39. Lewis, *In the Green Tree*, 47.

40. Scannell, *Not Without Glory*, 135.

41. Ibid.

42. Ibid., 138.

Chapter Three

1. Havighurst, *Britain in Transition*, 367.

2. Ibid.

3. Press, *A Map of Modern English Verse*, 253.

4. Ian Hamilton, "The Making of the Movement," in *British Poetry Since 1960*, 72.

5. Donald Davie, "Remembering the Movement," in *The Poet in the Imaginary Museum*, ed. Barry Alpert (New York: Persea Books, 1977), 72.

6. Blake Morrison, *The Movement: English Poetry and Fiction of the 1950s* (Oxford, 1980), 4.

7. Philip Larkin, *All What Jazz* (New York: St. Martin's Press, 1970), 17.

8. John Wain, *Professing Poetry* (New York: Viking Press, 1978), 16.

9. D. J. Enright, Introducton, *The Oxford Book of Contemporary Verse 1945–1980* (Oxford, 1980), xxviii.

10. Ibid., xxx.

11. Blake Morrison, "In Defense of Minimalism," *Critical Quarterly* 18, no. 2 (Summer 1976): 44.

12. Allan Austin, *Roy Fuller* (Boston, 1979), 22.

13. Peter Firchow, ed., *The Writer's Place: Interviews on the Literary Situation in Contemporary Britain* (Minneapolis: University of Minnesota Press, 1974), 127.

14. Austin, *Roy Fuller*, 20.

15. Roy Fuller, "Need for the Non-Literary," *TLS*, 10 Nov. 1972, 1363.

16. Roy Fuller, *Professors and Gods* (New York: St. Martin's Press, 1973), 108, 113.

17. Peter Orr, ed., *The Poet Speaks* (New York, 1966), 64.

18. Roy Fuller, *Owls and Artificers* (New York: Library Press, 1971), 72.

19. Fuller, *Professors and Gods*, 164.

20. Fuller, *Owls and Artificers*, 74.

21. Austin, *Roy Fuller*, 25.

22. Julien Gitzen, "The Evolution of Roy Fuller," *Contemporary Poetry* 3 (1943): 64.

23. Orr, *The Poet Speaks*, 63.

24. Roy Fuller, "Fetish of Speech Rhythms in Modern Poetry," *Southern Review* 15 (1979): 1–15.

25. Fuller, *Owls and Artificers*, 62.

26. Orr, *The Poet Speaks*, 64.

27. Firchow, *The Writer's Place*, 126.

28. Calvin Bedient, *Eight Contemporary Poets* (London, 1974), 94.

29. Henri Colette, "The Thought of *High Windows*," *Southern Review* 12 (1976): 439.

30. Davie, "Remembering the Movement," 64.

31. Hermann Peschmann, "Philip Larkin: Laureate of the Common Man," *English* 24 (1975): 49–58.

32. Eric Homberger, *The Art of the Real* (London: Dent, 1977), 76.

33. Davie, "Remembering the Movement," 65.

34. Philip Larkin, Introduction, *Jill* (London: Faber, 1964), 12.

35. Davie, "Remembering the Movement," 64.

36. See B. C. Bloomfield, *Philip Larkin. A Bibliography, 1933–1976* (London, 1979), 19–57.

37. Philip Larkin, "The Pleasure Principle," *Listen* 2 (Summer-Autumn 1956): 30.

38. See Larkin's recording of *The Whitsun Weddings* (Hessle, Yorkshire: Listen Records, 1965).

39. Larkin, *All What Jazz*, 96.

40. John Bayley, *The Uses of Division* (New York, 1976), 169–70.

41. Bedient, *Eight Contemporary Poets*, 78.

42. Anthony Thwaite, "The Poetry of Philip Larkin," in *The Survival of Poetry*, ed. Martin Dodsworth (London: Faber, 1970), 47.

43. See his recording of *The Whitsun Weddings*.

44. Grevel Lindop, "Being different from yourself: Philip Larkin in the 1970s," in *British Poetry Since 1970: A Critical Survey*, ed. Peter Jones and Michael Schmidt (New York, 1980), 52.

45. Geoffrey Thurley, *The Ironic Harvest: English Poetry in the Twentieth Century* (New York: St. Martin's Press, 1974), 141–49.

Chapter Four

1. A. Alvarez, "Introduction: The New Poetry, *or* Beyond the Gentility Principle," *The New Poetry* (Harmondsworth, Middlesex, England, 1962), 25.

2. Chad Walsh, "The Postwar Revolt in England Against Modern Poets," *Bucknell Review* 13 (1965): 105.

3. For examples, see M. L. Rosenthal, "Tuning in on Albion," *Nation* 188 (1959): 458–59, and *The New Poets*, ed. M. L. Rosenthal (New York, 1967).

4. Alvarez, "The New Poetry," 30.

5. Ibid., 29.

6. George Steiner, "Dying Is an Art," *Reporter* 33 (7 Oct. 1965): 51.

7. Quoted in Julian Symons, "Cooked and Raw," *New Statesman* 74 (21 July 1967): 87.

8. Anthony Thwaite, "Guts, Brain, Nerves," *New Statesman* 75 (1968): 659.

9. Alan Brownjohn, "Henry Himself," *New Statesman* 77 (1969): 776.

10. Martin Seymour-Smith, "Bones dream on," *Spectator*, 9 May 1969, 622.

11. Edward Lucie-Smith, Foreword, *A Group Anthology* (London, 1963), xv-xvii.

12. Michael Horovitz, cited in Grevel Lindop, "Poetry, Rhetoric and the Mass Audience: The Case of the Liverpool Poets," in *British Poetry Since 1960*, 93.

13. Lucie-Smith, *A Group Anthology*, 64.

14. Ibid.

15. Anthony Thwaite, *Twentieth-Century British Poetry* (London: Heinemann, 1978), 123.

16. Ted Hughes, *Poetry in the Making* (London: Faber, 1967), 15–17.

17. "For Sidney Bechet"

18. A. Kingsley Weatherhead, "Ted Hughes, 'Crow' and Pain," *Texas Quarterly* 19, no. 3 (Autumn 1976): 101.

19. Bedient, *Eight Contemporary Poets*, 95.

20. Ekbert Faas, *Ted Hughes: The Unaccommodated Universe* (Santa Barbara, 1980), 167.

21. Ibid., 203.

22. Thurley, *Ironic Harvest*, 180.

23. Ted Hughes, "Laura Riding" (1970), a previously unpublished essay included in Faas, 188–89.

24. Faas, *Ted Hughes*, 203.

25. Ibid., 62.

26. Ibid., 86.

27. Weatherhead, "Ted Hughes, 'Crow' and Pain," 106.

28. Ibid., 108.

29. Ibid., 106.

30. E.g., Faas, *Ted Hughes*, 104–116.

31. Ibid., 104.

32. Ibid., 116.

33. Ibid., 131–33.

34. Merle Brown, "Geoffrey Hill's 'Funeral Music,' " *Agenda* 17 (Spring 1979): 72–88; Stephen Utz, "The Realism of Geoffrey Hill," *Southern Review* 12 (1976): 426–33.

35. Geoffrey Hill, " 'Funeral Music': An Essay," in *Somewhere Is Such a Kingdom: Poems 1952–1958* (Boston, 1975), 125.

36. Thurley, *Ironic Harvest*, 159.

37. Hill, " 'Funeral Music,' " 125.

38. See Brown and Utz, cited in note 34 above.

39. Hill, " 'Funeral Music,' " 125–26.

40. Brown, " 'Funeral Music,' " 85–87.

41. Harold Bloom, "Introduction: The Survival of Strong Poetry," in *Somewhere Is Such a Kingdom*, xiii.

42. Donald Hall, "Poets of Stones and Fields," *Nation* 221 (1975): 601.

43. Bloom, "Survival of Strong Poetry," xiv.

44. "out of parenthesis?" *TLS*, 31 Oct. 1968, 1220.

45. " 'Decreation' in Geoffrey Hill's *Lachrimae*," *Agenda* 17 (1979): 61–71; Catherine Kazin, " 'Across a Wilderness of Retrospection': A Reading of Geoffrey Hill's *Lachrimae*," *Agenda* 17 (1979): 43–57.

Chapter Five

1. Louis Martz, *The Poetry of Meditation* (New Haven: Yale University Press, 1954).
2. Ibid., 324.
3. *TLS*, 9 March 1971, 16.
4. A. Alvarez, "Deadly funny," *Observer*, 3 August 1975, 21.
5. *Novel on Yellow Paper* (1936), *Over the Frontier* (1938), and *The Holiday* (1949)—all reprinted by Virago (London).
6. Stevie Smith, *Me Again. Uncollected Writings of Stevie Smith*, ed. Jack Barbera and William McBrien (New York: Farrar, Straus & Giroux, 1981).
7. *The Norton Anthology of English Literature*, ed. M. H. Abrams et al., 4th ed. (New York: Norton, 1979), vol. 2, 2361.
8. Quoted by James MacGibbon in Introduction to *Me Again*, 6.
9. "The Voice of Genteel Decay," *TLS*, 14 July 1972, 820.
10. In letters to Naomi Mitchison and Sally Chilver, *Me Again*, 274, 290.
11. Rev. Gerard Irvine, quoted by James MacGibbon in Preface to *The Collected Poems of Stevie Smith* (New York: Oxford University Press, 1976), 9.
12. See William James, *The Varieties of Religious Experience* (New York: Collier Books, 1961), 114–42. Originally published in 1902.
13. Kay Dick, *Ivy and Stevie* (London, 1971), 45.
14. James, *Varieties of Religious Experience*, 78–113.
15. D. J. Enright, "Did Nobody Teach You?" *Encounter*, June 1971, 57.
16. *British Poetry Since 1945*, ed. Edward Lucie-Smith (London, Harmondsworth, 1970), 136.
17. *Contemporary Poets*, ed. James Vinson, 2d ed. (New York: St. Martin's Press, 1979), 777; 3d ed. (1980), 789.

Chapter Six

1. Bedient, *Eight Contemporary Poets*, 1.
2. Charles Tomlinson, "Poetry Today," in *The Modern Age*, vol. 7, *Pelican Guide to English Literature*, ed. Boris Ford (Harmondsworth, Middlesex, England: Penguin, 1961), 458.
3. Charles Tomlinson, "The Middlebrow Muse," *Essays in Criticism* 7 (1957): 208–17.
4. Tomlinson, "Poetry Today," 458.

5. Jed Rasula and Mike Erwin, "An Interview with Charles Tomlinson," *Contemporary Literature* 16 (1975): 406.

6. Peter Orr, ed., *The Poet Speaks*, 250.

7. *The Genius of John Ruskin. Selections from His Writings*, ed. John D. Rosenberg (Boston: Houghton Mifflin, 1963), 24. Taken from *Modern Painters* (1843), vol. I, part 2, sec. 1, chap. 2.

8. Ibid., 28. Taken from *Modern Painters*, vol. I, part 2, sec. 2, chap. 5.

9. Ibid., 25. Taken from *Modern Painters*, vol. I, part 2, sec. 1, chap. 2.

10. Bedient, *Eight Contemporary Poets*, 1.

11. Orr, *The Poet Speaks*, 251.

12. John Press, *Rule and Energy* (London, 1963), 107; M. L. Rosenthal, *The New Poets*, 244.

13. Charles Tomlinson, *Some Americans. A Personal Record* (Berkeley: University of California Press, 1981), 12.

14. Bedient, *Eight Contemporary Poets*, 2.

15. P. R. King, *Nine Contemporary Poets* (London and New York, 1979), 74.

16. Ibid., 50–51.

17. Charles Tomlinson, *The Poem as Initiation* (Hamilton, N.Y., 1967), n.pag.

18. Rasula and Erwin, "An Interview with Charles Tomlinson," 406.

19. Lucio Piccolo, *Collected Poems*, trans. and ed. Brian Swann and Ruth Feldman (Princeton: Princeton University Press, 1972).

20. Calvin Bedient, "Poetry Comfortable and Uncomfortable," *Sewanee Review* 87 (1979): 302.

21. Kevin B. Nowlan, "On the Eve of the War" in *Ireland in the War Years and After, 1939–51*, ed. Kevin B. Nowlan and T. Desmond Williams (Notre Dame, Ind.: University of Notre Dame Press, 1970), 12.

22. Robert Kee, *Ireland: A History* (Boston: Little, Brown, 1980), 229–39.

23. Seamus Heaney, *Preoccupations: Selected Prose 1968–1978* (New York, 1980), 17–21.

24. Robert Buttel, *Seamus Heaney* (Lewisburg, Pa., 1975), 36.

25. James Randall, "An Interview with Seamus Heaney," *Ploughshares* 5, no. 3 (1975): 9.

26. Ibid., 8, 16.

27. Ibid., 8.

28. Frank Kinahan, "An Interview with Seamus Heaney," *Critical Inquiry* 8 (1982): 406.

29. Heaney, *Preoccupations*, 37.

30. Ibid., 34.

31. Kinahan, "Interview," 406.

32. Buttel, *Seamus Heaney,* 29–30.

33. See "Yeats as an Example?" in Heaney, *Preoccupations,* 98–114.

34. Ibid., 85.

35. "The Making of a Music," ibid., 61–78.

36. Jon Stallworthy, "Poet as Archeologist: W. B. Yeats and Seamus Heaney," *Review of English Studies,* n.s. 33 (1982): 165.

37. Heaney, *Preoccupations,* 57.

38. P. V. Glob, *The Bog People: Iron-Age Man Preserved,* trans. Rupert Bruce-Mitford (Ithaca, N.Y.: Cornell University Press, 1969), 151–53.

39. Heaney, *Preoccupations,* 56.

40. Ibid., 57.

41. Ibid., 60.

42. Ibid., 19.

43. Robert Fitzgerald, "Seamus Heaney: An Appreciation," *New Republic,* 27 March 1976, 27.

44. Heaney's terms, quoted in Fitzgerald, 29.

45. Heaney, *Preoccupations,* 54–55.

46. John W. Foster, "The Poetry of Seamus Heaney," *Critical Quarterly* 16 (1974): 44–45.

47. Stallworthy, "Poet as Archeologist," 174.

48. Calvin Bedient, "The Music of What Happens," *Parnassus* 8, no. 1 (Fall/Winter 1979): 109.

49. Kinahan, "Interview," 411.

50. Ibid., 412.

51. See Bedient, "The Music of What Happens," 113–18, and Seamus Heaney, "Current Unstated Assumptions about Poetry," *Critical Inquiry* 7 (1981): 648–49.

Chapter Seven

1. Robert Phillips, "The Art of Poetry XXX Philip Larkin," *Paris Review,* no. 84 (Summer 1982), 72.

2. Peter Jones and Michael Schmidt, introduction to *British Poetry Since 1970,* xv.

3. Phillips, "Art of Poetry," 60.

4. "A Voice of Our Time," *Observer Review,* 16 December 1979, 35.

5. Jones and Schmidt, *British Poetry Since 1970,* xxvi.

6. Michael Schmidt, "Short Back and Sides," *New Statesman* 99 (30 May 1980): 817.

7. Theodore Weiss, "Poetry from Porlock," *TLS*, 26 September 1980, 1059.

8. George Steiner, "Text and Context," *On Difficulty and Other Essays* (Oxford: Oxford University Press, 1978), 7.

Selected Bibliography

PRIMARY SOURCES

1. Significant Anthologies of British Poetry since 1939

Alvarez, A., ed. *The New Poetry*. Harmondsworth, England: Penguin, 1962.

Bold, Alan, ed. *The Cambridge Book of English Verse 1939–1975*. Cambridge: Cambridge University Press, 1976.

Conquest, Robert, ed. *New Lines*. London: Macmillan, 1956.

————. *New Lines II*. London: Macmillan, 1963.

Enright, D. J., ed. *The Oxford Book of Contemporary Verse 1945–1980*. Oxford: Oxford University Press, 1980.

Hall, Donald, Robert Pack, and Louis Simpson, eds. *New Poets of England and America*. Cleveland and New York: World Publishing Co., 1957.

Hamilton, Ian, ed. *The Poetry of War 1939–45*. London: Alan Ross, 1965.

Horovitz, Michael, ed. *Children of Albion: Poetry of the Underground in Britain*. Harmondsworth, England: Penguin, 1970.

Lucie-Smith, Edward, ed. *British Poetry since 1945*. Harmondsworth, England: Penguin, 1970.

————. *The Liverpool Scene*. London: Donald Carroll, 1967.

Lucie-Smith, Edward, and Philip Hobsbaum, eds. *A Group Anthology*. London: Oxford University Press, 1963.

Matthias, John, ed. *Twenty-three Modern British Poets*. Chicago: Swallow Press, 1971.

Robson, Jeremy, ed. *The Young British Poets*. London: Chatto & Windus, 1971.

2. Writings of Individual Poets

Note: the following attempts to be complete only in terms of poetry. Works in other genres are included selectively.

KEITH DOUGLAS (1920–44)

Poetry

Collected Poems. Edited by John Waller and G. S. Fraser. London: Nicholson & Watson, 1951.

Collected Poems. Edited by John Waller, G. S. Fraser, and J. C. Hall. London: Faber, 1966.

Complete Poems. Edited by Desmond Graham. Oxford: Oxford University Press, 1978.

Selected Poems, with J. C. Hall and Norman Nicholson. London: John Bale & Staples, 1943.

Selected Poems. Edited by Ted Hughes. London: Faber, 1964.

Prose

Alamein to Zem Zem. London: Nicholson & Watson, 1946. (autobiography)

ROY FULLER (b. 1912)

Poetry

Brutus's Orchard. London: Deutsch, 1957.
Buff. London: Deutsch, 1965.
Counterparts. London: Verschoyle, 1954.
Epitaphs and Occasions. London: Lehmann, 1949.
From the Joke Shop. London: Deutsch, 1975.
An Ill-Governed Coast: Poems. Sunderland: Ceolfrith Press, 1976.
The Joke-Shop Annex. Edinburgh: Tragara Press, 1975.
A Lost Season. London: Hogarth Press, 1944.
The Middle of a War. London: Hogarth Press, 1942.
New Poems. London: Deutsch, 1968.
Off Course. London: Turret, 1969.
An Old War. Edinburgh: Tragara Press, 1974.
Penguin Modern Poets 18, with A. Alvarez and Anthony Thwaite. London: Penguin, 1970.
Pergamon Poets 1, with R. S. Thomas. Edited by Evan Owen. Oxford: Pergamon Press, 1970.
Poems. London: Fortune Press, 1940.
Re-treads. Edinburgh: Tragara Press, 1979.
Song Cycle from a Record Sleeve. Oxford: Sycamore Press, 1972.
Tiny Tears. London: Deutsch, 1973.
To an Unknown Reader. London: Poem-of-the-Month Club, 1970.
Waiting for the Barbarians: A Poem. Richmond, Surrey: Keepsake Press, 1974.
Collected Poems 1936–1961. London: Deutsch, 1962.

Other

My Child, My Sister. London: Deutsch, 1965. (novel)
Owls and Artificers: Oxford Lectures on Poetry. London: Deutsch, 1971. (criticism)
Professors and Gods: Last Oxford Lectures on Poetry. London: Deutsch, 1973. (criticism)

The Ruined Boys. London: Deutsch, 1959.

SEAMUS HEANEY (b. 1939)

Poetry
Bog Poems. London: Rainbow Press, 1975.
Boy Driving His Father to Confession. Fresham, Surrey: Sceptre Press, 1970.
Death of a Naturalist. London: Faber, 1966.
Door into the Dark. London: Faber, 1969.
Eleven Poems. Belfast: Festival, 1965.
Field Work. London: Faber, 1979.
Land. London: Poem-of-the-Month Club, 1971.
A Lough Neagh Sequence. Manchester: Phoenix Pamphlet Poets Press, 1969.
Night Drive: Poems. Creditorn, Devon: Gilbertson, 1970.
North. London: Faber, 1975.
Room to Rhyme, with Dario Hammond and Michael Longley. Belfast: Arts Council of Northern Ireland, 1968.
Stations. Belfast: Ulsterman, 1975.
Wintering Out. London: Faber, 1972.

Prose
Preoccupations: Selected Prose 1968–1978. New York: Farrar, Straus & Giroux, 1980.

GEOFFREY HILL (b. 1932)

For the Unfallen: Poems 1952–1958. London: Deutsch, 1959.
King Log. London: Deutsch, 1968.
Mercian Hymns. London: Deutsch, 1971.
Penguin Modern Poets 8, with Edwin Brock and Stevie Smith. London: Penguin, 1966.
(Poems). Oxford: Fantasy Press, 1952.
Preghiere. Leeds: Northern House, 1964.
Tenebrae. London: Deutsch, 1978.
Somewhere Is Such a Kingdom: Poems 1952–1971. Boston: Houghton Mifflin, 1975.

TED HUGHES (b. 1930)

Poetry
Adam and the Sacred Nine. London: Rainbow Press, 1979.
All Around the Year. London: Murray, 1979.
Animal Poems. Crediton, Devon: Gilbertson, 1967.

The Burning of the Brothel. London: Turret, 1966.

Cave Birds. London: Scolar Press, 1975; rev. ed., London: Faber, 1978.

Chiasmadon. Baltimore: Charles Seluzicki, 1977.

Corgi Modern Poets in Focus 1, with others. Edited by Dannie Abse. London: Corgi, 1971.

Crow: From the Life and Songs of the Crow. London: Faber, 1970: rev. ed., Faber, 1972.

A Crow Hymn. Frensham, Surrey: Sceptre Press, 1970.

Crow Wakes. London: Poet and Printer, 1971.

Eat Crow. London: Rainbow Press, 1972.

Earth-Moon. London: Rainbow Press, 1976.

Eclipse. Knotting, Bedfordshire: Sceptre Press, 1976.

A Few Crows. Exeter: Rougemont Press, 1970.

Five Autumn Songs for Children's Voices. Crediton, Devon: Gilbertson, 1968.

Gaudette. London: Faber, 1977.

The Hawk in the Rain. London: Faber, 1957.

In the Little Girl's Angel Gaze. London: Steam Press, 1972.

Lupercal. London: Faber, 1960.

The Martyrdom of Bishop Farrer. Crediton, Devon: Gilbertson.

Moortown. London: Faber, 1979.

Moortown Elegies. London: Rainbow Press, 1978.

Orts. London: Rainbow Press, 1978.

Poems, with Ruth Fainlight and Alan Sillitoe. London: Rainbow Press, 1971.

Prometheus on His Crag: 21 Poems. London: Rainbow Press, 1973.

Recklings. London: Turret, 1966.

Remains of Elmet. London: Rainbow Press, 1979.

River. New York: Harper & Row, 1983.

Scapegoats and Rabies: A Poem in Five Parts. London: Poet and Printer, 1967.

A Solstice. Knotting, Bedfordshire: Sceptre Press, 1978.

Spring, Summer, Autumn, Winter. London: Rainbow Press, 1973.

Sunstruck. Knotting, Bedfordshire: Sceptre Press, 1977.

Wodwo. London: Faber, 1967.

Selected Poems, with Thom Gunn. London: Faber, 1962.

Selected Poems 1957–1967. London: Faber, 1972.

New Selected Poems. New York: Harper & Row, 1982.

Other

The Earth-Owl and Other Moon-People. London: Faber, 1963. (juvenile)

Meet My Folks! London: Faber, 1961. (juvenile)

Moon-Whales and Other Moon Poems. New York: Viking Press, 1976. (juvenile)

Nessie the Mannerless Monster. London: Faber, 1964. (juvenile)

Poetry in the Making. London: Faber, 1967.
Seneca's Oedipus. London: Faber, 1969. (play produced London, 1968)
The Story of Vasco. Music by Gordon Crosse. Adaptation of a play by Georges Schehade (produced London, 1974). London: Oxford University Press, 1974.

ELIZABETH JENNINGS (b. 1926)

The Animals' Arrival. London: Macmillan, 1967.
The Child and the Seashell. San Francisco: Poems in Folio, 1957.
Consequently I Rejoice. Manchester: Carcanet, 1977.
Growing-Points: New Poems. Manchester: Carcanet, 1975.
Hurt. London: Poems-of-the-Month Club, 1970.
Lucidities. London: Macmillan, 1970.
The Mind Has Mountains. London: Macmillan, 1966.
Moments of Grace: New Poems. Manchester: Carcanet, 1979.
Penguin Modern Poets 1, with Lawrence Durrell and R. S. Thomas. London: Penguin, 1962.
The Secret Brother and Other Poems for Children. London: Macmillan, 1966.
A Sense of the World. London: Deutsch, 1958.
Song for a Birth or a Death and Other Poems. London: Deutsch, 1961.
A Way of Looking. London: Deutsch, 1955.

PHILIP LARKIN (b. 1922)

Poetry
Corgi Modern Poets in Focus 5, with others. Edited by Jeremy Robson. London: Corgi, 1971.
The Explosion. London: Poem-of-the-Month Club, 1970.
High Windows. London: Faber, 1974.
The Less Deceived. Hessle, Yorkshire: Marvell Press, 1955.
The North Ship. London: Fortune Press, 1945; rev. ed., London: Faber, 1966.
(Poems). Oxford: Fantasy Press, 1954.
XX Poems. Privately printed, 1951.
The Whitsun Weddings. London: Faber, 1964.

Other
All What Jazz: A Record Diary 1961–68. London: Faber, 1970. (reviews)
Jill. London: Fortune Press, 1946; rev. ed., London: Faber, 1964.
A Girl in Winter. London: Faber, 1947.
Required Writing. Miscellaneous Pieces 1955–1982. London: Faber, 1983. (essays and criticism)

ALUN LEWIS (1915–44)

Poetry
Ha! Ha! Among The Trumpets. London: Allen & Unwin, 1945.
Raiders' Dawn. London: Allen & Unwin, 1942.
Selected Poetry and Prose. Edited by Ian Hamilton. London: Allen & Unwin, 1966.

Other
In the Green Tree. London: Allen & Unwin, 1948. (stories and letters)
The Last Inspection. London: Allen & Unwin, 1942. (stories)
Letters from India. Cardiff: Penmark Press, 1946.

HENRY REED (b. 1914)

A Map of Verona. London: Cape, 1946.
Lessons of the War. New York: Chilmark Press, 1970.

STEVIE SMITH (1902–71)

Poetry
The Best Beast. New York: Knopf, 1969.
Corgi Modern Poets in Focus 4. Edited by Jeremy Robson. London: Corgi, 1971.
Francesca in Winter. London: Poem-of-the-Month Club, 1970.
The Frog Prince and Other Poems. London: Longman, 1966.
A Good Time Was Had by All. London: Cape, 1937.
Harold's Leap. London: Chapman & Hall, 1950.
Mother, What Is Man? London: Cape, 1942.
Not Waving But Drowning. London: Deutsch, 1957.
Penguin Modern Poets 8, with Edwin Brock and Geoffrey Hill. London: Penguin, 1966.
Scorpion and Other Poems. London: Longman, 1972.
Tender Only to One. London: Cape, 1938.
The Collected Poems of Stevie Smith. Edited by James MacGibbon. New York: Oxford University Press, 1976.
Me Again. Uncollected Writings of Stevie Smith. Edited by Jack Barbera and William McBrian. New York: Farrar, Straus & Giroux, 1983.
Selected Poems. London: Longman, 1962.
Selected Poems. Edited by James MacGibbon. London: Penguin, 1978.
Two in One: Selected Poems and The Frog Prince and Other Poems. London: Longman, 1971.

Other

Cats in Colour. London: Batsford, 1959. (sketches)

The Holiday. London: Chapman & Hall, 1949. (novel)

Novel on Yellow Paper; or, Work It Out for Yourself. London: Cape, 1937.

Over the Frontier. London: Cape, 1938. (novel)

CHARLES TOMLINSON (b. 1927)

Poetry

American West Southwest. Cerillos, N.M.: San Marcos Press, 1969.

American Scenes and Other Poems. London: Oxford University Press, 1966.

The Mattachines. Cerrillos, N.M.: San Marcos Press, 1968.

The Necklace. Oxford: Fantasy Press, 1955; rev. ed., London: Oxford University Press, 1966.

Penguin Modern Poets 14, with Alan Brownjohn and Michael Hamburger. London: Penguin, 1969.

A Peopled Landscape. London: Oxford University Press, 1963.

Relations and Contraries. Aldington, Kent: Hand and Flower Press, 1951.

Seeing Is Believing. New York: McDowell Obolensky, 1958.

The Shaft. London: Oxford University Press, 1974.

Solo for a Glass Harmonica. San Francisco: Poems in Folio, 1957.

To Be Engraved on the Skull of a Cormorant. London: Unaccompanied Serpent, 1968.

The Way In and Other Poems. London: Oxford University Press, 1974.

Words and Images. London: Covent Garden Press, 1972.

Written on Water. London: Oxford University Press, 1972.

Selected Poems 1951–1974. London: Oxford University Press, 1978.

Other

The Poem as Initiation. Hamilton, N.Y.: Colgate University Press, 1967. (lecture)

SECONDARY SOURCES

1.Concerning British Poetry Since 1939

Bedient, Calvin. *Eight Contemporary Poets.* London: Oxford University Press, 1974. Stimulating, self-contained essays on each of the eight, which include Tomlinson, Davie, Larkin, and Hughes.

Brown, Merle. *Double Lyric. Divisiveness and Communal Creativity in Recent English Poetry.* New York: Columbia University, 1980. Stimulating appraisals of several prominent figures.

Jones, Peter, and Michael Schmidt, eds. *British Poetry since 1970: A Critical Survey.* New York: Persea Books, 1980. Similar in intention and format to the earlier volume below, by Schmidt and Lindop.

King, P. R. *Nine Contemporary Poets.* London and New York: Methuen, 1979. Close readings of the works of Hughes, Larkin, Heaney, and a half dozen other significant recent British poets.

Morrison, Blake. *The Movement: English Poetry and Fiction of the 1950s.* Oxford: Oxford University Press, 1980. Essentially a history of the Movement, particularly valuable in terms of background factors and relations among key figures.

Orr, Peter, ed. *The Poet Speaks.* New York: Barnes & Noble, 1966. Interviews with many contemporary British poets.

Press, John. *A Map of Modern English Verse.* London: Oxford University Press, 1969. While largely concerned with poetry earlier in the century, contains useful discussion of World War II poets and the Movement.

————. *Rule and Energy: Trends in British Poetry since the Second World War.* London: Oxford University Press, 1963. An early attempt to examine the relationship between modernism and postwar British poetry.

Rosenthal, M. L. *The New Poets. American and British Poetry Since World War II.* New York: Oxford University Press, 1967. Influential and provocative; highly critical of the Movement.

Scannell, Vernon. *Not Without Glory: Poets of the Second World War.* London: Woburn Press, 1976. Useful discussions of several poets.

Schmidt, Michael, and Grevel Lindop, eds. *British Poetry since 1960: A Critical Survey.* Oxford: Carcanet, 1972. Contains many useful essays on developments and key figures in British poetry of the 1960s, plus an especially informative bibliography of poetry books published in Britain since the early 1950s.

Sherry, Vincent B., Jr., ed. *Poets of Great Britain and Ireland, 1945–1960.* Dictionary of Literary Biography, vol. 27. Detroit: Bruccoli Clark, 1984. Contains essays on dozens of poets of the forties and fifties— including Douglas, Jennings, Larkin, and Reed; especially helpful in relating the poetry of the time to poets' lives and careers.

Stanford, Donald E., ed. *British Poets, 1914–1945.* Dictionary of Literary Biography, vol. 20. Detroit: Bruccoli Clark, 1983. Includes essays on Fuller and Smith, as well as many others, that give a biographically based perspective on the poets and their careers.

Weatherhead, A. Kingsley. *The British Dissonance.* Columbia: University of Missouri Press, 1983. Essays on ten contemporary poets.

2. Concerning Individual Poets

KEITH DOUGLAS

Fuller, Roy. "The Warrior Bard: Keith Douglas After Thirty Years."

Encounter, September 1974, 75–79. Perceptively places Douglas in relation to the other war poets.

Graham, Desmond. *Keith Douglas.* London: Oxford University Press, 1974. A close study of the man and the poet; of considerable biographical and critical value.

Hughes, Ted. "The Poetry of Keith Douglas." *Critical Quarterly* 5 (1963): 43–48. An appreciative but pointed evaluation of his work.

Scannell, Vernon. "Keith Douglas." In *Not Without Glory* (see above under "Secondary Sources Concerning British Poetry Since 1939"), 23–51. Thoughtfully examines the continuity in Douglas's shift from civilian to soldier-poet.

Waller, John. "The Poetry of Keith Douglas." *Accent* 8 (1948): 226–35. A brief but thoughtful account of Douglas's chief poetic concerns.

ROY FULLER

Austin, Allan. *Roy Fuller.* Boston: Twayne, 1979. An introductory study to all of Fuller's writing. Useful on the relationship between his fiction and his poetry.

Gitzen, Julien. "The Evolution of Roy Fuller." *Contemporary Poetry* 3 (1977): 56–69. Sees more evolution than radical shift between Fuller's war poetry and his postwar writings.

"Roy Fuller: An Interview." *Minnesota Review* 10 (Spring 1978): 87–94. Contains many revealing remarks on his attitude toward politics, poetry, and his writing career.

SEAMUS HEANEY

Buttel, Robert. *Seamus Heaney.* Lewisburg, Pa.: Bucknell University Press, 1975. An introductory study covering Heaney's first three collections. Much useful biographical information, plus extended discussion of particular poems.

Des Pres, Terrence. "Emblems of Adversity." *Harper's* 262 (March 1981): 73–77. A sensitive examination of Heaney's wrestling with politics and poetics.

Fitzgerald, Robert. "Seamus Heaney: An Appreciation." *New Republic,* 27 March 1976, 27–29. Describes Heaney's use of bog-people lore.

Foster, John W. "The Poetry of Seamus Heaney." *Critical Quarterly* 16 (1974): 35–48. Examines Heaney's being suspended between English and Irish traditions.

Kinahan, Frank. "An Interview with Seamus Heaney." *Critical Inquiry* 8 (1982): 405–14. Especially interesting on Heaney's literary background and the implications of his move to the South.

McGuinness, Arthur E. " 'Hoarder of Common Ground': Tradition and Ritual in Seamus Heaney's Poetry." *Eire* 13, no. 2 (Summer 1978): 71–92. Heaney's search for a ritual vision studied in detail.

Morrison, Blake. "Speech and Reticence: Seamus Heaney's *North.*" In *British Poetry Since 1970* (see above under "Secondary Sources Concerning British Poetry Since 1939"), 103–11. Argues provocatively that a political-religious viewpoint exists beneath the neutral appearance of Heaney's writing.

Parini, Jay. "Seamus Heaney: The Ground Possessed." *Sewanee Review* 16 (1980): 100–23. Studies the evolution of Heaney's pastoralism.

Randall, James. "An Interview with Seamus Heaney." *Ploughshares* 5, no. 3 (Spring 1979): 7–34.

Stallworthy, Jon. "Poet as Archeologist: W. B. Yeats and Seamus Heaney." *Review of English Studies* n.s. 33 (1982): 158–74. Significant differences and similarities between the two noted.

GEOFFREY HILL

Brown, Merle. "Flesh of Abnegation: The Poems of Geoffrey Hill." In *Double Lyric,* (see above under "Secondary Sources Concerning British Poetry Since 1939"), 20–34. Compares Hill with Eliot.

———. "Geoffrey Hill's 'Funeral Music.' " *Agenda* 17 (Spring 1979): 72–88. Deals with the problem of organization in this important sequence. This issue of *Agenda* is devoted exclusively to Hill and contains several other essays on his work.

Heaney, Seamus. "Now and In England." *Critical Inquiry* 3 (1975): 471–88. Compares Hill's style and viewpoint with those of Larkin and Hughes.

Utz, Stephen. "The Realism of Geoffrey Hill." *Southern Review* 12 (1976): 426–33. Describes Hill's search for a "new realism" to replace the old in dealing with the moral predicament posed by contemporary history.

TED HUGHES

Faas, Ekbert. *Ted Hughes: The Unaccommodated Universe.* Santa Barbara: Black Sparrow Press, 1980. A lengthy, detailed examination of the origins and poetics of Hughes's quest as a writer of nature; especially interesting in mapping out the domain of each successive Hughes volume.

Fernandez, Charles V. "*Crow*: A Mythology of the Demonic." *Modern Poetry Studies* 6, no. 2 (Autumn 1975): 144–56. Hughes's mixing of Eskimo mythology and Christianity.

Hahn, Claire. *"Crow* and the Biblical Creation Narratives." *Critical Quarterly* 19, no. 1 (Spring 1977): 43–52. Traces the biblical element in *Crow,* especially its reliance on Genesis.

Heaney, Seamus. "Now and in England." (see above under "Geoffrey Hill")

Weatherhead, A. Kingsley. "Ted Hughes, 'Crow' and Pain." *Texas Quarterly* 19, no. 3 (Autumn 1976): 95–108. A most interesting study of Hughes's shift of style as he moves toward *Crow.*

PHILIP LARKIN

a. Bibliography
Bloomfield, B. C. *Philip Larkin. A Bibliography, 1933–1976,* London: Faber, 1979.

b. Critical Studies
"The Art of Poetry XXX Philip Larkin." *Paris Review,* no. 84 (Summer 1982), 42–72. The longest and most detailed interview with Larkin to date; extremely witty and interesting.

Bayley, John. *The Uses of Division.* New York: Viking Press, 1976. Pp. 157–82. Larkin's poetic and viewpoint in relation to those of other modern poets, including Eliot and Lowell.

King, P. R. "Without Illusion." In *Nine Contemporary Poets.* London and New York: Methuen, 1979, 1–43. A thoughtful critical introduction to Larkin's poems.

Kuby, Lolette. *An Uncommon Poet for the Common Man. A Study of Philip Larkin's Poetry.* The Hague: Mouton, 1974. A detailed examination of the humanistic elements in Larkin's writing. Very thorough.

Larkin at Sixty. Edited by Anthony Thwaite. London: Faber, 1982. Essays rich in biographical and anecdotal material.

Martin, Bruce K. *Philip Larkin.* Boston: Twayne, 1978. Examines the world and structures of his writing, as well as the connections between his poetry and his prose works.

Naremore, James. "Philip Larkin's 'Lost World,' " *Contemporary Literature* 15 (1974): 331–43. Detects romantic longing even in Larkin's most cynical poems.

Timms, David. *Philip Larkin.* New York: Barnes & Noble, 1973. A brief but reliable introduction to Larkin's life and writings.

Weatherhead, A. Kingsley. "Philip Larkin of England." *ELH* 38 (1971): 616–30. Examines Larkin's relationship to the larger patterns of English poetry.

Whalen, Terry. "Philip Larkin's Imagist Bias: His Poetry of Observation." *Critical Quarterly* 23 (Summer 1981): 29–46.

ALUN LEWIS

Bangeree, A. "Alun Lewis." In *Spirit Above Wars*. London: Macmillan, 1976, 136–71. Appraises the strengths and weaknesses of Lewis's poetry.

John, Alun. *Alun Lewis*. Mystic, Conn.: Verry, 1970. An introduction to his life and works.

Maclaren-Ross, Julien. "Second Lt. Lewis." In *Memoirs of the Forties*. London: Ross, 1965, 225–34.

Scannell, Vernon. "Alun Lewis." In *Not Without Glory* (see above under "Keith Douglas"), 52–73. Contrasts Lewis with Keith Douglas.

HENRY REED

Scannell, Vernon. "Henry Reed and Others." In *Not Without Glory* (see above under "Keith Douglas"), 134–41. Explores the paradox of Reed as an "Ariel-dominated poet" writing famous war poems.

STEVIE SMITH

Bedient, Calvin. "Stevie Smith." In *Eight Contemporary Poets* (see above under "Secondary Sources Concerning British Poetry Since 1939"), 139–58. Perceptive discussion of Stevie's central concerns and techniques.

Dick, Kay. "Talking to Stevie." In *Ivy and Stevie*. London: Duckworth, 1971, 35–60. Wide-ranging interview in which Stevie Smith discusses her life and the writing of poetry.

Enright, D. J. "Did Nobody Teach You?" *Encounter* 36 (June 1971): 53–57. Review-essay appreciative of Stevie Smith's characteristic strategies.

Holming, Stevie. "Delivered for a Time from Silence." *Parnassus* 6 (1977): 314–30. Review of her *Collected Poems*; useful discussion of style and persona in her poetry.

Larkin, Philip. "Stevie, good-bye." *Observer*, 23 January 1972, 23. A fellow poet expresses his admiration.

Wade Stephen. "Stevie Smith and the Untruth of Myth." *Agenda* (London) 15 (1973): 102–6. Sees Stevie cutting myth down to manageable proportions.

CHARLES TOMLINSON

Edwards, Michael. "Charles Tomlinson: Notes on Tradition and Impersonality." *Critical Quarterly* 15 (1975): 405–16. Review-article stressing the "Augustan decorum" of Tomlinson's verse.

"Fifteen Ways of Looking at Charles Tomlinson." *PN Review* 5 (1977): 40–50. Provocative responses to his writings by fifteen contemporary poets.

Gitzen, Julian. "Charles Tomlinson and the Plenitude of Fact." *Critical Quarterly* 13 (1971): 355–62. Explores Tomlinson's concern with the issue of epistemology in a mutable world.

Grogan, Ruth. "Charles Tomlinson: The Way of His World." *Contemporary Literature* 19 (1978): 472–96. Examines Tomlinson's "Endless adroitness" at rendering the world's flux.

————. "Charles Tomlinson: Poet as Painter." *Critical Quarterly* 19 (1977): 71–77. Discusses the painter's humility before nature in Tomlinson's writing.

Rasula, Jed and Mike Erwin. "An Interview with Charles Tomlinson." *Contemporary Literature* 16 (1975): 405–16. Tomlinson discusses his poetic.

Index

Abse, Dannie, 86, 173
"Against Romanticism" (Amis), 51
Alexandria Quartet, The (Durrell), 27
Alvarez, A., 83–85, 120
Amis, Kingsley, 37, 47, 50, 112, 136, 140,
  143, 172
Apocalyptics, 17, 50, 82, 142
Ariel (Plath), 85
Arts Council, 176
Auden, W. H., 2, 3–6, 8, 10, 11, 16, 20,
  21, 23, 47, 53, 80, 81, 83, 150, 156,
  159, 171, 173; *Collected Poems,* 4; "Epi-
  taph on a Tyrant," 6; "James Honeyman,"
  5; "Johnny," 5; "Miss Gee," 5; "Musée
  des Beaux Arts," 6; "Spain, 1937," 5;
  "Unknown Citizen, The," 6, 62, 115;
  "Victor," 5
Auden Group, 3, 5, 8, 10, 16, 17, 18, 33,
  47, 63, 71, 155, 173

Barker, George, 8, 17, 173
Bayley, John, 79
Beckett, Samuel, 175
Bedient, Calvin, 79, 96, 143, 155
Bergonzi, Bernard, 4, 5
Berryman, John, 79, 84, 85, 86
Betjeman, John, 74, 109
Black Mountain School, 146, 150
Blake, William, 104, 126
Bloom, Harold, 104, 111, 114
Blunden, Edmund, 19
Bog People, The (P. V. Glob), 163, 164
Bowen, Elizabeth, 52, 175
Browning, Robert, 131
Brownjohn, Alan, 86

Campbell, Roy, 8
Carroll, Lewis, 121
Caudwell, Christopher (Christopher St. John
  Sprig), 8
Causley, Charles, 173
"Christ Climbed Down" (Ferlinghetti), 37
Coleridge, Samuel Taylor, 55, 147
Confessional Poets, 84–85, 88
Connolly, Cyril, 15
Conquest, Robert, 50, 83, 134

Cornford, John, 8
Coward, Noel, 1–2, 5, 87
Crashaw, Richard, 117
Creeley, Robert, 146

Deane, Seamus, 159
Davie, Donald, 50, 75, 84, 172, 174
De La Mare, Walter, 40
Dickinson, Emily, 117, 119, 121, 126, 129
Donne, John, 23, 104, 108, 117, 119, 138
Douglas, Keith, 13, 17–31, 32, 33, 34, 35,
  37, 40, 46, 47; background and educa-
  tion, 19; feeling of inferiority toward
  World War I poets, 17–19; Middle East
  poems and mature style, 25–28; Oxford
  and early army poems, 22–25; school
  poems, 19–22; shift in stance toward
  War, 28–31

WORKS—EDITIONS:
Collected Poems, 19
Complete Poems, 19

WORKS—PROSE:
Alamein to Zem Zem, 19, 29, 47

WORKS—VERSE:
"Actors Waiting in the Wings of Eu-
  rope," 31
"Adams," 25, 26
"Behavior of Fish in an Egyptian Tea Gar-
  den," 28
Bête Noir, 31
"Cairo Jag," 28
"Christodoulos," 28
"Dead Men," 20, 29
"Dejections," 20
"Devils," 20, 28
"Distraction," 20
"Encounter with a God," 21–22
"Famous Men," 20–21
"Gallantry," 18, 29
"Hand, The," 20, 26, 27
"How to Kill," 30
"Images," 20
"Jerusalem," 26

"Kristen," 20
"Landscape with Figures," 30
"Love and Gorizia," 20
"Mummers," 21
"Negative Information," 26
"Offensive, The," 26
"On a Return from Egypt," 31
"On Leaving School," 20, 21
"Pleasures," 20
"Point of View," 20
"Russians," 22
"Sea Bird, The," 20, 25, 26
"Simplify Me When I'm Dead," 22, 23, 24–25
"Sportsmen," 29
"Storm, A," 20
"Syria," 26
"Tel Aviv," 20, 26
"This is the Dream," 20
"Those grasses, ancient enemies," 26
".303," 20
"Time Eating," 22, 23–24
"To Curse Her," 22–23
"Trumpet," 29
"Vergissmeinnicht," 30
"Villanelle of Gorizia," 21
"Youth," 20, 21

Duncan, Robert, 146
Dunn, Douglas, 173
Durrell, Lawrence, 27
Dylan, Bob, 87

Eliot, T. S., 1, 4, 9, 10, 11, 16, 20, 21, 41, 44, 84, 112, 115, 119, 163, 171, 172; *Four Quartets,* 16, 110; "Little Gidding," 16; "Journey of the Magi," 112; *The Waste Land,* 115
Empson, William, 8
Enright, D. J., 50, 51, 133, 172, 177
Ewart, Gavin, 173

Ferlinghetti, Lawrence, 87
Forster, E. M., 40
Frost, Robert, 160
Fuller, Roy, 4, 28, 47, 52–64, 67, 75, 76, 77, 78, 82, 104, 134, 140, 172; background and education, 54–55; changes in persona, 56–57; early shift to empiricism, 53–54; prosody, syntax, and diction, 59–60; range of subjects and attitudes, 55–56; singularity among recent poets, 52–53; tendency toward concrete exposi-

tion, 57–59; treatment of love, 63–64; treatment of nature, 62–63; treatment of politics, 62; views on art, 60–62

WORKS—VERSE:
"At a Warwickshire Mansion," 61
"Autobiography of a Lungworm," 56
Brutus's Orchard, 55
"Coast, The," 57
"Day, The," 58
"Departures," 61
"Dialogue of the Poet and His Talent," 62
"Epitaph on a Bombing Victim," 62
"Fifties, The," 62
From the Joke Shop, 59
"Historian, The" (sequence), 59
"Jag and Hangover," 60–61
"Legions, The," 57
Lost Season, A, 54
"Meredithian Sonnets" (sequence), 59
"Middle of a War, The," 54
Middle of the War, The, 54
"Mythological Sonnets" (sequence), 59
"Painter, The," 61
"Perturbations of Uranus," 58–59
Poems, 53
"Pure Poet, The," 61
"Reading *The Bostonians* in Algeciras Bay," 62
"Rhetoric of a Journey," 61
"Royal Navy Air Station," 54
"Shore Leave Lorry," 54
"Soliloquy in an Air Raid," 54
"Spring 1942," 54
"Times of War and Revolution," 62
"To My Brother," 53
"Wife's Unease, A," 58
"Winter in Camp" (sequence), 59

Gascoyne, David, 17
Ginsberg, Allen, 85, 87
Graham, W. S., 173
Graves, Robert, 16
Greene, Graham, 2, 52, 119, 175
Group Anthology, A, 86
Gunn, Thom, 84, 174
Gurney, Ivor, 13

H. D. (Hilda Doolittle), 94
Hall, Donald, 111, 134
Hamburger, Michael, 174
Hardy, Thomas, 72, 80, 81, 110, 114, 125, 134

Hartley, L. P., 52
Heaney, Seamus, 142, 155–71, 172, 173,
    174; depiction of Irish political tensions,
    157–58; Irish–British mix in literary sen-
    sibility, 158–60; Modern Irish back-
    ground, 155–57; recent retreat from
    public role, 169–71; search for appropri-
    ate poetic response to contemporary Ire-
    land, 163–69; sense of bardic role and
    related problems, 160–63

    WORKS—VERSE:
    "Advancement of Learning, An," 164
    "Afterwards, An," 170
    "Antaeus," 169
    "At a Potato Digging," 158
    "At the Water's Edge," 157
    "Backward Look, The," 168
    "Badgers, The," 170
    "Belderg," 169
    "Bog Queen," 169
    "Bogland," 167
    "Bone Dreams," 179
    "Broagh," 168
    "Casualty," 157
    "Constable Calls, A," 162
    "Cow in Calf," 164
    "Death of a Naturalist," 163
    Death of a Naturalist, 163–65
    "Digging," 164–65
    "Digging Shadow, The," 169
    Door into the Dark, 165–66, 167
    "Dream," 165
    "Early Purges, The," 164
    "Elegy," 171
    "Exposure," 161, 162–63, 170
    Field Work, 157, 170–71
    "Follower," 164
    "Forge, The," 166
    "Fosterage," 162
    "Funeral Rites," 157
    "Gifts of Rain," 167–68
    "Glanmere Sonnets," 170
    "Harvest Bow, The," 170
    "In Memoriam Sean O'Riada," 170
    "Kinship," 158
    "Last Mummer, The," 166–67
    "Lilting," 166
    "Linen Town," 157
    "Lough Neagh Sequence," 166
    "New Song, A," 168
    "North," 161, 164
    North, 157, 158, 169–70

    "Northern Hoard, A," 157
    "Orange Drums, Tyrone, 1969," 162
    "Other Side, The," 158
    "Otter, The," 170
    "Outlaw, The," 165–66
    "Oysters," 170
    "Polder," 170
    "Punishment," 157
    "Requiem for the Croppies," 158
    "Salmon Fisher to the Salmon," 166
    "Servant Boy," 166
    "Singing School" (sequence), 161–63
    "Summer 1969," 162
    "Thatcher," 166
    "Tolland Man, The," 167
    "Toombe," 168
    "Toombe Road, The," 157
    "Traditions," 158
    "Trout," 164
    "Turkeys Observed," 164
    "Viking Dublin: Trial Pieces," 169
    "Vision," 166
    "Waterfall," 164
    "Whatever You Say Say Nothing," 157
    Wintering Out, 157, 166–69

Henri, Adrian, 86
Hill, Geoffrey, 107–18, 142, 172; compared
    with Hughes, 111–14; difficulty of read-
    ing, 107–109; oblique humanism, 114–
    17; recent developments, 117–18; use of
    the past in his poetry, 109–11

    WORKS—VERSE:
    "Baroque Meditations, The," 108
    "Bidden Guest, The," 112
    "Canticle for Good Friday," 112
    "Crowning of Offa," 115–16
    For the Unfallen, 107–108, 112
    "Four Poems Regarding the Endurance of
        Poets," 113
    "Funeral Music," 109–11
    "Genesis," 112
    "History as Poetry," 111
    "I Had Hope When Violence Was
        Ceas't," 115
    "In Memory of Jane Fraser," 144
    King Log, 109
    "King Offa's Laws," 116
    Lacrimae, 117
    "Lacrimae Coactae," 117
    Mercian Hymns, 109–12, 115–17
    "Metamorphoses," 108

"Offa's Coins," 116
"Offa's Laws," 116
"Ovid in the Third Reich," 114–15, 116
"Picture of a Nativity," 112
"Requiem for the Plantagenet Kings," 108
"September Song," 115
Songbook of Sebastian Airunuz, 113
Tenebrae, 112, 117–18
"Troublesome Reign, The," 113
"Turtle Dove," 112–13
"Two Formal Elegies," 108

Hopkins, Gerard Manley, 5, 89, 108, 112, 117, 119, 120, 124, 133, 145, 160; "God's Grandeur," 148; "Pied Beauty," 145; "Spring," 145; "Windover, The," 145
Horizon, 15
Housbaum, Philip, 86
Hughes, Ted, 28, 84, 88–107, 109, 111, 112, 113, 114, 116, 117, 118, 121, 123, 142, 150, 159, 160, 172, 174; conception of nature, 96–97; controversy surrounding, 88–89; compared with Larkin, 92–93; counterproposals for human existence, 101–103; depiction of human achievement, 98–101; depiction of human nature, 97–98; depiction of man in nature, 89–92; principal developments, 104–107; principles of discovery, 93–96; stylistic tendencies, 103–104

WORKS—VERSE:
"Ancient Heroes and the Bomber Pilot, The," 100
"Battle of Osfrontalis, The," 94
"Bayonet Charge," 99
"Bear, The," 103
"Bowled Over," 90
"Bull Moses, The," 91, 93, 96, 165
"Bullfrog," 103
Cave Birds, 106
"Childish Prank," 100
"Churches Topple," 106–107
"Cleopatra to the Asp," 104
"Contender, The," 100
"Crag Jack's Apostasy," 100
Crow, 89–91, 94, 97, 99, 100, 102, 103, 105–106, 107
"Crow Alights," 91
"Crow and the Birds," 103
"Crow Communes," 94

"Crow Goes Hunting," 94
"Crow Tries the Media," 94
"Crow Tyrannosaurus," 100
"Crow's Account of St. George," 105
"Crow's Elephant Totem Song," 91
"Crow's First Lesson," 100
"Dawn's Rose," 91
"Dove-Breeder," 103
"Earth-Numb," 106
"Egg Head," 97–98
"Examination at the Womb-Door," 97
"February," 93
"Fourth of July," 100–101
"Full Moon and Little Frieda," 94–95, 98
Gaudette, 106–107, 112
"Gnat Psalm," 93
"Gog," 102
"Griefs for Dead Soldiers," 99
"Harvesting, The," 98
"Hawk in the Rain, The," 89, 93
Hawk in the Rain, The, 89, 91, 98, 104
"Hawk Roosting," 101–102
"Her Husband," 103
"Kreutzer Sonata," 101
"Law in the Country of the Cats," 98
"Ludwig's Death Mask," 101
Lupercal, 91, 98, 104
"Lupercalia," 104
"Macaw and Little Miss," 98
"Man Seeking Experience Enquires His Way of a Drop of Water, The," 93–94
"March morning unlike others," 92
"Martyrdom of Bishop Farrar, The," 102–103
"Mayday on Holderness," 103
"Meeting," 98
"Modest Proposal, A," 103
Moortown, 92, 106
"New Moon in January," 103
"October Dawn," 90, 91, 93
"Phaetons," 104
"Pibroch," 102
"Pike," 91, 93, 98, 164
"Prometheus," 106
"Robin Song," 91
"Scapegoats and Rabies," 99
Season Songs, 92
Selected Poems 1956–67, 105
"Six Young Men," 99
"Strawberry Hill," 98
"Sugar Loaf," 90
"Sunstroke," 98
"Thistles," 103

"Thought-Fox, The," 95–96, 169
"Thrushes," 101
"To Paint a Water Lily," 97
"Two Legends," 97
"Vampire," 98
"View of a Pig," 91, 93
"Wind," 90
"Wodwo," 102
Wodwo, 90, 98, 99, 104, 105
"Wound, The," 99

Hurry on Down (Wain), 30
Huxley, Aldous, 2

"In the Movement" (*Spectator*, 1954), 50
International Poetry Incarnation, 87
"Is Verse a Dying Technique?" (Edmund
   Wilson), 1
Isherwood, Christopher, 2

James, William, 125, 133
Jarrell, Randall, 85
Jennings, Elizabeth, 50, 119, 120, 133–41,
   172; anti-empiricist tendencies, 135–36;
   Movement roots, 133–35; related treat-
   ment of love and human relations, 138–
   41; religious outlook, 136–38

WORKS—VERSE:
"Afternoon in Florence," 135
"Annunciation, The," 137
"Chorus, A," 138
"Consequently, I Rejoice," 138
"Education, An," 136
"Family Affairs," 139
"Father," 139
"Forgiveness," 138
"Ghosts," 136
"Identity," 134
"In the Night," 135
"In This Time," 136–37
"Italian Light," 135
"Losing and Finding," 140
Moments of Grace, 138
"My Grandmother," 139
"Never Such Peace," 138
"New Patience, A," 139
"Old Man," 135
"One Flesh," 139–40
"Parting, The," 134
"Resemblances," 135
"Resurrection, The," 138
"Song at the Beginning of Autumn," 134

"Teresa of Auila," 138
"Thomas Aquinas," 138
"To My Mother at 73," 140
"Warning to Parents," 139

Joyce, James, 1, 78, 160

Kafka, Franz, 60
Kavanaugh, Patrick, 160
Keats, John, 21, 139, 160
Kunitz, Stanley, 85

Langley, Michael, 159
Larkin, Philip, 47, 50, 64–81, 82, 84, 92,
   101, 104, 107, 109, 111, 117, 120,
   134–35, 140, 143, 153, 159, 172, 173,
   174, 176, 178; anti-romanticism, 69–71;
   compared with Roy Fuller, 75–79; em-
   phasis upon continuity and custom, 74–
   75; empiricist plotting in key poems, 64–
   69; realism and historicism, 71–72; recent
   developments, 80–81; reticence and wari-
   ness, 79–80

WORKS—PROSE:
All What Jazz, 51, 76
Jill, 75, 92

WORKS—VERSE:
"Arundel Tomb, An," 70
"At Grass," 71
"Broadcast," 70
"Building, The," 81
"Card-Players," 81
"Church Going," 66–67, 71, 77, 80,
   136, 137
"Deceptions," 72
"Days," 72
"Dockery and Son," 73
"Dry Point," 71
"Essential Beauty," 71, 80
"Explosion, The," 72
"Faith Healing," 77–78
"Going, Going," 71
"Here," 71
"High Windows," 64–66, 67, 70, 71, 74
High Windows, 75, 80–81
"I Remember, I Remember," 69
"If My Darling," 71
"Large Cool Store, The," 71
"Latest Face," 70
Less Deceived, The, 50, 66, 75, 80
"Lines on a Young Lady's Photograph Al-
   bum," 70

"Livings," 72
"Love Songs in Age," 71
"Maiden Name," 71
"MCMXIV," 72, 75
"Mr. Bleaney," 68, 70, 71
"Next, Please," 73–74
North Ship, The, 75, 80
"Sad Steps," 81
"Self's the Man," 67–68
"Show Saturday," 75
"Solar," 81
"Sunny Prestatyn," 80
"Old Fools, The," 70
"Take One Home for the Kiddies," 69
"Talking in Bed," 71
"This Be the Verse," 81
"To the Sea," 74–75, 178
"Toads," 79
"Toads Revisited," 79
"Triple Time," 72, 135, 172
"Vers de Société," 79
"Waiting for Breakfast. . . ," 71
"Wants," 79
"Wedding Winds," 71
"Whatever Happened?" 73
Whitsun Weddings, The, 67, 75
"Whitsun Weddings, The," 68–69, 70, 74
"Wild Oats," 71

Lawrence, D. H., 84, 89, 96, 104, 121
Lear, Edward, 121
Lehmann, John, 17, 50
Lennon, John, 87
Lewis, Alun, 31–40, 46, 47, 112; affinity to Edward Thomas, 32–33; background, 31–32; central poems, 35–37; compared with Keith Douglas, 31–35; complex attitude toward the East, 37–40; realism and ideology in his writing, 33–35

WORKS—VERSE:
"After Dunkirk," 35–36
"All Day it has Rained," 32
"Burma Casualty," 36–37, 39
"Crucifixion, The," 37, 100
"Dawn on the East Coast," 35
"Destruction," 33, 34
"Home Thoughts from Abroad," 38
"In Hospital: Poona (2)," 33, 36
"Karanje Village," 33, 38
"Jungle, The," 39–40
"Mahratta Ghats, The," 37–38

"Midnight in India," 38
"Mountain Over Aberdare," 33
"Peasant Song," 38–39
"Peasants, The," 38
"Rhondda, The," 33, 34
"River Temple: Wai, The," 38
"Sacco Writes to His Son," 37
"To Edward Thomas," 32–33

Lewis, C. Day, 2, 3, 7, 8, 173; "Bombers, The," 7; "February, 1936," 7; *From Feathers to Iron,* 3; "Landscapes," 7; *Magnetic Mountain, The,* 3, 7; "Maple and Sumach," 7; *Overtures of Death,* 7; "Sex Crimes," 7; *Transitional Poem,* 3
Liverpool group, 86–87
Logue, Christopher, 87
Loneliness of the Long-Distance Runner (Sillitoe), 44
Look Back in Anger (Osborne), 52
Lowell, Robert, 79, 84–85, 109, 120, 171
Lucie-Smith, Edward, 86, 87
Lucky Jim (Amis), 50, 92

McCarthy, Desmond, 120
McGough, Roger, 86
Macbeth, George, 86, 173, 174
MacNeice, Louis, 2, 7–8, 16; "Eclogue for Christmas," 7; "Turf-stacks," 8
Mahon, Derek, 159
Manning, Olivia, 27
Marvell, Andrew, 23
Mavericks, 86
Mitchell, Adrian, 87, 177
Moore, Marianne, 145, 146
Movement, the, 47, 50–51, 52, 63, 66, 82, 83, 84, 86, 134, 135, 136, 142, 144, 173, 174
Muir, Edwin, 16
Murdoch, Iris, 52

Nash, Ogden, 120
New Country, 3
New Criticism, 176
New Lines, 50, 86, 134, 143
New Lines II, 83
New Poetry, The, 83–84
New Poetry of England and America, 134
New Signatures, 3

Objectivism, 146
Olson, Charles, 146
Oppen, George, 146

Orwell, George, 2, 5, 15, 84
Osborne, John, 174
Owen, Wilfred, 13, 18, 23, 32
Oxford Anthology of Contemporary Verse 1945–1980, The, 51, 177
Oxford Poetry 1927, 3

Pater, Walter, 145
Patten, Brian, 86, 172
Piccolo, Lucio, 155
Pinter, Harold, 172, 174
Plath, Sylvia, 84, 85, 87, 104, 120
Poetry (London), 15, 19
Porter, Cole, 5
Pound, Ezra, 4, 9, 11, 16, 20, 94, 146, 150; Pisan Cantos, 16
Purity of Diction in English Verse (Davie), 51

Raine, Kathleen, 17
Ransom, John Crowe, 88
Reed, Henry, 41–46, 47; lesser poems and drift toward drama, 45–46; "Lessons of War," 41–44; poetry surveyed, 40–41

WORKS—VERSE:
"Chard Whitlow," 41, 44
"Chrysothemis," 41, 45
"Desert, The," 41, 45
"Iseult Blaunches-mains," 45
"Iseult La Belle," 45
"Judging Distances" ("Lessons of War"), 42–43
"King Mark," 45
"Lessons of War" (sequence), 41
"Lives," 41
Map of Verona, A, 40–46
"Naming of Parts," 40, 41–42
"Philoctetes," 41, 45
"Tintagel," 41
"Tristram," 45
"Unarmed Combat" ("Lessons of War"), 43–44

Roberts, Michael, 3
Roethke, Theodore, 85
Room at the Top (Braine), 52
Rosenberg, Isaac, 13, 18, 32
Rosenthal, M. L., 84
Rudolf, Anthony, 177
Ruskin, John, 144–45

Sassoon, Siegfried, 18, 23, 32
Scannell, Vernon, 24, 43, 173

Schwartz, Delmore, 85
Sexton, Anne, 84
Seymour-Smith, Martin, 86
Shaffer, Peter, 175
Silkin, Jon, 173
Sillitoe, Alan, 44, 52
Sitwell, Edith, 16, 20; "Still Falls the Rain," 16; "The Poet Laments the Coming of Old Age," 16; "Three Poems of the Atomic Age," 16
Smith, Stevie, 112, 119, 120–33, 172; meditations on death, 129–30; misleading surface simplicity, 121–23; religious struggles, 125–28; reputation, 120–21; strategy of nonsense, 123–24; treatment of human relations, 130–33; 136

WORKS—EDITIONS:
Collected Poems, 120, 123, 124, 129

WORKS—PROSE:
Me Again, 120
"Some Impediments to Christian Commitment," 125

WORKS—VERSE:
"After-thought, The," 123
"Agnostic, An," 127
"Ah, will the Savior . . . ?," 126
"Ass, The," 122
"Autumn," 132
"Away, Melancholy," 127
"Bag-Snatching in Dublin," 123
"Bereaved Swan, The," 122
"Blood Flows Back, The," 126
"Brickenden, Hertfordshire," 123
"Castle, The," 121
"Children of the Cross, The," 126
"Come Death," 129
"Correspondence between Mr. Harrison in Newcastle and Mr. Sholto Peach Harrison in Hull," 123
"Dear Child of God," 126
"Dear Female Heart," 123
"Death Came to Me," 122
"Death of the Dog Belvoir," 123
"Distractions and the Human Crowd," 127
"Do Take Muriel Out," 131
"Edmonton, thy cemetary . . . .," 127
"Egocentric," 125
"Engine Drain, The," 122
"Exeat," 130

"Frog Prince, The," 121
"Frozen Lake, The," 121
"God the Eater," 127
Good Time Was Had By All, A, 125
"Grange, The," 123
"Harold's Leap," 129
"Heber," 122
"Hostage, The," 129
"I Am," 130
"I Hate this Girl," 131
"Jew Is Angry with his Friend who does
   not Believe in Circumcision, A," 126
"Lads of the Village, The," 123
"Lot's Wife," 129
"Love Me!," 131
"Mother, among the Dustbins," 127
Mother, What is Man?, 130
"Mrs. Simpkins," 125
"Murderer, The," 131
"No Categories!," 127
"Not Waving But Drowning," 132–33
"O Pug," 121
"One of Many," 126
"Orphan Reformed, The," 123
"Persephone," 121
"Pleasures of Friendship, The," 132
"Portrait," 131
"Religious Man, A," 127
"Study to Deserve Death," 129–30
"Tableau de 'Inconstance des Mauvais
   Anges,' " 126
"Tender Only to One," 129
Tender Only to One, 129, 130
"Tenuous and Precarious," 123–24
"To Carry the Child," 123
"To the Dog Belvoir," 123
"Valuable," 132
"Violent Hand, The," 126
"Was He Married?," 37, 100, 128
"Weak Monk, The," 126
"Wedding Photograph, The," 131
"Who Shot Eugenie," 123
"Why do I . . .," 129
"Why do you rage?," 127
"Zoo, The," 126

Snodgrass, W. D., 85
Sons and Lovers (Lawrence), 103
Southwell, Robert, 117
Spark, Muriel, 52
Spencer, Bernard, 27
Spender, Stephen, 2, 5, 6–7, 10–11, 16,
   150; "Express, The," 6; "Landscape Near

an Aerodrome," 6; *Love-Hate Relations,*
   174; "Uncreating Chaos, The," 6; *Vienna,*
   7; "W. B. Yeats as a Realist," 10–11
Stallworthy, Jon, 163, 170
Steiner, George, 177
Stevens, Wallace, 55, 119, 145
Stevie (Whitebread), 120
Stoppard, Tom, 175
Swift, Jonathan, 98

Tambimutto, M. J., 15, 19
Taylor, A. J. P., 2
Tennyson, Alfred Lord, 39, 45
Thomas, Dylan, 8–9, 17, 47, 89, 145; *18
   Poems,* 8, 9; "A Refusal to Mourn the
   Death, by Fire, of a Child in London,"
   17; "Altarwise by owl-light," 9; *Collected
   Poems,* 49; *Deaths and Entrances,* 17; "Fern
   Hill," 17; "Force that through the green
   fuse drives the flower, The," 9; "I see the
   boys of summer," 9; "Vision and Prayer,"
   17
Thomas, Edward, 32, 33
Thomas, R. S., 119, 172
Thwaite, Anthony, 86, 87
Tiller, Terrence, 27
Tomlinson, Charles, 142–55, 159, 164,
   174; anti-empiricist aesthetic, 142–45;
   blending of inner and outer, 148–49; cen-
   tral poems, 152–54; developments, 154–
   55; dominant scenes and settings, 149–
   50; poems about artists, 146–47; poetic
   affinities, 145–46; technical dimension of
   aesthetic, 150–52

WORKS—VERSE:
"Aesthetic," 144
American Scenes, 154–55
"Arizona Desert," 150
"Atlantic, The," 150
"Before the Dance," 151
"Canal," 151
"Composition," 147
"Crane, The," 150
"Crow," 150
"Death in the Desert, A," 150
"Face and Image," 148
"Fiascherino," 148–49
"Garland for Thomas Eakins," 146–47
"Grass Grain," 152
"John Maydew *or* the Allotment," 151–52
"Meditation on John Constable, A," 148
"Mediterranean, The," 150

"More Foreign Cities," 143
Necklace, The, 154
"Observation of Facts," 144
"Ode to Arnold Schoenberg," 147
"Oxen: Ploughing at Fiesole," 151
"Paring the Apple," 152
Peopled Landscape, A, 154
Relations and Contraries, 154
"Saving the Appearance," 151
"Sea Change," 149–50
Seeing is Believing, 146, 154
"Sense of Distance, A," 152
Shaft, The, 155
"Swimming Chenango Lake," 149
"Through Binoculars," 152
"Tramontana at Lerici," 152
"Up at La Serra," 152–53
Way In, The, 155
"Written on Water," 153–54
Written on Water, 153, 155

Traherne, Thomas, 136
Transatlantic Patterns (Martin Green), 174

Ulster Group, 159
Ulster Revival, 160

Wain, John, 47, 50, 51
Waiting for Godot (Beckett), 175
Walsh, Chad, 84
Watkins, Vernon, 17
Waugh, Evelyn, 2, 52, 119, 175
Weatherhead, A. Kingsley, 105, 106
Wesker, Arnold, 175
White Goddess, The (Graves), 106
Whitman, Walt, 146
Wilbur, Richard, 88
Williams, William Carlos, 145, 146, 150
Wilson, Angus, 52
Woolf, Virginia, 1
Wordsworth, William, 55, 98, 109, 119,
    136, 148, 160, 161, 171

Yeats, W. B., 3, 6, 9–10, 11, 16, 20, 38,
    47, 59, 80, 81, 104, 119, 127, 160,
    161, 171, 172, 173, 178; "Among School
    Children," 10; Autobiographies, 162; "By-
    zantium," 10; Full Moon in March, A, 10;
    Last Poems and Plays, 16; "Magi, The,"
    112; "Sailing to Byzantium," 10; Tower,
    The, 10; Winding Stair, The, 10; Vision,
    A, 10

Zukovsky, Charles, 146